AUTOMOTIVE BRAKES

Vent port
close on Breaden gluges.

AUTOMOTIVE
BRAKES

FRANK C. DERATO

GREGG DIVISION

McGRAW-HILL BOOK COMPANY

New York ■ Atlanta ■ Dallas ■ St. Louis ■ San Francisco ■ Auckland ■ Bogotá
Guatemala ■ Hamburg ■ Lisbon ■ London ■ Madrid
Mexico ■ Milan ■ Montreal ■ New Delhi ■ Panama ■ Paris ■ San Juan ■ São Paulo
Singapore ■ Sydney ■ Tokyo ■ Toronto

About the Author

Frank C. Derato teaches automotive mechanics at Westhill High School, Stamford, Connecticut. He received the Bachelor of Engineering and Master of Science degrees in electrical engineering from Stevens Institute of Technology and attended New York University, where he received a Certificate of Advanced Study in technology and industrial education.

A member of the Society of Automotive Engineers, he has written training material on vehicle maintenance for the U.S. Post Office Department, and has served on the Connecticut State Committee to revise the Power/Automotive Mechanics curriculum.

Mr. Derato has taught courses in electronics and automotive mechanics on both the secondary and the postsecondary levels.

Sponsoring Editor: D. Eugene Gilmore
Editing Supervisor: Kelly A. Warsak
Design and Art Supervisor: Meri Shardin
Production Supervisor: Kathleen Donnelly

Interior Design: Pencil Point Studio/Gene Garone
Cover Design: Sulpizio Associates Graphic Design

Series Consultant: Donald L. Anglin

Library of Congress Cataloging-in-Publication Data

Derato, Frank C.
   Automotive brakes.

   Includes index.
   I. Automobiles—Brakes.   2. Automobiles—Brakes—
Maintenance and repair—Handbooks, manuals, etc.
I. Title.
TL269.D47   1988   629.2'46   88-5471
ISBN 0-07-016502-5   (TEXT)
ISBN 0-07-016503-3   (SHOP MANUAL)
ISBN 0-07-909010-9   (SET)

The manuscript for this book was processed electronically.

Automotive Brakes

1234567890 SEMSEM 8954321098

ISBN 0-07-016502-5 {TEXT}
ISBN 0-07-016503-3 {SHOP MANUAL}
ISBN 0-07-909010-9 {SET}

CONTENTS

FOREWORD

Automotive Brakes by Frank C. Derato is another two-volume text in the McGraw-Hill Basic Automotive Series. The series offers a fresh start in automotive service training. Each book is totally new and not a revision of any previous book or manual.

Each text was prepared by an outstanding teacher in the subject-matter area and then reviewed by other experts in automotive service training. The result is a two-book set—a textbook and a shop manual—that provides the needed basics both for the classroom and for the shop.

The textbooks in the Basic Automotive Series will cover each area of the National Institute for Automotive Service Excellence (ASE) certification tests for Master Automobile Technician. The content of each was selected after careful analysis of the latest available task lists, ASE test-preparation guidelines, manufacturers' service recommendations, and, most importantly, the needs and experiences of automotive teachers.

Pedagogically, each two-book set in the McGraw-Hill Basic Automotive Series is a thoroughly researched and field-tested textbook and shop manual. Each task leads the student toward the development of skills which can be measured objectively.

For schools seeking program certification by the National Automotive Technicians Education Foundation (NATEF), every attempt has been made to include the *high-priority* items from their task list. At least ninety percent of these must be included in the curriculum to meet the minimum standards for certification.

The style of the series has been designed to attract the student, cultivate interest, and enhance learning. Review questions at the end of each chapter reinforce key points, while providing practice with ASE-type questions. Key words are defined in the text, and again in the chapter vocabulary review.

The author of each book has included the latest information and service procedures available from the automotive and test equipment manufacturers. In addition, a complete new illustration program has been prepared for each book. These illustrations provide new insights into the construction and operation of the latest and most advanced automotive components.

Donald L. Anglin
Series Consultant

PREFACE

The automobile brake system has gradually evolved over the years. The first cars had mechanical service brakes that operated on only two wheels. These brakes were sufficient when cars were light in weight and speeds were low. But as weight and speed increased, four-wheel brakes became necessary. Hydraulic brakes were introduced in the 1920s, and by the late 1930s had completely replaced mechanical service brakes on passenger cars. Power brakes became widely used in the 1950s, and disc brakes in the 1960s. With each change in brake system technology, brake service technicians had to learn new theories and new service skills.

Now in the 1980s, microprocessor-controlled antilock brake systems are becoming commonplace. Complex electronic systems are now part of the brake system, and the service technician must have a knowledge of electronics. Again, the technician must learn new theories and new service skills.

This two-book set, textbook and shop manual, provides information on the latest brake systems. These books have been designed to prepare a technician for the ASE Brakes Test. The information provided is relevant to that required for the test, and the end-of-chapter questions are similar in format to questions found in the test.

The textbook presents a background of basic brake and hydraulic theory. Then, drum brakes, disc brakes, and the various types of parking brakes are covered in detail. Three types of power brake systems are included, and the theory of operation of the Bosch and Teves antilock brake systems is described.

The shop manual covers the service aspect of the systems listed above. In addition, a chapter on the hazards of asbestos and the proper methods of working with asbestos dust is presented.

These two books provide automotive students with the means to learn brake systems from basic concepts to the advanced antilock systems. They also provide experienced technicians the opportunity to learn the latest troubleshooting methods and repair procedures.

The author wishes to acknowledge some of the people who helped in the preparation of these books. Donald L. Anglin helped in the planning of the books, read the manuscripts, and suggested many improvements in both the technical content and the manner of presentation. Jack LaRosa reviewed the manuscripts and offered many suggestions for improving them. Harry R. Abbott, Ted Armstrong, Howard Buzzutto, Bill Campana, John Cilento, David J. Norton, and everyone at Joe Rysz and Company (especially Peter Rysz and Ruth Ashmore) provided valuable assistance. Joseph N. Catino and Jeffery Faski aided in preparing some of the illustrations, with the cooperation of Kenneth W. Miller.

Frank C. Derato

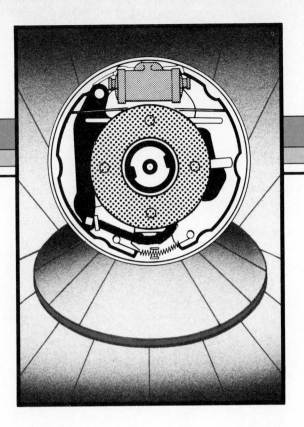

CHAPTER 1

INTRODUCTION TO BRAKES

OBJECTIVES

After you have studied this chapter, you should be able to:

1. Describe friction and its relationship to automotive brakes.

2. Name the parts of a drum-brake system.

3. Describe the basic operation of drum brakes.

4. Name the parts of a disc-brake system.

5. Describe the basic operation of disc brakes.

6. Describe the characteristics of brake-lining materials.

Brakes are devices that convert mechanical energy into heat energy. They slow or stop a moving vehicle or prevent a vehicle from rolling. All cars have two independent brake systems (Fig. 1-1). The *service brakes* are used to stop the vehicle under normal driving conditions. The *parking brakes* are used to prevent the car from rolling while it is parked. The parking brake can also be used in an emergency if the service brakes fail; however, the parking brake is not as effective as the service brakes in stopping a moving vehicle.

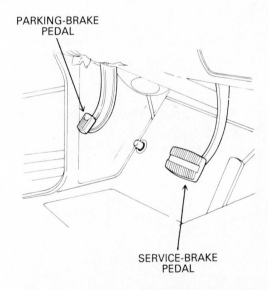

Fig 1-1. The locations of the service-brake pedal and parking-brake pedal. *(Ford Motor Company)*

ENERGY

All moving vehicles have energy. *Energy* is the ability to do work. The amount of energy that a vehicle has depends on its weight and speed. The heavier the vehicle and the faster it goes, the more energy it has. This energy of motion is called *kinetic energy*.

Energy can neither be created nor destroyed, but it can be changed into other forms. Therefore, when the

$E \propto w \cdot p_2$

$K = \frac{1}{2} m v^2$

brakes are used to reduce the speed of a moving automobile, the kinetic energy is changed into heat energy by friction.

FRICTION

Friction is the resistance to motion between two objects that are in contact with each other. Figure 1-2 shows a block being pulled along a flat surface. A force is required to move the block because the friction between the block and the surface opposes the motion. A *force* is a push or pull. It is usually measured in pounds (lb) or in newtons (N); 1 lb of force equals 4.45 N. The force that opposes the motion between two objects that are in contact with each other is called the *friction force*.

It is easier to keep the block moving than it is to start it moving. Therefore, there are two types of friction: *static friction* and *kinetic friction*. *Static friction* is the friction between two objects which are in contact, but which are not moving. *Kinetic friction* is the friction between two objects when one object is sliding on or against the other.

Kinetic friction is always less than static friction. When the block in Fig. 1-2 is moving, the friction force is caused by kinetic friction. This is the same as when the service brakes are used to stop a moving car. However, when the parking brake is used to keep the car from rolling while it is parked, static friction holds the car still.

When a second block is placed on top of the first block in Fig. 1-2, the force required to move the blocks is greater (Fig. 1-3). This is because the weight (or force) pushing downward increases the friction force. The force pushing downward on the surface is called the *normal force*.

The friction force is also affected by the types of materials that are in contact. For example, a rubber block requires more force to pull it across the same surface than does a wood block. The effect of the materials on the amount of friction is called the *coefficient of friction*. This is the ratio of the friction force to the normal force:

$$\text{Coefficient of friction} = \frac{\text{friction force}}{\text{normal force}}$$

For example, Fig. 1-4 shows a block of steel with a weight (normal force) of 100 lb [445 N]. It takes a force of 50 lb [223 N] to move the block along the surface. Therefore, the coefficient of friction is

$$\frac{50 \text{ lb}}{100 \text{ lb}} = 0.5$$

$$\left[\frac{223 \text{ N}}{445 \text{ N}} = 0.5 \right]$$

If a 75-lb [334-N] pull is required to move the block (Fig. 1-5), the coefficient of friction is

$$\frac{75 \text{ lb}}{100 \text{ lb}} = 0.75$$

$$\left[\frac{334 \text{ N}}{445 \text{ N}} = 0.75 \right]$$

The greater the force needed to move the block, the greater is the coefficient of friction.

In automotive brakes, the friction is usually caused by asbestos or a similar friction material rubbing against cast iron. The coefficient of friction of these materials ranges from about 0.3 to 0.5 under normal conditions.

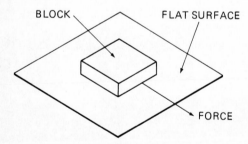

Fig. 1-2. A block being pulled along a flat surface.

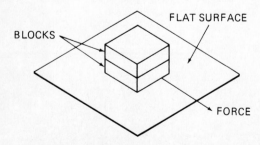

Fig. 1-3. Two blocks being pulled along a flat surface.

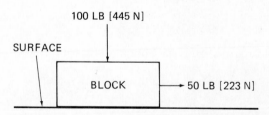

Fig. 1-4. If a force of 50 lb [223 N] is required to pull a 100-lb [445-N] block along a surface, the coefficient of friction of the surfaces is 0.5.

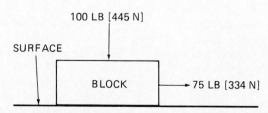

Fig. 1-5. If a force of 75 lb [334 N] is required to pull a 100-lb [445-N] block along a surface, the coefficient of friction of the surfaces is 0.75.

AUTOMOTIVE BRAKES

An early type of brake used on horse-drawn wagons had a block of friction material that was pushed against a moving wheel (Fig. 1-6). The resulting friction force slowed and stopped the wheel (Fig. 1-7). The greater the normal force or the higher the coefficient of friction, the greater is the friction force and the shorter the stopping distance.

Early cars had brakes on only the two rear wheels. These cars were light in weight and their speeds were low. As cars became heavier and their speeds increased, four-wheel brakes were needed.

The wagon brake was used on some of the first cars, but when rubber tires were introduced, the wagon brake was not practical. An improvement over the wagon brake was a band of friction material wrapped around part of the wheel (Fig. 1-8). As the brake was applied, the friction material wrapped tighter around the wheel, slowing its rotation. This was called an *external-contracting* brake. However, external brakes were easily contaminated by dirt, water, and ice. Soon they were replaced by enclosed internal brakes.

Figure 1-9 shows a basic *internal-expanding* type of *drum brake*. Two curved sections of friction material are located inside a rotating *brake drum* (Fig. 1-10). The drum is made of cast iron, and the drum and wheel are bolted together.

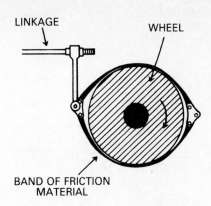

Fig. 1-8. An external-contracting drum brake. (*Bendix Aftermarket Brake Division*)

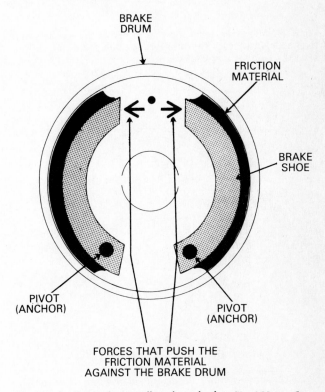

Fig. 1-9. An internal-expanding drum brake. (*Ford Motor Company*)

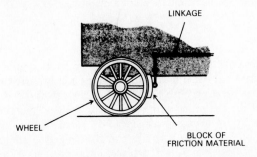

Fig. 1-6. A wagon-wheel brake. (*Bendix Aftermarket Brake Division*)

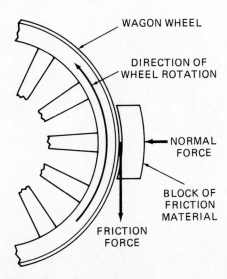

Fig. 1-7. The friction force applied to the wagon wheel by the friction material.

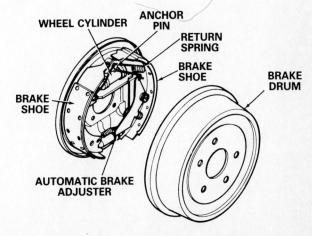

Fig. 1-10. The brake drum removed from the brake assembly. (*Chevrolet Motor Division of General Motors Corporation*)

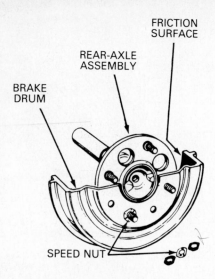

Fig. 1-11. The brake drum shown attached to the rear axle of a rear-wheel-drive car. The brake components are not shown. *(EIS Division of Parker Hannifin Corporation)*

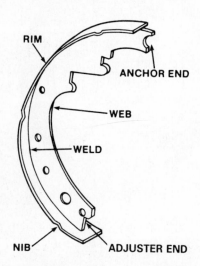

Fig. 1-12. A brake shoe. *(Bendix Aftermarket Brake Division)*

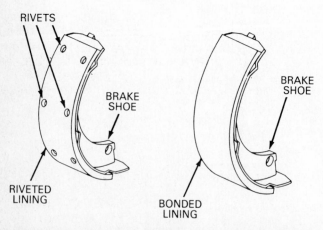

Fig. 1-13. Riveted and bonded brake linings. *(Chevrolet Motor Division of General Motors Corporation)*

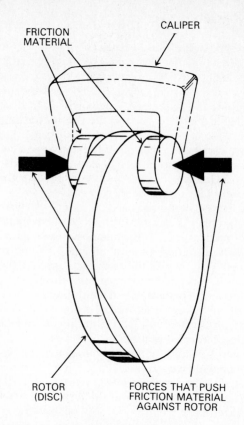

Fig. 1-14. The basic operation of a disc brake. *(EIS Division of Parker Hannifin Corporation)*

When the brakes are applied, the friction material is pushed against the drum. This action slows the drum, which is rotating with the wheel, and stops the car. The part of the drum in contact with the friction material is called the *friction surface* (Fig. 1-11). The friction material, called *brake lining*, is attached to curved metal *brake shoes* (Fig. 1-12). A brake shoe consists of a rim and a web that are welded together. The lining is attached to the rim of the shoe either with rivets (riveted linings) or with an adhesive (bonded linings). Figure 1-13 shows the two types of linings.

In the 1960s the *disc brake* (Fig. 1-14) became widely used on automobiles. Two flat pieces of friction material are held close to the sides of a rotating *disc*. The disc is made of cast iron, and the wheel is bolted to it (Fig. 1-15). The friction material is held in a clamplike device called a *caliper*. When the brakes are applied, the caliper forces the friction material against the disc. This slows and stops the rotation of the wheel.

The disc is often called a *rotor*. The friction material, or lining, is called a *brake pad*. It is attached to a metal shoe or plate (Fig. 1-16) to form the pad-and-plate assembly. The word *pad* is often used to mean the lining-and-shoe assembly.

HEAT DISSIPATION

Friction produces heat. In the brakes, the heat causes the temperature of the brake parts to rise. If the temperature goes too high, the brakes will not stop the car.

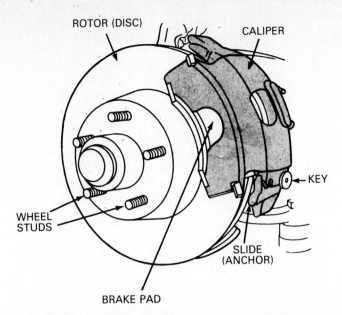

Fig. 1-15. A disc-brake assembly. (*Bendix Aftermarket Brake Division*)

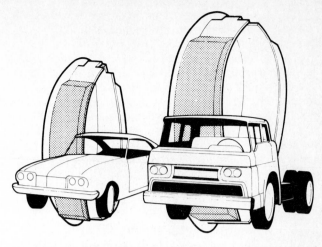

Fig. 1-17. Trucks require larger brakes than cars because of their greater kinetic energy, which produces more heat during braking. (*Ford Motor Company*)

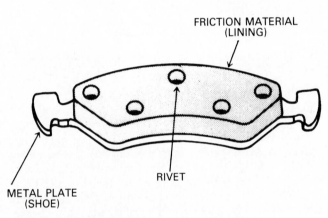

Fig. 1-16. A disc-brake pad. (*Chrysler Corporation*)

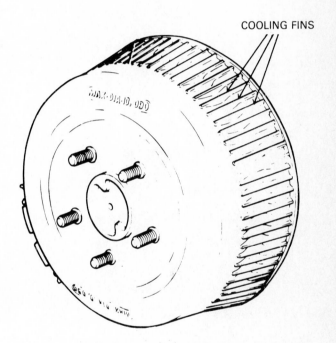

Fig. 1-18. A brake drum with cooling fins. (*Chrysler Corporation*)

One reason is that the coefficient of friction of the brake lining decreases with increasing temperature. At high temperatures there is less friction and less stopping ability. To prevent this from happening, the brakes must dissipate excess heat to the surrounding air.

A heavy truck has larger brakes than does a lightweight vehicle (Fig. 1-17). The heavier truck has more kinetic energy, which produces more heat during braking; therefore, a larger brake surface area is needed to dissipate the heat. Truck brake drums and rotors are larger than those for the smaller passenger cars, and their brake linings have a greater surface area.

In drum brakes, much of the heat is absorbed by the brake drum; therefore, the brake drum must dissipate the heat. Some brake drums have small cooling fins (Fig. 1-18) that increase the surface area over which the cooling air flows.

Disc brakes provide better heat dissipation than drum brakes do. Air circulates more freely around disc-

brake parts because they are more exposed to the air than drum-brake parts are. In addition, the disc usually has an opening between the two friction surfaces (Fig. 1-19). These surfaces are joined by cooling fins, or *louvers*. As the disc turns, air flows through the louvers and helps cool the disc.

OPERATING THE BRAKES

To operate the brakes, the driver applies a force to the brake pedal that must be transmitted to each brake assembly. Early cars used *mechanical brakes*. Metal rods and cables connected the brake pedal to the brake as-

5

sembly at each wheel. When the driver depressed the brake pedal, linkage pulled a lever at each wheel-brake assembly to apply the brake (Fig. 1-20).

Mechanical service brakes were difficult to adjust to make the braking force equal at each wheel. Often the car would pull to one side when braking; this was because one brake was adjusted differently than the others. In addition, the mechanical brake parts were affected by dirt, water, and ice. Cars no longer use mechanical brakes for the service brakes. However, a cable-operated mechanical brake is still used for the parking brake (Fig. 1-21).

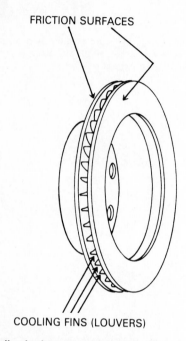

Fig. 1-19. A disc-brake rotor with cooling fins. *(EIS Division of Parker Hannifin Corporation)*

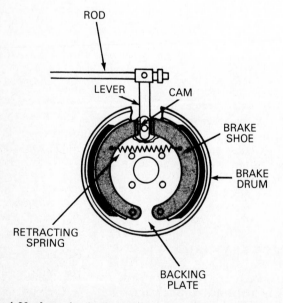

Fig. 1-20. A mechanically operated drum brake. *(Bendix Aftermarket Brake Division)*

6

In the 1930s *hydraulic brakes* became widely used. In the hydraulic brake system, the force applied by the driver's foot is transmitted to each wheel-brake assembly by a liquid under pressure (Fig. 1-22). The liquid is called *brake fluid*.

When the driver depresses the brake pedal, the brake fluid is pressurized by the *master cylinder*. In drum brakes the pressure is transmitted through hoses and tubing to hydraulic cylinders, or *wheel cylinders*, located in each wheel-brake assembly. Pistons in the wheel cylinders are forced outward by the brake fluid. The pistons push against links (pins) that force the brake shoe and lining outward to contact the drum (Fig. 1-23). As the brake shoes move outward, they must overcome the tension of the brake-shoe retracting springs. When the brake pedal is released, the retracting springs pull the shoes and linings away from the drum, allowing it to turn freely.

In disc brakes the hydraulic unit is the caliper (Fig. 1-24). Brake fluid pushes against one or more pistons in the caliper. When the pistons are pushed outward, the brake pads are forced against the rotor. When the brake pedal is released, the pistons are pulled back slightly by the action of a rubber seal in the caliper assembly. This allows the rotor to turn freely again. This action is described in Chap. 5.

A TYPICAL BRAKE SYSTEM

When the brakes are applied on a moving car, some of the car's weight is transferred to the front wheels. The front of the car tends to dip toward the road, and the rear of the car tends to lift (Fig. 1-25). Because of this effect, the front brakes must provide up to 85 percent of the braking (on front-engine front-wheel-drive cars). Most cars now have disc brakes in the front and drum brakes in the rear. Disc brakes are used in the front of the car because of their greater ability than drum brakes to dissipate heat. Drum brakes are sufficient for the rear because they provide as little as 15 percent of the total braking.

In addition, disc brakes are not always used at the rear because of the complexity of adding a parking brake to a disc-brake assembly. However, some cars do have four-wheel disc brakes.

STOPPING A VEHICLE

When the brakes are applied to stop a vehicle, there is friction between the braking surfaces and also between the tires and the road surface. The friction between the braking surfaces causes the wheel and tire to rotate at a slower speed, and the friction between the tire and the road surface causes the car to slow down.

When a tire is rolling over the road surface, the friction between the tire and the road is static friction. This is because the part of the tire in contact with the road is not sliding on the road surface. As the tire rolls, different parts of the tire come into contact with different parts of the road surface.

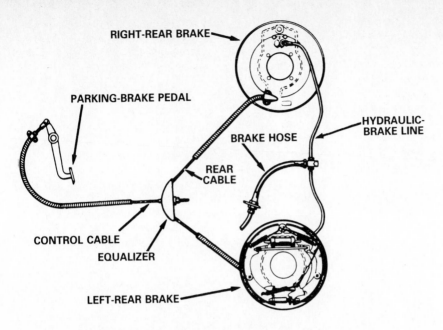

Fig. 1-21. A cable-operated parking-brake system. *(Bendix Aftermarket Brake Division)*

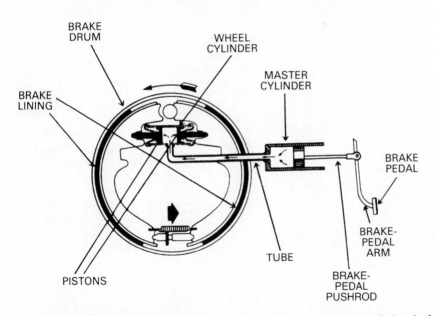

Fig. 1-22. A hydraulically operated drum brake. *(Wagner Division, Cooper Industries Inc.)*

However, if a tire is skidding (slipping or sliding on the road surface), the tire may not be rotating. Instead, one section of the tire remains in contact with the road and slides over it. When this occurs, the friction between the tire and road is kinetic friction. The vehicle will not stop as quickly when the tires are skidding, because kinetic friction is less than static friction.

A vehicle stops in the shortest distance when the brakes are applied just hard enough to get the highest possible static-friction force between the tires and the road. If the brakes are applied any harder than this, the wheels will lock (stop rotating) and skid. The car will then require a longer distance to stop.

BRAKE-LINING MATERIALS

Brake lining must be able to withstand high temperatures. Stopping a car from a speed of 55 miles per hour (mph) [88 kilometers per hour (kph)] can increase the lining temperature to 450°F (degrees Fahrenheit) [232°C (degrees Celsius)] or higher. The lining should not char (burn) at high temperature, and the coefficient of friction should remain fairly constant.

There is a slight reduction in the brake-lining coefficient of friction as temperature increases. Therefore, the brakes are less effective as they get hot, and the driver

7

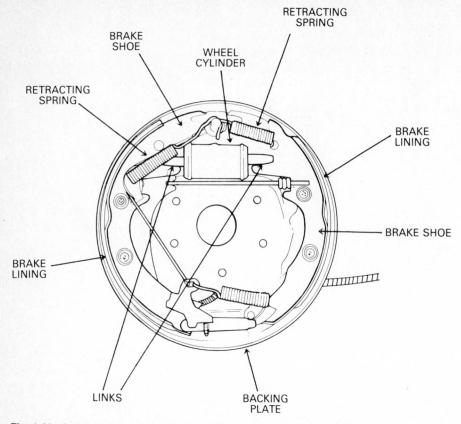

Fig. 1-23. A drum-brake assembly for a right-rear wheel, shown without the drum. *(Ford Motor Company)*

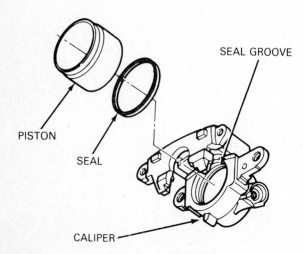

Fig. 1-24. A disassembled disc-brake caliper. *(Chevrolet Motor Division of General Motors Corporation)*

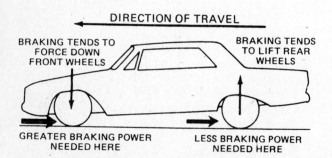

Fig. 1-25. Weight transfer in a car during braking. *(Wagner Division, Cooper Industries Inc.)*

has to press harder on the brake pedal to stop the car. The reduction in braking ability at high temperatures is called *heat fade*. If heat fade occurs, the lining should recover quickly as it cools so that normal braking is restored.

Figure 1-26 is a graph of the coefficient of friction and how it changes with temperature for two different brake-lining materials. One lining fades only slightly at high temperature and is considered acceptable. The other lining fades severely and is not acceptable.

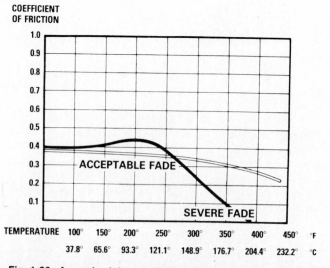

Fig. 1-26. A graph of the coefficient of friction over a range of temperatures for two different lining materials. *(Ford Motor Company)*

Another type of brake fade is *water fade*. It reduces braking ability because water (which acts as a lubricant) gets between the brake lining and the friction surface. This greatly reduces the coefficient of friction. Brake lining should recover quickly from water fade as the lining dries.

Brake lining should also have good wear characteristics and long life (not wear away quickly). As the brakes are used, the rubbing of the brake lining against the friction surface causes the lining to wear away. With each normal brake application, part of the lining becomes dust. With drum brakes, much of the dust remains inside the drum. Some dust drops on the road. With disc brakes, almost all the dust drops on the road. As a general rule, a friction material with a low coefficient of friction is relatively hard and has a long life. A friction material with a high coefficient of friction is relatively soft and has a shorter life.

There are three types of friction materials used as brake lining: asbestos, nonasbestos, and semimetallic. As-bestos has been used as a friction material for many years. Asbestos fibers are mixed with a filler material and then bound together with an adhesive. However, asbestos is a health hazard because it is a carcinogen. A *carcinogen* is a cancer-causing material. Breathing asbestos dust can cause lung cancer, and handling asbestos can cause skin irritation.

Other materials are replacing asbestos for use in brake linings. Nonasbestos linings use fiberglass or synthetic (manufactured) fibers mixed with a filler and a binder. Both asbestos linings and nonasbestos linings (fiberglass or synthetic) are called *organic linings*.

A third type of friction material uses iron powder and iron fibers with a filler and a binder. These linings are called *semimetallic linings*. Semimetallic linings provide better braking than organic linings at high temperature. But at low temperature, organic linings provide better braking than semimetallic linings. The lining material used on a vehicle depends on the temperature at which the brakes are designed to operate.

VOCABULARY REVIEW

Bonded lining A brake lining that is attached to the shoe with an adhesive.

Brake drum The part of a brake assembly, shaped like a cylinder, to which the wheel is attached. The drum rotates with the wheel, and the brake shoes are pressed against the friction surface of the drum to slow or stop the vehicle.

Brake fluid The liquid used in a hydraulic brake system.

Brake lining The friction material attached to a brake shoe.

Brake pad The friction material attached to a metal plate and pressed against the disc in a disc-brake assembly.

Brake shoes The metal parts to which the brake linings are attached.

Caliper The clamplike device that houses (or holds) the piston (or pistons) and brake pads in a disc-brake hydraulic system.

Coefficient of friction The ratio of the friction force to the normal force when one object slides on or against another object.

Disc The rotating part of a disc-brake assembly against which the friction material is pressed. Also called a *rotor*.

Disc brake A brake in which pads of friction material are pressed against both sides of a rotating disc (or rotor).

Drum brake A brake using curved brake shoes and linings that press against the inside surface of a rotating drum.

Energy The ability to do work.

Force A push or a pull.

Friction The resistance to motion between two objects in contact with each other.

Friction force The force that opposes the motion between two objects when one object slides on or against the other.

Friction surface The part of a brake drum or rotor that is in contact with the brake lining.

Heat fade The reduction in braking effectiveness caused by a high temperature at the brake lining and friction surface.

Hydraulic brake system A brake system operated by a liquid under pressure.

Kinetic energy The energy of motion.

Kinetic friction The friction between two objects when one object is sliding on or against the other.

Louvers The cooling fins between the surfaces of a disc-brake rotor.

Master cylinder The part of the hydraulic system, which is operated by a force applied by the driver's foot, and in which the brake fluid is pressurized.

Mechanical brake system A brake system operated by rods, cables, and levers.

Normal force The force between two moving objects that pushes them together.

Organic lining Brake lining that does not contain metal particles or fibers.

Parking brakes The brakes used to prevent a car from rolling while it is parked.

Riveted lining Brake lining that is attached to the shoe with rivets.

Rotor Another name for the disc in a disc-brake assembly.

Semimetallic lining Brake lining containing iron powder or fibers.

Service brakes The brakes used to stop a car under normal driving conditions.

Static friction The friction between two objects which are in contact, but which are not moving.

Water fade The reduction in braking effectiveness caused by water between the brake lining and the friction surface.

Wheel cylinder The hydraulic cylinder in a drum brake, with pistons that force the brake shoes against the brake drum. Also called a *brake cylinder*.

REVIEW QUESTIONS

Select the *one* correct, best, or most probable answer to each question.

1. When the brakes are used to stop the car, the energy of motion is converted into:
   a. heat energy.
   b. kinetic energy.
   c. friction.
   d. potential energy.

2. When one object slides on or against another object, the friction force is increased when:
   a. the normal force is reduced.
   b. the coefficient of friction is reduced.
   c. the normal force is increased.
   d. the pull on the object is increased.

3. If a force of 25 lb [111 N] is required to pull a 100-lb [445-N] object across a surface, what is the coefficient of friction of the surfaces?
   a. 4
   b. 25
   c. 0.25
   d. 2,500

4. The brake hydraulic system includes all of the following *except*:
   a. A master cylinder
   b. A caliper
   c. A wheel cylinder
   d. Brake lining

5. A drum brake includes all of the following *except*:
   a. A wheel cylinder
   b. A brake pad
   c. A brake shoe
   d. Brake lining

6. A disc brake includes all of the following *except*:
   a. A rotor
   b. A brake drum
   c. A brake pad
   d. A caliper

7. Technician A says that a heavier car has more kinetic energy than a lighter car if they are both traveling at the same speed. Technician B says that the front wheels and the rear wheels each provide 50 percent of the braking force. Who is right?
   a. A only
   b. B only
   c. Both A and B
   d. Neither A nor B

8. Heat fade means:
   a. the brakes grab at high temperature.
   b. less braking force is required when the brakes are hot.
   c. the coefficient of friction increases at high temperature.
   d. the coefficient of friction decreases at high temperature.

9. The use of which brake-lining material is being discontinued because it is considered a health hazard?
   a. Asbestos material
   b. Fiberglass material
   c. Semimetallic material
   d. Synthetic material

10. Technician A says that when the parking brake is applied, the car is prevented from rolling by static friction. Technician B says that when a tire is rolling over a road surface, there is static friction between the tire and the road. Who is right?
    a. A only
    b. B only
    c. Both A and B
    d. Neither A nor B

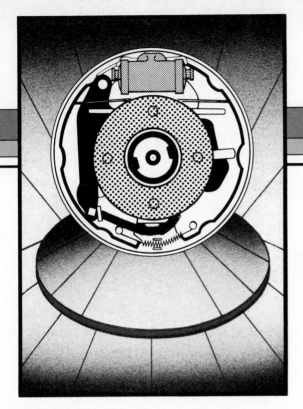

CHAPTER 2

FUNDAMENTALS OF HYDRAULICS

OBJECTIVES

After you have studied this chapter, you should be able to:

1. Define force and pressure.

2. Explain the basic principles of hydraulics.

3. Name the parts of a hydraulic brake system.

4. Describe a typical hydraulic brake system.

5. Describe the properties and types of brake fluid.

Hydraulics is the use of a liquid to transmit force and motion. The liquid is called the *hydraulic fluid*. Blaise Pascal, a French philosopher and mathematician, studied liquids in the 1600s. The results of his studies are summarized in Pascal's law, which states that *a confined liquid transmits an externally applied pressure uniformly in all directions.*

The basics of hydraulics, and the applications of hydraulics to an automobile brake system, are described in the following sections.

PRESSURE

Pressure is a force divided by the area on which it acts, or the force per unit area. For example, Fig. 2-1 shows a force of 10 pounds (lb) [44.5 newtons (N)] being applied to 1 square inch (in.^{2}) [6.45 square centimeters

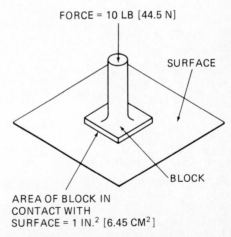

Fig. 2-1. A force of 10 lb [44.5 N] applied to 1 in.^{2} [6.45 cm^2] produces a pressure of 10 psi [6.9 N/cm^2].

(cm^2)] of surface area. The pressure on the surface is 10 pounds per square inch (psi) [6.9 newtons per square centimeter (N/cm^2)].

$$\frac{force}{area} = pressure$$

$$\frac{10\ lb}{1\ in.^2} = 10\ psi$$

$$\left[\frac{44.5\ N}{6.45\ cm^2} = 6.9\ N/cm^2\right]$$

> NOTE   In the metric system, pressure is usually expressed in kilopascals (kPa). One newton per square centimeter equals 10 kilopascals; therefore, 6.9 N/cm^2 = 69 kPa
> When converting pressure from the U.S. Customary System to the metric system, a pressure of 1 psi equals 6.9 kPa.

Figure 2-2 shows a force of 10 lb [44.5 N] being applied to 5 in.^{2} [32.3 cm^2] of surface area. The pressure is

$$\frac{10\ lb}{5\ in.^2} = 2\ psi$$

$$\left[\frac{44.5\ N}{32.3\ cm^2} = 1.38\ N/cm^2\ or\ 13.8\ kPa\right]$$

Therefore, if the same force is applied to a larger area, the pressure on the surface is reduced.

Figure 2-3 shows a force of 10 lb [44.5 N] being applied to 0.5 in.^{2} [3.23 cm^2] of surface area. The pressure is

$$\frac{10\ lb}{0.5\ in.^2} = 20\ psi$$

$$\left[\frac{44.5\ N}{3.23\ cm^2} = 13.8\ N/cm^2\ or\ 138\ kPa\right]$$

When the same force is applied to a smaller area, the pressure on the surface is increased.

COMPRESSIBILITY OF LIQUIDS AND GASES

Liquids and gases are made of molecules. A *molecule* is the smallest particle of a substance that has all the properties of that substance. In liquids the molecules are constantly moving and are as close together as possible. In gases, the molecules are also constantly moving, but the distances between them are much larger than in liquids.

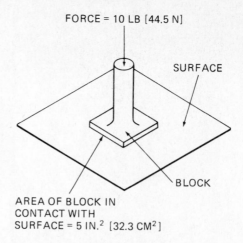

FORCE = 10 LB [44.5 N]

SURFACE

BLOCK

AREA OF BLOCK IN CONTACT WITH SURFACE = 5 IN.^{2} [32.3 CM^2]

Fig. 2-2. A force of 10 lb [44.5 N] applied to 5 in.^{2} [32.3 cm^2] produces a pressure of 2 psi [1.38 N/cm^2, or 13.8 kPa].

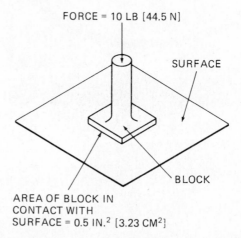

FORCE = 10 LB [44.5 N]

SURFACE

BLOCK

AREA OF BLOCK IN CONTACT WITH SURFACE = 0.5 IN.^{2} [3.23 CM^2]

Fig. 2-3. A force of 10 lb [44.5 N] applied to 0.5 in.^{2} [3.23 cm^2] produces a pressure of 20 psi [13.8 N/cm^2, or 138 kPa].

Compressibility is the ability of a material to be compressed, or made smaller. Some materials are compressed when acted on by a force. Figure 2-4a shows a piston in the top of a cylinder that is filled with a gas, such as air. The piston fits tightly in the cylinder so that air cannot escape between the piston and the cylinder. When the piston is forced into the cylinder, the molecules of air are pushed closer together. This compresses the air, which now occupies a smaller space and has a higher pressure (Fig. 2-4b).

The molecules of a liquid are already as close together as possible. Therefore, if the cylinder is filled with liquid, the piston cannot be pushed into the cylinder (Fig. 2-5). Under most conditions, liquids are incompressible. Because liquids are incompressible, they can be used to transmit force and motion.

USING LIQUIDS TO TRANSMIT MOTION

Figure 2-6a shows a cylinder with two pistons. The space between the pistons is filled with liquid. If piston A is pushed to the right, piston B will move the same dis-

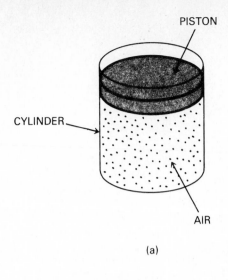

(a)

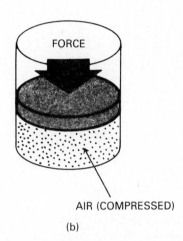

FORCE

AIR (COMPRESSED)

(b)

Fig. 2-4. When a force is applied to a piston in a cylinder filled with air, the air compresses. *(Chevrolet Motor Division of General Motors Corporation)*

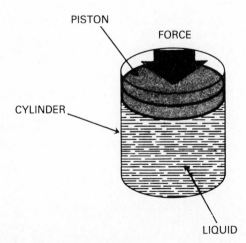

Fig. 2-5. When a force is applied to a piston in a cylinder filled with liquid, the liquid is not compressed. *(Chevrolet Motor Division of General Motors Corporation)*

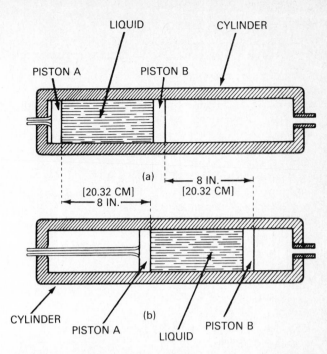

(a)

[20.32 CM]
8 IN.

8 IN.
[20.32 CM]

(b)

Fig. 2-6. A cylinder with two pistons. *(a)* **When no force is applied to piston A;** *(b)* **when piston A is forced to the right, the motion is transferred through the liquid to piston B.** *(Chrysler Corporation)*

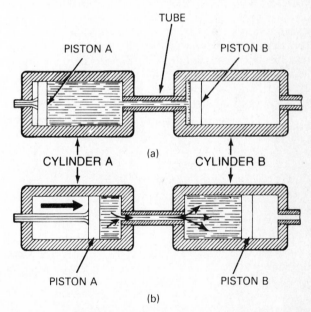

TUBE

PISTON A   PISTON B

CYLINDER A   (a)   CYLINDER B

PISTON A   PISTON B

(b)

Fig. 2-7. Two cylinders connected by a tube. *(a)* **When no force is applied to piston A;** *(b)* **when piston A is forced to the right, the motion is transferred through the liquid to piston B in cylinder B.** *(Chrysler Corporation)*

tance to the right (Fig. 2-6b). The liquid between the pistons transmits the motion from piston A to piston B.

Figure 2-7a shows two cylinders connected by a tube. Both cylinders are the same size. Piston A is in cylinder A, and piston B is in cylinder B. The space between the pistons is filled with liquid. If piston A is pushed to the right, piston B will move the same distance to the right (Fig. 2-7b). This shows that liquids can transmit motion from one cylinder to another over a distance.

13

USING LIQUIDS TO TRANSMIT FORCE

When pressure is applied to a confined liquid, instead of being compressed, the liquid pushes back against the piston with an equal and opposite pressure. The liquid is said to be "pressurized," or "under pressure." When this occurs, the liquid pushes back at the piston—and also pushes out against the sides and bottom of the cylinder—with the same pressure.

Figure 2-8 shows a piston being pushed down with a force of 10 lb [44.5 N] on a liquid in a cylinder. The area of the piston in contact with the liquid is 2 in.^{2} [12.9 cm^2]. Therefore, the pressure on the liquid is

$$\frac{force}{area} = pressure$$

$$\frac{10 \text{ lb}}{2 \text{ in.}^2} = 5 \text{ psi}$$

$$\left[\frac{44.5 \text{ N}}{12.9 \text{ cm}^2} = 3.45 \text{ N/cm}^2 \text{ or } 34.5 \text{ kPa} \right]$$

The liquid transmits this pressure to all the surfaces it touches.

The fact that a liquid pushes outward on its container with the same pressure that is applied to it is very useful. Figure 2-9 shows a hydraulic system that has four cylinders connected by small pipes or tubes. Each cylinder has a piston. Piston 1 is the input piston, because an external force is applied to it to pressurize the liquid. Assume that piston 1 is pushed inward with a force of 100 lb [445 N] and that the surface area of the piston is 1 in.^{2} [6.45 cm^2]; therefore, the pressure in cylinder 1 is

$$\frac{force}{area} = pressure$$

$$\frac{100 \text{ lb}}{1 \text{ in.}^2} = 100 \text{ psi}$$

$$\left[\frac{445 \text{ N}}{6.45 \text{ cm}^2} = 68.9 \text{ N/cm}^2 \text{ or } 689 \text{ kPa} \right]$$

Because the liquid pushes outward with the same pressure on all surfaces, the pressure in the connecting

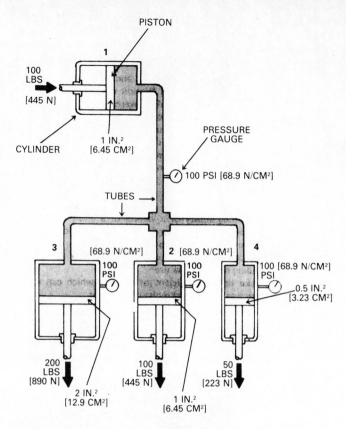

Fig. 2-9. A cylinder connected by tubes to three other cylinders. The force applied to piston 1 is multiplied or reduced, depending on the size of the other pistons. *(Wagner Division, Cooper Industries Inc.)*

tubes and in the other cylinders is also 100 psi [68.9 N/cm^2]. Pressure gauges in Fig. 2-9 indicate this pressure. If piston 2 has a surface area of 1 in.^{2} [6.45 cm^2], then the liquid pushes against piston 2 with a force of 100 lb [445 N]:

$$Pressure \times area = force$$
$$100 \text{ psi} \times 1 \text{ in.}^2 = 100 \text{ lb}$$
$$[68.9 \text{ N/cm}^2 \times 6.45 \text{ cm}^2 = 445 \text{ N}]$$

Piston 2 could be connected to a mechanical device. The pressure on piston 2 could cause it to move and operate the device. Piston 2 is an output piston, because the pressurized liquid can cause it to apply force to move an object. If a long tube is used, cylinder 2 can be located some distance from cylinder 1. The tube allows the liquid to transfer a force over a distance.

In Fig. 2-9, cylinder 3 and its piston are larger than cylinder 1 and its piston. Piston 3 has a surface area of 2 in.^{2} [12.9 cm^2]. Because the pressure of 100 psi [68.9 N/cm^2] is acting on 2 in.^{2} [12.9 cm^2] of surface, the force on piston 3 is 200 lb [890 N]:

$$Pressure \times area = force$$
$$100 \text{ psi} \times 2 \text{ in.}^2 = 200 \text{ lb}$$
$$[68.9 \text{ N/cm}^2 \times 12.9 \text{ cm}^2 = 890 \text{ N}]$$

Because the force on piston 3 is twice as great as the force applied to piston 1, the applied force has been multiplied. This is because the output piston has a greater surface area than the input piston.

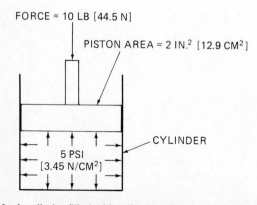

Fig. 2-8. A cylinder filled with a liquid that is under a pressure of 5 psi [3.45 n/cm², or 34.5 kPa].

14

In Fig. 2-9, piston 4 has a surface area of 0.5 in.^{2} [3.23 cm^2]. Because the pressure of 100 psi [68.9 N/cm^2] is acting on 0.5 in.^{2} [3.23 cm^2] of surface, the force on piston 4 is 50 lb [223 N]:

$$\text{Pressure} \times \text{area} = \text{force}$$
$$100 \text{ psi} \times 0.5 \text{ in.}^2 = 50 \text{ lb}$$
$$[68.9 \text{ N/cm}^2 \times 3.23 \text{ cm}^2 = 223 \text{ N}]$$

The force is reduced because the output piston has a smaller surface area than the input piston.

Therefore, by using pistons of different sizes, the force can be multiplied or reduced in a hydraulic system.

AUTOMOTIVE HYDRAULIC SYSTEMS

On the automobile, the service brakes are operated by the hydraulic system (Fig. 2-10). The input piston is located in the *master cylinder* and is operated when the driver applies force to the brake pedal. The output pistons are located in cylinders that are part of the brake assembly at each wheel. These pistons apply force that operates the brakes to provide the braking action.

Prior to 1968, most cars used a master cylinder with a single piston (Fig. 2-11). The construction of a single-piston master cylinder is shown in Fig. 2-12. If a leak developed and the pressure in the hydraulic system dropped to zero, the brakes would fail. Since 1968, all cars have a dual master cylinder and a hydraulic system split into two sections (Fig. 2-13). A dual master cylinder

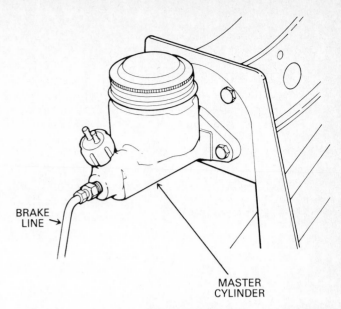

BRAKE LINE →

MASTER CYLINDER

Fig. 2-11. A single-piston master cylinder. *(Ford Motor Company)*

has two pistons (Fig. 2-14). If one section leaks, the other section of the system continues to operate. This allows the brakes at two wheels to stop the car.

Figure 2-15 shows a brake system in which the front wheels are in one section of the hydraulic system and the rear wheels are in another. This is called a *front/rear–split system*. Figure 2-16 shows a system in which diagonal wheels are in the same section of the hydraulic system. This is called a *diagonally split system*. The manufacturer of the vehicle chooses the type of system based

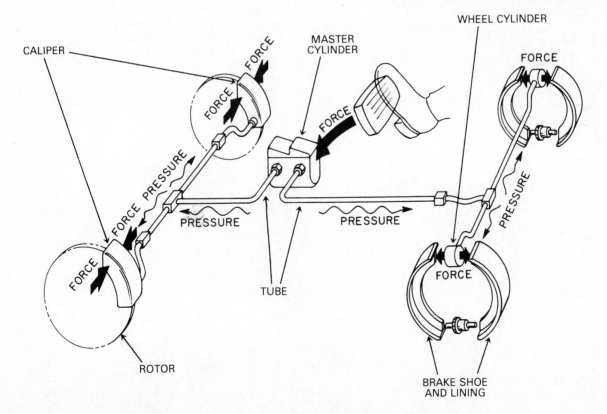

CALIPER

FORCE

FORCE

FORCE

MASTER CYLINDER

FORCE

FORCE PRESSURE

PRESSURE

PRESSURE

FORCE

TUBE

ROTOR

WHEEL CYLINDER

FORCE

PRESSURE

FORCE

BRAKE SHOE AND LINING

Fig. 2-10. The basic hydraulic system for automotive service brakes. *(EIS Division of Parker Hannifin Corporation)*

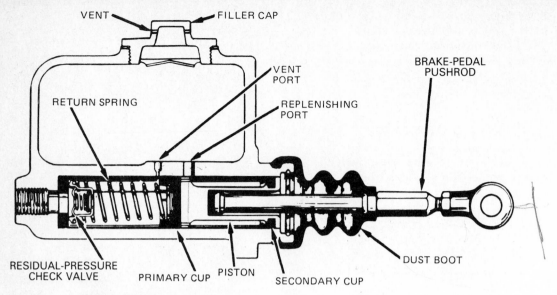

Fig. 2-12. The construction of a single-piston master cylinder. *(Wagner Division, Cooper Industries Inc.)*

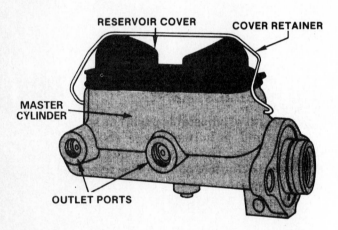

Fig. 2-13. A dual master cylinder. *(Bendix Aftermarket Brake Division)*

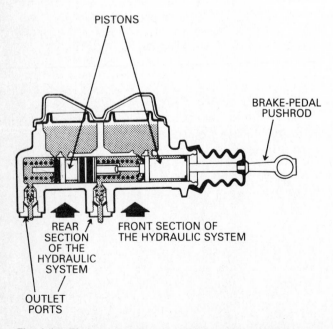

Fig. 2-14. The construction of a dual master cylinder. *(Ford Motor Company)*

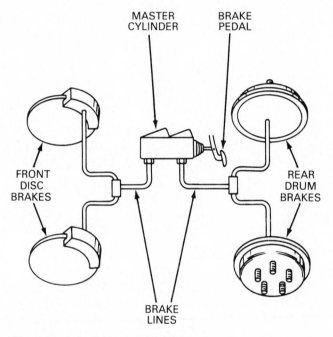

Fig. 2-15. A front/rear-split hydraulic system. *(EIS Division of Parker Hannifin Corporation)*

on the weight distribution and the handling properties of the vehicle. The object is to permit the vehicle to stop in as straight a line as possible whenever a failure occurs in one section of the hydraulic system.

Diagonally split systems are used mostly on front-wheel-drive vehicles. Front/rear–split systems are usually used on rear-wheel-drive vehicles.

Wheel Cylinders and Calipers

On cars with drum brakes, the output cylinders are called *wheel cylinders* (Fig. 2-17). Each wheel cylinder has two pistons (Fig. 2-18). The pistons move outward to force the brake shoes and linings against the drum.

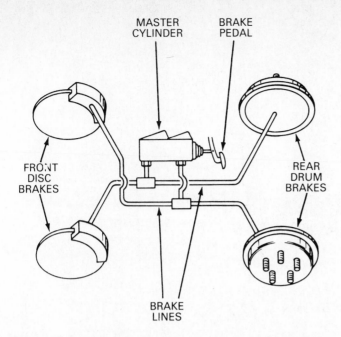

Fig. 2-16. A diagonally split hydraulic system. (*EIS Division of Parker Hannifin Corporation*)

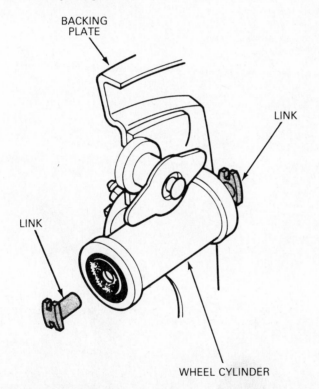

Fig. 2-17. A wheel cylinder mounted on the backing plate. (*Chevrolet Motor Division of General Motors Corporation*)

On cars with disc brakes, the output cylinders are located in the calipers (Fig. 2-19). On most cars the caliper has only one piston. Tubes or pipes called *brake lines* and *brake hoses* connect the master cylinder to the wheel cylinders or calipers (Fig. 2-20). Brake lines are usually preformed steel tubes that attach to the frame or floorpan of the car. Flexible brake hose attaches a brake line to a cylinder, or other brake line, that moves with the suspension of the car.

Automotive brake systems provide greater braking force at the front wheels than at the rear wheels. Larger-diameter pistons are often used at the front wheels, with smaller-diameter pistons at the rear wheels. Because the pressure in the hydraulic system is the same everywhere, the larger pistons will apply greater braking force than will the smaller pistons.

Older cars used drum brakes at all four wheels. Typically, the master cylinder had a 1-in. [2.54-cm] diameter piston, the front-wheel cylinders had 1 1/4-in. [3.18-cm] diameter pistons, and the rear-wheel cylinders had 7/8-in. [2.22-cm] diameter pistons. This gave a force multiplication at the front wheels and a force reduction at the rear wheels.

Most cars use disc brakes at the front wheels and drum brakes at the rear wheels. The pistons in the disc-brake calipers are larger than the pistons in wheel cylinders. This is because a greater force is required to operate a disc brake than a drum brake. Caliper pistons vary in size from 2 to 3 in. [5.08 to 7.62 cm] in diameter, depending on the car. On cars with four-wheel disc brakes, the front calipers have larger pistons than do the rear calipers.

Brake-Pedal Force

In a typical hydraulic brake system, the piston in the master cylinder has a surface area of approximately 0.8 in.^{2} [5.16 cm^2]. Assume that when the brakes are applied to stop the car, a pressure of 600 psi [414 N/cm^2] is required in the hydraulic system. This means that 480 lb [2,136 N] of force must be applied to the master-cylinder piston:

$$\text{Pressure} \times \text{area} = \text{force}$$
$$600 \text{ psi} \times 0.8 \text{ in.}^2 = 480 \text{ lb}$$
$$[414 \text{ N/cm}^2 \times 5.16 \text{ cm}^2 = 2,136 \text{ N}]$$

To enable the driver to apply this force, the brake-pedal arm acts as a lever. Figure 2-21 shows a typical master-cylinder-and-brake-pedal installation. The master cylinder is mounted inside the engine compartment on the bulkhead, or *firewall*; this is the part of the body of the vehicle that separates the engine compartment from the passenger compartment. The brake-pedal arm (or lever) swings on a pivot, or *fulcrum*, located under the instrument panel. The length of the pedal arm is shown as the distance A in Fig. 2-21. A pushrod (the brake-pedal pushrod) contacts the master-cylinder piston. The other end of the pushrod attaches to the brake-pedal arm at a distance B from the fulcrum. Assume that on a particular car the distance A divided by the distance B is 6:

$$\frac{\text{Distance A}}{\text{Distance B}} = 6$$

This number is the *mechanical advantage* of the lever. The mechanical advantage is the number of times the lever multiplies the applied force. In this example, the driver needs to apply only 80 lb [356 N] of force to the brake pedal. The mechanical advantage of the lever multiplies that force by 6. Therefore, the lever applies 480

17

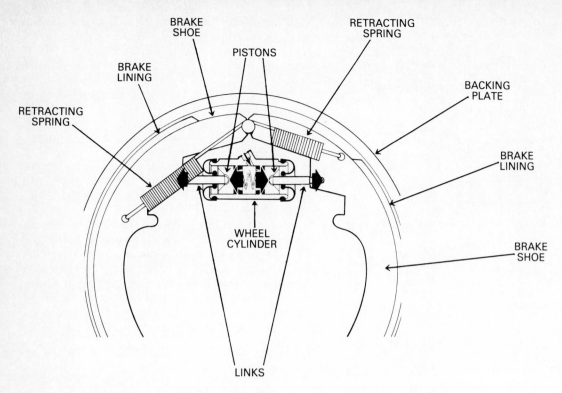

Fig. 2-18. As the hydraulic pressure increases, it forces the wheel-cylinder pistons to move outward, pushing the brake lining against the brake drum. *(Ford Motor Company)*

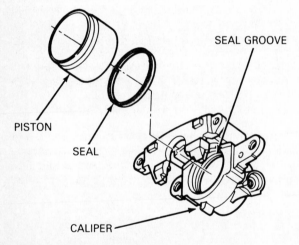

Fig. 2-19. A caliper-and-piston assembly. *(Chevrolet Motor Division of General Motors Corporation)*

lb (80 lb x 6)[2,136 N (356 N x 6)] to the brake-pedal pushrod. The mechanical advantage of the brake-pedal arm ranges from 3 on some cars to 7 on other cars.

To reduce driver fatigue, many cars have some type of power-brake unit (Fig. 2-22). The power-brake unit is usually located between the brake-pedal pushrod and the master cylinder. The power-brake unit multiplies the force of the brake-pedal arm, and then this greater force is applied to the master cylinder. With power brakes, the driver must apply much less force at the brake pedal than without power brakes. Power brakes are discussed in Chaps. 7, 8, and 9.

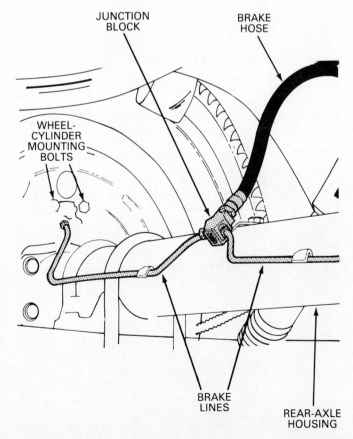

Fig. 2-20. Brake lines and a brake hose. *(Ford Motor Company)*

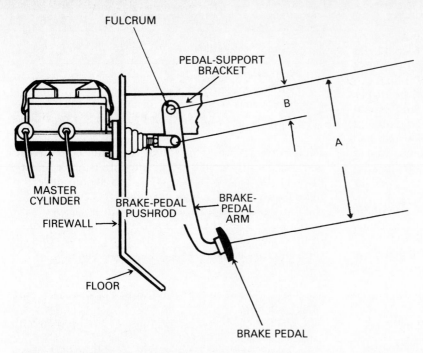

Fig. 2-21. A master cylinder and brake pedal, showing the brake-pedal arm used as a lever. *(Bendix Aftermarket Brake Division)*

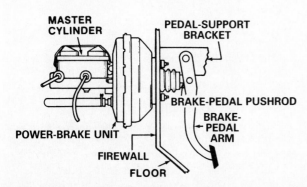

Fig. 2-22. The location of the power-brake unit. *(Bendix Aftermarket Brake Division)*

BRAKE FLUID ▬▬▬▬

The hydraulic fluid used in the automobile brake system is called *brake fluid*. Brake fluid must meet requirements set by the Society of Automotive Engineers (SAE) and by the federal government through the Department of Transportation (DOT). The most important requirement is the operating-temperature range. Brake fluid must remain liquid over a wide range of temperature. Its freezing point must be appoximately -100°F (degrees Fahrenheit) [-73°C (degrees Celsius)] and its boiling point must be approximately 450°F [232°C].

During braking, the kinetic energy of motion is converted into heat. As the brake fluid absorbs some of this heat, the fluid temperature increases. If the brake fluid boils, it becomes a gas or vapor. Because a gas is compressible, the gas bubbles compress when the driver depresses the brake pedal. Then no pressure develops in the brake fluid, and the brakes do not apply.

Brake fluid is *hygroscopic*, which means that it absorbs water. Water has a lower boiling point (212°F [100°C]) than brake fluid; therefore, when brake fluid absorbs water, the boiling point of the brake fluid is lowered. The boiling point of brake fluid with a certain small percentage of water is called the *wet boiling point*. The *dry boiling point* is the boiling point of the brake fluid with no absorbed water. The wet boiling point is always lower than the dry boiling point.

Some additional requirements of brake fluid are:

- Brake fluid must have a low viscosity over its operating temperature range. *Viscosity* is the tendency of a liquid to resist flow. A low viscosity means that the brake fluid flows freely through the hydraulic system.

- Brake fluid must lubricate the hydraulic system's moving parts, such as pistons and seals.

- Brake fluid must help resist corrosion in the hydraulic system.

- Brake fluid must not evaporate easily.

- Brake fluid must be compatible with the rubber seals and components in the hydraulic system. Some liquids, such as gasoline, kerosene, and oil, attack rubber seals and cause them to swell.

- Brake fluid must be able to absorb water. If it did not absorb water, any water that did enter the system could freeze and cause brake failure. The freezing temperature of water is 32°F [0°C].

There are three classifications of brake fluid: DOT 3, DOT 4, and DOT 5. DOT 3 and DOT 4 fluids are similar in type but differ in boiling point. They are *glycol-*

based fluids; a glycol is a type of alcohol. DOT 4 fluid has a higher boiling point than DOT 3 fluid. DOT 4 fluids were developed for disc brakes, which operate at higher temperatures than drum brakes. Both these fluids are clear to amber in color when new. DOT 4 fluid can be used in place of DOT 3 fluid because of the higher boiling point of DOT 4 fluid, but DOT 3 fluid should never be used in place of DOT 4 fluid. DOT 5 fluid has a higher boiling point than DOT 3 or DOT 4 fluid and is usually a silicone-based brake fluid. Silicone fluid is purple in color when new. Figure 2-23 is a table showing the three types of brake fluid and their wet and dry boiling points.

Silicone brake fluid does not absorb water. With no absorbed water, it should be less corrosive to hydraulic-system components than are DOT 3 or DOT 4 fluids. However, if water does enter the system, the water is

	Dot 3	Dot 4	Dot 5
Dry boiling point	401°F [205°C]	446°F [230°C]	500°F [260°C]
Wet boiling point	284°F [140°C]	311°F [155°C]	356°F [180°C]

Fig. 2-23. The wet and dry boiling points for various types of brake fluid.

not absorbed by the brake fluid. The water could freeze and cause a brake failure. Silicone fluid is not compatible with DOT 3 or DOT 4 fluids and should never be mixed with them. If a hydraulic system is converted for use with silicone fluid, the system must be flushed with alcohol, and all rubber parts must be replaced. Because of this, use only the brake-fluid type recommended by the vehicle manufacturer.

VOCABULARY REVIEW

Brake fluid   The hydraulic fluid used in an automobile brake system.

Brake hose   A flexible hose that transfers hydraulic pressure from a brake line to a wheel cylinder or caliper or to another brake line that moves with the suspension of the car.

Brake line   A steel tube or pipe that transfers hydraulic pressure from the master cylinder to the wheel cylinders or calipers.

Compressibility   The ability of a material to be compressed.

Diagonally split system   A brake system in which diagonal wheels are in the same section of the hydraulic system.

Dry boiling point   The boiling point of brake fluid with no absorbed water.

Dual master cylinder   A master cylinder that has two pistons. Each piston controls one-half of the hydraulic system.

Firewall   The part of the body of the vehicle that separates the engine compartment from the passenger compartment.

Front/rear–split system   A brake system in which the front-wheel brakes are operated by one piston in the master cylinder, and the rear-wheel brakes are operated by the other piston.

Fulcrum   The pivot point of a lever.

Glycol   A type of alcohol.

Hydraulic fluid   The liquid used in a hydraulic system.

Hydraulics   Using liquids to transmit force and motion.

Hygroscopic   The tendency to absorb water.

Mechanical advantage   The number of times that a simple machine (such as a lever) multiplies a force.

Molecule   The smallest particle of a substance that has all the properties of the substance.

Pressure   The force divided by the area on which it acts.

Viscosity   The tendency of a liquid to resist flow.

Wet boiling point   The boiling point of brake fluid with a certain amount of absorbed water.

REVIEW QUESTIONS

Select the *one* correct, best, or most probable answer to each question.

1. A force is applied to a surface. If the area on which the force acts is decreased, while the force remains the same, the pressure:
   a. decreases.
   b. increases.
   c. remains the same.
   d. causes the force to increase.

2. All of the following apply to the operation of hydraulic systems *except*:
   a. Liquids are incompressible
   b. Liquids transmit pressure equally in all directions
   c. Hydraulic systems can be used to multiply force
   d. Hydraulic systems can be used to multiply pressure

3. If a force of 50 lb [223 N] is applied to a hydraulic piston with a surface area of 2 in.² [12.9 cm²], the resulting pressure is:
   a. 100 psi [68.9 N/cm²].
   b. 52 psi [35.8 N/cm²].
   c. 25 psi [17.2 N/cm²].
   d. 50 psi [34.5 N/cm²].

4. In a hydraulic system, the wheel cylinder with the largest diameter:
   a. receives the highest pressure.
   b. has the greatest force applied to its pistons.
   c. has the least force applied to its pistons.
   d. receives the lowest pressure.

5. On a car with a dual master cylinder, if a brake line cracks at a wheel cylinder:
   a. one wheel will stop the car.
   b. the pressure in both sections of the hydraulic system will drop to zero.
   c. two wheels will stop the car.
   d. none of the brakes will operate.

6. What is the wet boiling point of DOT 4 brake fluid?
   a. 311°F [155°C]
   b. 401°F [205°C]
   c. 284°F [140°C]
   d. 446°F [223°C]

7. What happens if heavy braking causes the brake fluid to boil?
   a. The gas bubbles expand and apply the brakes.
   b. The pressure in the system increases.
   c. The brakes operate normally.
   d. The brakes fail to stop the car because the gas bubbles are compressed.

8. The input piston in an automobile hydraulic system is located in the:
   a. master cylinder.
   b. wheel cylinder.
   c. brake cylinder.
   d. caliper.

9. In a car with front disc brakes and rear drum brakes, the largest hydraulic piston is located in the:
   a. master cylinder.
   b. caliper.
   c. brake cylinder.
   d. wheel cylinder.

10. A hydraulic system has a brake-fluid pressure of 300 psi [206.7 N/cm²]. A piston with a 3-in.² [19.4 cm²] surface area would have a force of:
    a. 100 lb [445 N].
    b. 300 lb [1,335 N].
    c. 150 lb [667.5 N].
    d. 900 lb [4,005 N].

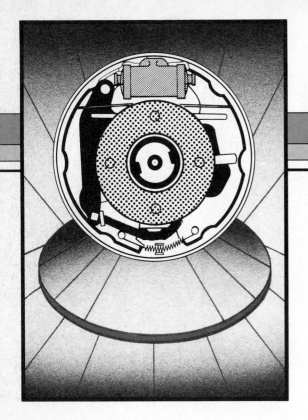

CHAPTER 3

HYDRAULIC-BRAKE-SYSTEM COMPONENTS

OBJECTIVES

After you have studied this chapter, you should be able to:

1. Describe the operation of master cylinders.

2. Describe the operation of fast-fill master cylinders.

3. Describe the operation of wheel cylinders and calipers.

4. Describe the operation of the pressure-differential switch, metering valve, and proportioning valve.

5. Describe the operation of stoplamp switches.

A complete hydraulic brake system on a car with front disc brakes and rear drum brakes is shown in Fig. 3-1. The system includes the master cylinder, calipers, wheel cylinders, and the components used to control the system operation. These components are the *pressure-differential switch*, the *metering valve*, and the *proportioning valve*. In many cars these components are combined in a single unit, called a *combination valve* or *brake control valve*. However, not all cars have a metering valve or a proportioning valve.

MASTER CYLINDERS

A dual master cylinder is shown in Fig. 3-2. The master cylinder houses the hydraulic-system input pistons (Fig. 3-3). The pistons are located in a drilled (or bored) hole in the master-cylinder housing called the *cylinder bore*.

The brake-pedal pushrod connects from the brake-pedal arm to the master cylinder (Fig. 3-2). The pushrod fits through an opening in the dust boot, and the dust boot fits over the end of the master cylinder. The dust boot prevents dirt from entering the master cylinder.

Master-Cylinder Reservoirs

The master cylinder shown in Fig. 3-3 has a two-chamber fluid reservoir that holds a quantity of brake fluid. A dual master cylinder has two separate chambers: the *primary reservoir* and the *secondary reservoir*. A master cylinder in which the cylinder bore and reservoir are part of the same housing is called an *integral* master cylinder. Integral master cylinders are usually made of cast iron. A reservoir cover prevents dirt from contaminating the

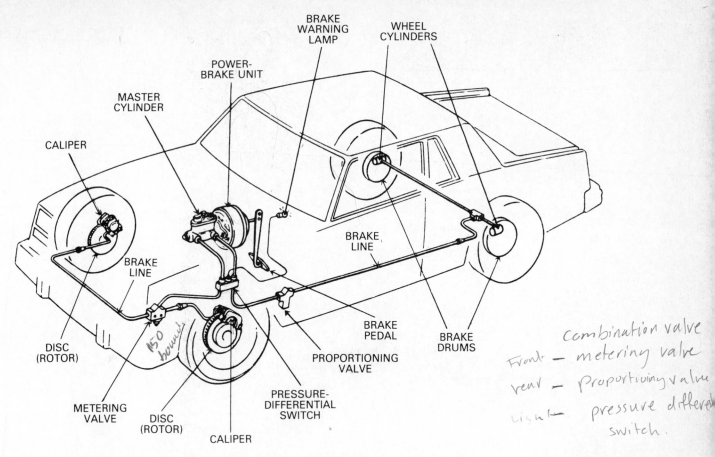

BRAKE WARNING LAMP

WHEEL CYLINDERS

POWER-BRAKE UNIT

MASTER CYLINDER

CALIPER

BRAKE LINE

BRAKE LINE

BRAKE PEDAL

BRAKE DRUMS

DISC (ROTOR)

M50 *brownel*

PROPORTIONING VALUE

METERING VALVE

DISC (ROTOR)

PRESSURE-DIFFERENTIAL SWITCH

CALIPER

Combination valve
Front — metering valve
rear — Proportioning valve
light — pressure differel
switch.

Fig. 3-1. A hydraulic brake system on a vehicle with front disc brakes and rear drum brakes.
(EIS Division of Parker Hannifin Corporation)

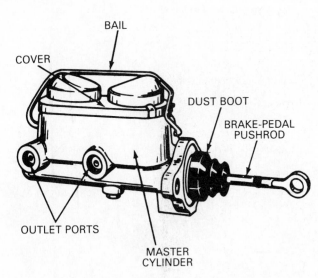

BAIL

COVER

DUST BOOT

BRAKE-PEDAL PUSHROD

OUTLET PORTS

MASTER CYLINDER

Fig. 3-2. A dual master cylinder. *(Wagner Division, Cooper Industries Inc.)*

brake fluid. The cover is held on with a bail (Fig. 3-2) or a bolt.

A *composite* master cylinder is one in which the reservoir is separate from the master-cylinder housing (Fig. 3-4). The reservoir is attached to the master-cylinder housing with rubber seals or grommets. The reservoirs used on some composite master cylinders are

plastic or nylon. These reservoirs are often translucent, or have translucent windows, so that the level of brake fluid can be seen without removing the cover (Fig. 3-5). A *translucent* material is one that is partially transparent and allows light to pass through it. The reservoir cover shown in Fig. 3-5 is also made of plastic, and it is held on the reservoir with locking tabs.

A reservoir with a fluid-level switch is shown in Fig. 3-6. When the brake fluid drops below a safe level, the switch contacts close. This turns on the brake warning lamp on the instrument panel.

Figure 3-7 shows a master cylinder that has the fluid reservoirs remotely located, away from the master-cylinder body. Hoses connect the reservoir to the master-cylinder body.

The reservoir that supplies brake fluid to the disc brakes is usually larger than the reservoir that supplies fluid to the drum brakes (Fig. 3-8). Caliper pistons are larger than wheel-cylinder pistons, so a larger quantity of brake fluid is transferred to the calipers as the lining wears.

Master-Cylinder Pistons

Two pistons are located in the master-cylinder bore (Fig. 3-3). The pushrod acts on the *primary piston* (Fig. 3-9), which is the piston closest to the firewall. The piston

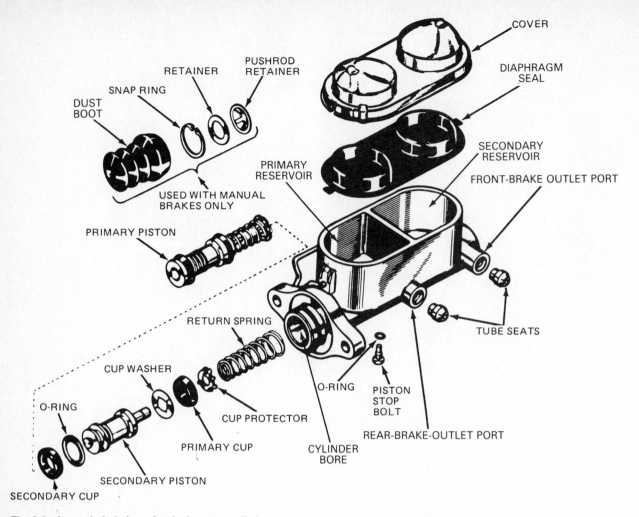

Fig. 3-3. An exploded view of a dual master cylinder. *(Wagner Division, Cooper Industries Inc.)*

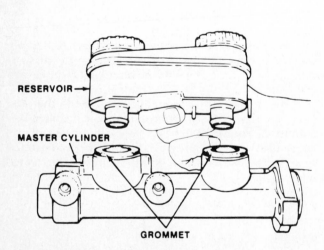

Fig. 3-4. A composite master cylinder, shown with the reservoir removed from the master-cylinder housing. *(Chrysler Corporation)*

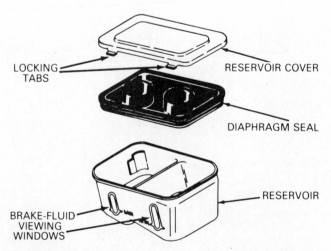

Fig. 3-5. A composite master-cylinder reservoir with translucent brake-fluid viewing windows. *(Chevrolet Motor Division of General Motors Corporation)*

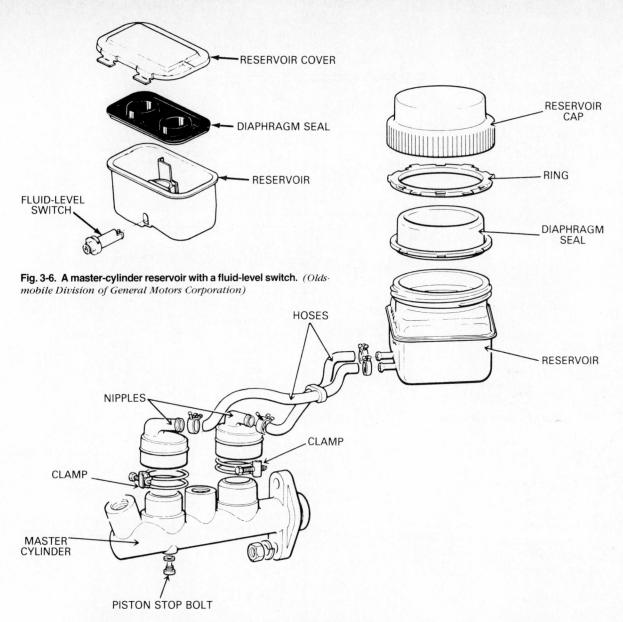

Fig. 3-6. A master-cylinder reservoir with a fluid-level switch. (*Oldsmobile Division of General Motors Corporation*)

Fig. 3-7. A master-cylinder reservoir that is remotely located from the master cylinder. (*Chrysler Corporation*)

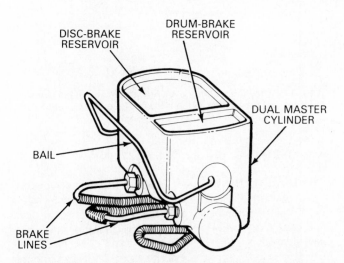

Fig. 3-8. A dual master cylinder, showing the relative sizes of the reservoirs. (*Ford Motor Company*)

closest to the front of the car is the *secondary piston*. The two pistons are in *tandem*, one behind the other. The pistons are spool-shaped, with two large-diameter parts called *lands* and a small-diameter part called a *groove* (Fig. 3-10).

The front end of the piston is the *face*, and the rear end is the *base*. The parts of the cylinder bore ahead of the pistons are the *high-pressure chambers* (Fig. 3-9). These chambers are filled with brake fluid. When the brakes are applied, the pushrod pushes the pistons forward, and the fluid in these chambers is pressurized. The parts of the bore around piston grooves are also filled with brake fluid. The fluid in these parts of the bore is not pressurized when the brakes are applied; therefore, they are called *low-pressure chambers*.

Each piston has a piston return spring located in the cylinder bore (Fig. 3-9). The secondary-piston return spring is between the closed end of the cylinder bore

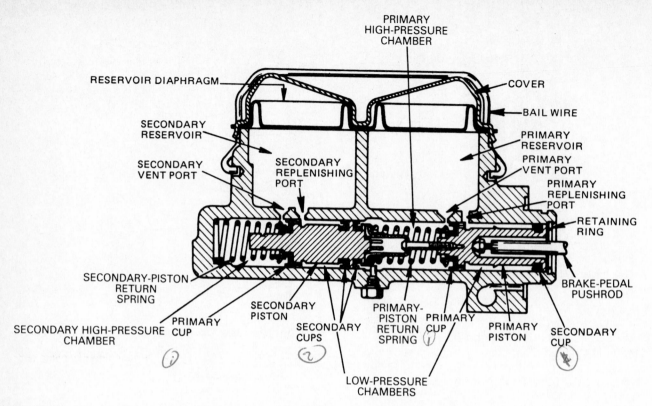

Fig. 3-9. The construction of a dual master cylinder. *(Wagner Division, Cooper Industries Inc.)*

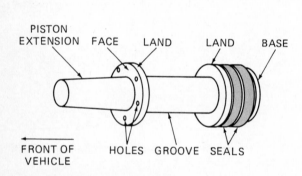

Fig. 3-10. A master-cylinder piston.

and the secondary piston. The primary-piston return spring is between the pistons. A retaining ring fits in a groove near the open end of the cylinder bore. The ring holds the pistons and return springs in the bore.

Piston Seals

The pistons have rubber seals, called *cups*, at each end (Fig. 3-9). The cups at the front of the pistons are called *primary cups*. The cups at the rear of the pistons are called *secondary cups*. The primary cups are positioned so that their open ends, or lips, face forward and fill with brake fluid. When the piston moves forward (Fig. 3-11), the brake fluid forces the lip of the cup tightly against the cylinder bore, making a tighter seal. Unless the lip of the cup or the cylinder bore is damaged, the lip prevents fluid from flowing past the cup. Cup seals prevent fluid flow in one direction only. When the piston moves

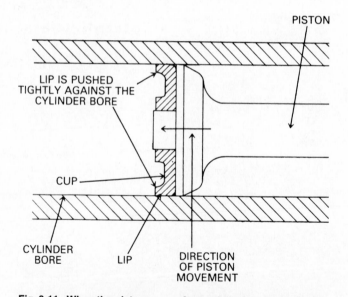

Fig. 3-11. When the piston moves forward, the lip of the cup seal is forced tightly against the cylinder bore, making a tight seal. *(EIS Division of Parker Hannifin Corporation)*

rearward, the cup deflects (Fig. 3-12) and fluid flows past the cup.

The lip of the secondary cup on the primary piston faces forward (Fig. 3-13), toward the low-pressure chamber. This prevents brake fluid from leaking past the seal and out of the cylinder bore. The secondary piston has two secondary-cup seals (Figs. 3-9 and 3-14). The lip of the rear cup faces rearward. On some master cylinders the rear seal is a cup seal and the front seal is an O-ring. O-ring seals prevent fluid flow in both directions of piston movement.

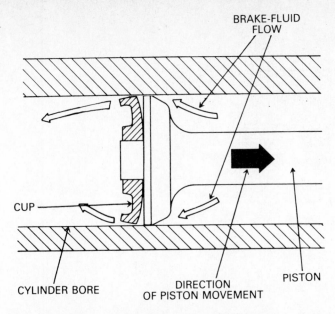

BRAKE-FLUID FLOW

CUP

CYLINDER BORE

DIRECTION OF PISTON MOVEMENT

PISTON

Fig. 3-12. When the piston moves rearward, the cup seal deflects, allowing brake fluid to flow past the seal. *(EIS Division of Parker Hannifin Corporation)*

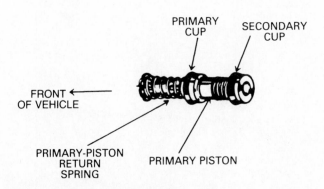

PRIMARY CUP

SECONDARY CUP

FRONT OF VEHICLE

PRIMARY-PISTON RETURN SPRING

PRIMARY PISTON

Fig. 3-13. A master-cylinder primary piston. *(Wagner Division, Cooper Industries Inc.)*

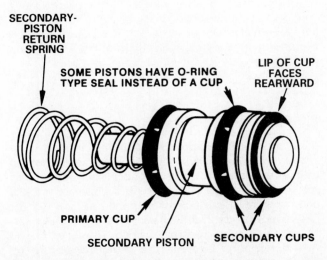

SECONDARY-PISTON RETURN SPRING

SOME PISTONS HAVE O-RING TYPE SEAL INSTEAD OF A CUP

LIP OF CUP FACES REARWARD

PRIMARY CUP

SECONDARY PISTON

SECONDARY CUPS

Fig. 3-14. A master-cylinder secondary piston. *(Bendix Aftermarket Brake Division)*

Master-Cylinder Reservoir Ports

In the master cylinder shown in Fig. 3-9 the fluid reservoirs are located above the cylinder bore. The primary reservoir is above the primary piston, and the secondary reservoir is above the secondary piston. Two holes, called *ports*, connect the bottom of each reservoir to the cylinder bore. The front ports are *vent ports*, and the rear ports are *replenishing ports*. The replenishing ports are larger than the vent ports. When the pistons are in their normal at-rest positions, the primary cup of each piston is between the vent port and the replenishing port (Fig. 3-15).

When Rebuilding a master cylinder.

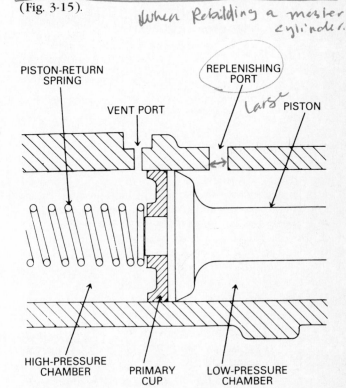

PISTON-RETURN SPRING

REPLENISHING PORT

VENT PORT

Large **PISTON**

HIGH-PRESSURE CHAMBER

PRIMARY CUP

LOW-PRESSURE CHAMBER

Fig. 3-15. The normal, or rest, position of a piston in the master cylinder. *(EIS Division of Parker Hannifin Corporation)*

NOTE Manufacturers have called master-cylinder ports by various names. Following the SAE Recommended Practice, this book uses the names "vent port" and "representing port."

MASTER-CYLINDER OPERATION
Applying the Brakes

As the brake pedal is depressed, force is applied to the brake-pedal pushrod (Fig. 3-16). The pushrod, in turn,

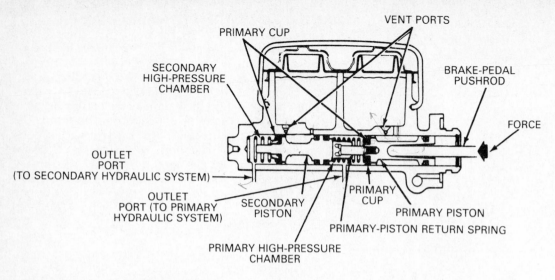

Fig. 3-16. The position of the pistons in the master cylinder when the brakes are applied. *(Wagner Division, Cooper Industries Inc.)*

applies force to the primary piston. This pushes the piston forward in the cylinder bore. Initially, no pressure is built up ahead of the piston in the high-pressure chamber. This is because fluid is pushed through the vent port into the reservoir. But as the lip of the primary cup moves past the vent port, the fluid ahead of the piston is trapped between the pistons and pressurized.

The secondary piston is pushed forward in the cylinder bore by a combination of two forces:

- The primary piston pushes the primary-piston return spring against the secondary piston.

- As the primary piston moves forward, the brake fluid trapped in the cylinder bore between the pistons pushes against the secondary piston.

Pressure is built up in the secondary high-pressure chamber in the same manner as in the primary high-pressure chamber. Outlet ports in each chamber allow brake lines to be attached to the master cylinder (Fig. 3-16). The hydraulic pressure in both high-pressure chambers is transmitted through the brake lines to operate the brakes at the wheels. Each high-pressure chamber controls one section of the hydraulic brake system.

The section of the system that is connected to the primary high-pressure chamber is the *primary hydraulic system*. The section connected to the secondary high-pressure chamber is the *secondary hydraulic system*. On some vehicles with front/rear–split hydraulic systems, the primary hydraulic system operates the front brakes. On others, it operates the rear brakes.

Drum brakes have retracting springs that hold the brake shoes away from the drum while the brakes are released (Fig. 3-17). When the brakes are applied, hydraulic pressure increases in the wheel cylinders until the pistons begin to move outward. As the pistons move outward to push the brake shoes against the drums, brake fluid is pushed out of the master cylinder. The fluid flows from the master cylinder, through the brake lines, and into the wheel cylinders.

When disc brakes are in the released position, the caliper pistons are pulled back slightly by the piston seals

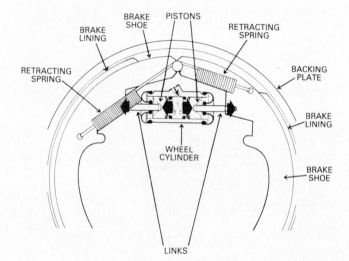

Fig. 3-17. Drum-brake components. *(Ford Motor Company)*

in the caliper bores (Fig. 3-18). When the brakes are applied, hydraulic pressure increases in the calipers until the pistons begin to move outward. As the pistons move outward to push the brake pads against the rotors, brake fluid is pushed out of the master cylinder. The fluid flows from the master cylinder, through the brake lines, and into the calipers.

Releasing the Brakes

After the brakes are applied and the brake pedal is released, brake fluid flows from the wheel cylinders and calipers back into the master cylinder. The piston return springs in the master cylinder push the primary and secondary pistons back to their normal positions (Fig. 3-19). The pistons move faster than the fluid, so a vacuum tries to develop in the high-pressure chambers. However, the replenishing ports prevent this from happening by keeping the low-pressure chambers filled with brake fluid.

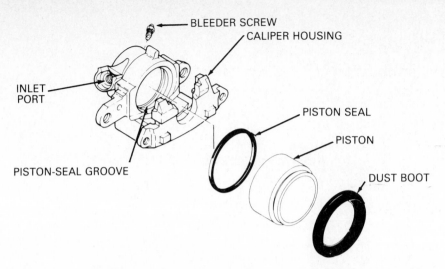

Fig. 3-18. **An exploded view of a caliper assembly .** *(Delco Moraine Division of General Motors Corporation)*

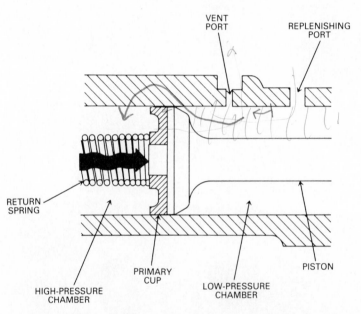

Fig. 3-19. **The return spring pushing back the piston when the brake pedal is released.**
(EIS Division of Parker Hannifin Corporation)

As the pistons move back, the brake fluid in the low-pressure chambers moves past the primary cups into the high-pressure chambers (Fig. 3-20). Because the lips of the primary cups face away from the motion of the piston, the fluid flows easily past the cups.

There are holes in the piston faces that help the fluid flow into the high-pressure chambers (Fig. 3-10). This keeps the high-pressure chambers filled. In some master cylinders, instead of holes in the piston faces, the piston faces have a smaller diameter. This allows a greater clearance between the piston face and the cylinder bore to permit a sufficient fluid flow. To replenish the fluid lost from the low-pressure chamber, brake fluid flows from the reservoir, through the replenishing port, and into the low-pressure chamber (Fig. 3-21).

As the pistons reach their normal at-rest positions, the primary cups uncover the vent ports. This allows any excess fluid returning to the master cylinder from the brake lines to flow into the reservoirs through the vent ports (Fig. 3-22).

The vent ports serve another purpose. Heavy brake usage creates high temperatures in the wheel cylinders and calipers, and this causes the brake fluid to expand. The vent ports allow the excess fluid to flow into the master-cylinder reservoirs; otherwise, the expanding fluid would partially apply the brakes.

RESIDUAL-PRESSURE CHECK VALVES

In some cars, a pressure of from 6 to 25 pounds per square inch (psi) [41.4 to 172.5 kilopascals (kPa)] is

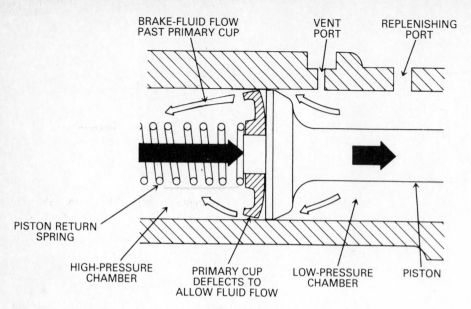

Fig. 3-20. Brake fluid moving past the primary cup as the piston returns to its rest position.
(EIS Division of Parker Hannifin Corporation)

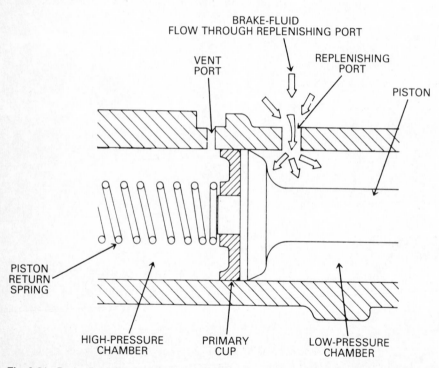

Fig. 3-21. Brake fluid flowing from the reservoir into the low-pressure chamber. *(EIS Division of Parker Hannifin Corporation)*

maintained in the brake lines leading to the drum brakes. This pressure keeps the wheel-cylinder cup seals held tightly against the cylinder bores. This prevents brake-fluid leakage out of the wheel cylinders and air leakage into the wheel cylinders.

Residual line pressure is maintained by a one-way check valve in the master-cylinder outlet (Fig. 3-23). This valve is the *residual pressure check valve.* A spring in the check valve normally holds the valve closed. When the brake pedal is depressed, fluid flows easily

through the valve and out the master-cylinder outlet port.

When the brake pedal is released, the fluid pressure in the brake lines overcomes the spring tension in the check valve and pushes the valve off its seat. Fluid then flows back into the master cylinder. When the brake fluid in the lines drops to a certain pressure, the spring forces the valve closed. Then, additional fluid is prevented from returning to the master cylinder. The fluid remains in the brake lines at the residual line pressure determined by the check-valve spring.

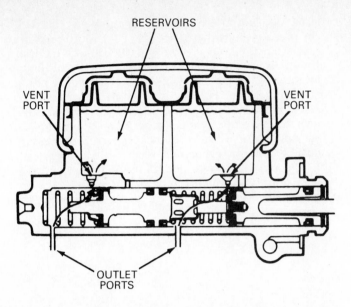

Fig. 3-22. **Brake fluid returning to the master cylinder and flowing back into the reservoirs.** *(Wagner Division, Cooper Industries Inc.)*

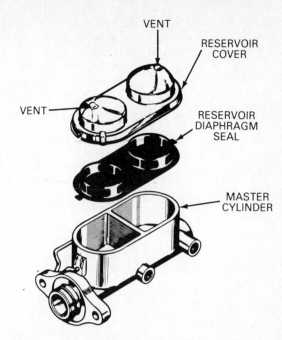

Fig. 3-24. **A master-cylinder reservoir cover and diagram seal.** *(EIS Division of Parker Hannifin Corporation)*

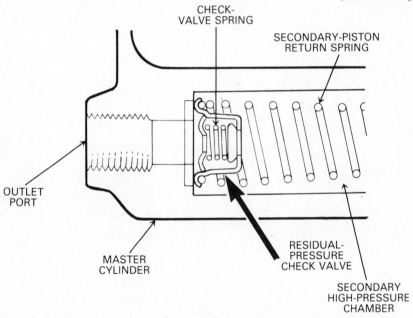

Fig. 3-23. **A residual-pressure check valve.** *(EIS Division of Parker Hannifin Corporation)*

VENTING THE MASTER CYLINDER

The brake-fluid level in the master cylinder changes as the brakes are applied and released. In addition, as the brake linings wear, fluid transfers from the master cylinder to the wheel cylinders and calipers. Because of this fluid movement, the top of the master cylinder cannot be sealed. If it were sealed, a vacuum would be created in the reservoir as brake fluid flowed out of the reservoir. The vacuum would not allow the brake fluid to flow freely out of the master cylinder.

To prevent a vacuum from forming, the master cylinder cover is vented to the atmosphere. This allows air to flow into the reservoirs as the fluid levels drop. However, the cover must be vented in a way that prevents outside air from contacting the brake fluid. Air carries dirt particles and moisture, which would contaminate the brake fluid.

To prevent air from contacting the brake fluid, most cars have a diaphragm-type seal between the master cylinder and its cover (Fig. 3-24). The seal has expandable sections, and the cover has small vent openings. Therefore, as the fluid levels drop, air is drawn in through the vent openings in the cover, and the seal moves downward. The air remains above the diaphragm. In this way, a vacuum is not formed in the reservoirs, and the air does not contaminate the brake fluid.

HYDRAULIC-SYSTEM LEAKS

If a leak occurs in one half of the hydraulic system, the master cylinder will pressurize the fluid in the other half of the system. Figure 3-25 shows a leak in the secondary hydraulic system. When the brake pedal is depressed, the primary piston moves forward and begins to pres-

surize the fluid in the primary high-pressure chamber. The primary return spring, and the fluid under pressure, push against the secondary piston. Because of the leak, the secondary piston moves forward and pushes brake fluid out of the master cylinder. The secondary piston has an extension (Fig. 3-25). When there is a leak, the piston moves farther than normal, and the extension contacts the end of the cylinder bore. Now the primary piston builds up pressure in the primary high-pressure chamber, and the primary hydraulic system operates.

Figure 3-26 shows the leak in the primary hydraulic system. When the brake pedal is depressed, the primary piston moves forward and pushes fluid out of the

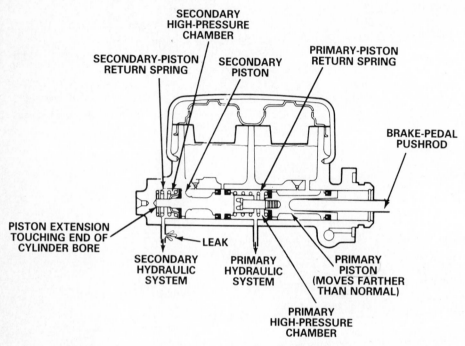

Fig. 3-25. The position of the pistons in a dual master cylinder when there is a leak in the secondary hydraulic system. *(Chevrolet Motor Division of General Motors Corporation)*

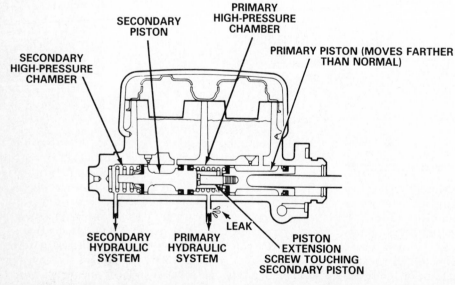

Fig. 3-26. The position of the pistons in a dual master cylinder when there is a leak in the primary hydraulic system. *(Chevrolet Motor Division of General Motors Corporation)*

32

master cylinder. Because of the leak, pressure does not build up in the primary high-pressure chamber. The primary piston has an extension, usually a screw extension. As the piston moves forward, the extension stops against the secondary piston. Therefore, brake pedal force is applied directly to the secondary piston. This pushes the secondary piston forward to pressurize the fluid in the secondary high-pressure chamber. Then the secondary hydraulic system will operate.

When a failure occurs, the brake pedal must be pushed closer to the floor to stop the car. This is because the pistons move farther than normal in the cylinder bore.

FAST-FILL MASTER CYLINDERS

On most cars with disc brakes, the brake pads rest lightly against the rotors when the brakes are not applied. Then, when the brakes are applied, very little brake-pedal movement is needed to push the brake pads against the rotor. A disadvantage is the slight drag on the rotors, which increases fuel consumption.

To improve fuel economy, some cars have *low-drag disc brakes*. With these brakes, the brake pads are pulled away from the rotor when the brakes are not applied. Therefore, when the brakes are applied, a large quantity of brake fluid must quickly flow to the calipers to move the pads into contact with the rotor. To do this with the type of master cylinder described above would require a large brake-pedal movement.

A *fast-fill*, or *quick-takeup, master cylinder* is shown in Fig. 3-27. The cylinder has a *stepbore* of two different diameters. A short length of the bore near the open end has a larger diameter than at the closed end. The face of the primary piston fits into the smaller bore, and the base of the piston fits into the larger bore. The secondary part of the fast-fill master cylinder is the same as in other master cylinders.

The primary reservoir has a fluid control valve (or quick-takeup valve) between the reservoir and the vent and replenishing ports. This valve is a ball check valve, held in its seat by a small spring. The valve also has a

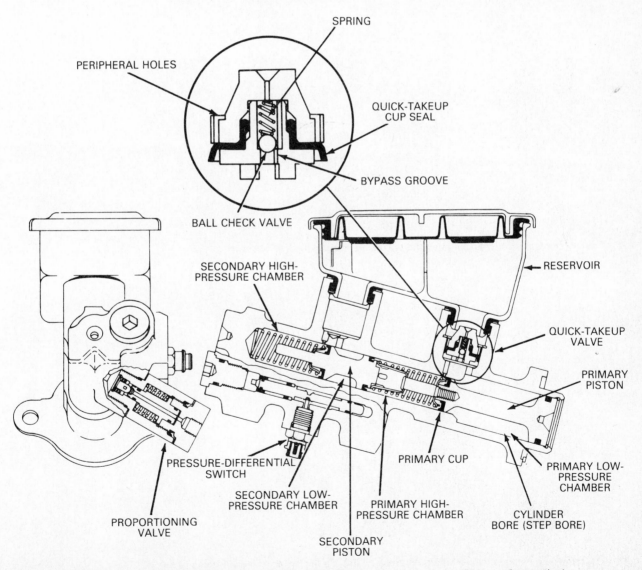

Fig. 3-27. A Delco Moraine quick-takeup master cylinder. *(Delco Moraine Division of General Motors Corporation)*

cup seal. Fluid is allowed to flow from the reservoir through small peripheral holes around the edge of the valve, and past the cup to the cylinder bore. But the valve does not allow fluid to flow from the cylinder bore to the reservoir unless a certain pressure is reached in the bore. When this pressure is reached, the pressure in the bore overcomes the tension of the check-valve spring and pushes the ball check valve off its seat.

When the brakes are applied, the primary piston moves forward into the smaller-diameter part of the cylinder bore (Fig. 3-28). This causes the brake fluid in the low-pressure chamber to build up pressure, because the base of the piston pushes the fluid into a smaller volume than it originally occupied. As the pressure increases, brake fluid is forced past the primary cup into the high-pressure chamber ahead of the piston. This causes the pressure in the high-pressure chamber to build up quickly. When this occurs, the secondary piston moves

to pressurize the fluid in the secondary high-pressure chamber. With a relatively small brake-pedal movement, a large quantity of brake fluid is moved quickly to build up pressure in both high-pressure chambers.

When the brake fluid in the low-pressure chamber reaches a certain pressure, the quick-takeup valve opens. Excess fluid flows into the reservoir (Fig. 3-29). This limits the maximum pressure in the low-pressure chamber.

When the brake pedal is released, replenishing in the secondary section takes place in the same way as in other master cylinders (Fig. 3-30). Replenishing in the primary section takes place through the vent and replenishing ports and the quick-takeup valve. Fluid flows from the reservoir through the peripheral holes in the valve, past the valve cup seal (Fig. 3-27), and through the replenishing port into the low-pressure chamber. From there, the fluid flows past the primary cup into the high-pressure chamber.

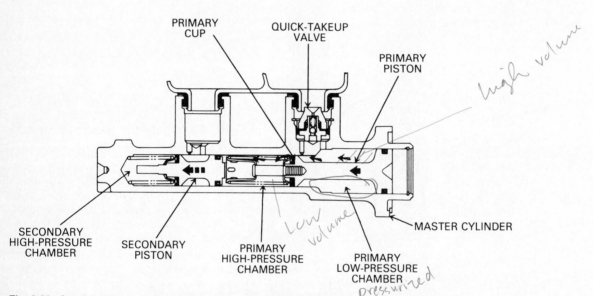

Fig. 3-28. A quick-takeup master cylinder when the brakes are initially applied. (*Delco Moraine Division of General Motors Corporation*)

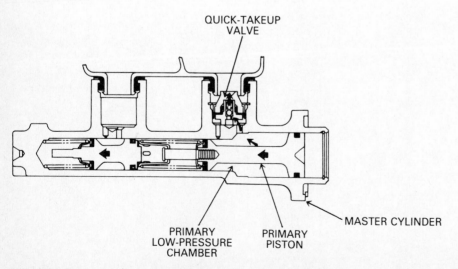

Fig. 3-29. A quick-takeup master cylinder when the pressure in the primary low-pressure chamber is high enough to open the quick-takeup valve. (*Delco Moraine Division of General Motors Corporation*)

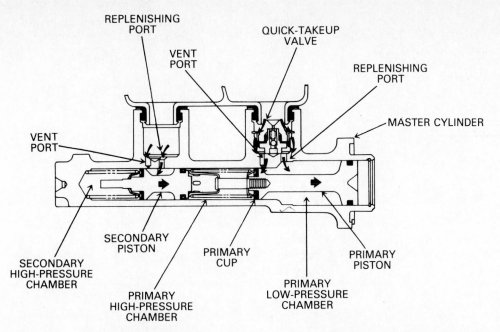

Fig. 3-30. A quick-takeup master cylinder when the brakes are released and the pistons are moving toward their normal, or rest, positions. *(Delco Moraine Division of General Motors Corporation)*

There is a small bypass groove in the quick-takeup check valve to allow for brake-fluid expansion caused by high temperature. If the brake fluid expands, it flows through the vent valve, through the groove in the quick-takeup valve, and into the reservoir.

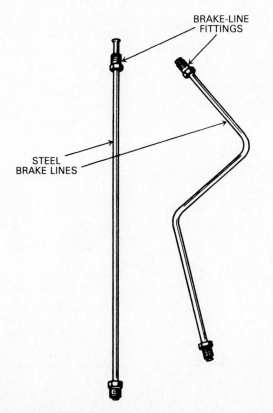

Fig. 3-31. Steel brake lines. *(Wagner Division, Cooper Industries Inc.)*

BRAKE LINES AND BRAKE HOSES

Brake lines (Fig. 3-31) and brake hoses (Fig. 3-32) connect the hydraulic-system components together. They transmit hydraulic pressure from the master cylinder to the wheel cylinders and calipers. The typical brake lines and hoses for a car with front disc brakes and rear drum brakes are shown in Fig. 3-33. Brake lines are made of steel, bent to fit along the frame or underbody of the car. The lines are routed so that they are protected from damage from road debris that may strike the underside of the car. Brake lines are usually clamped to the frame or underbody, to hold them in position.

Brake hoses are flexible and connect brake lines to parts of the hydraulic system that move with the car's suspension. Therefore, a hose is used at each front wheel to connect the brake line to the caliper. Another hose is used at the rear-axle assembly. It connects a brake line routed along the frame or underbody to a brake line routed along the axle assembly. The line along the axle assembly connects to wheel cylinders, or calipers, depending on the type of brakes used on the rear wheels.

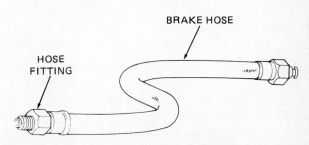

Fig. 3-32. A flexible brake hose. *(EIS Division of Parker Hannifin Corporation)*

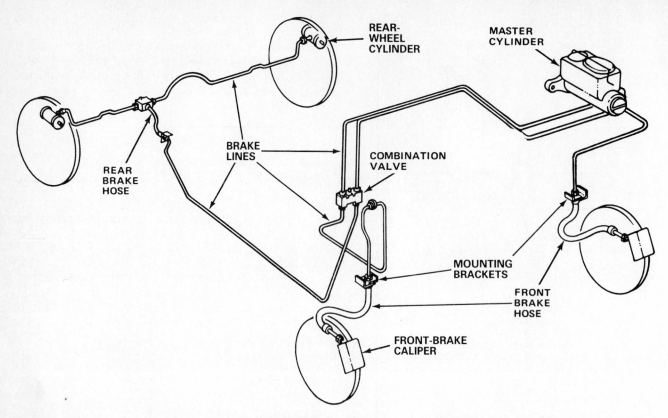

Fig. 3-33. The location of the brake lines on a rear-wheel-drive vehicle. *(American Motors Corporation)*

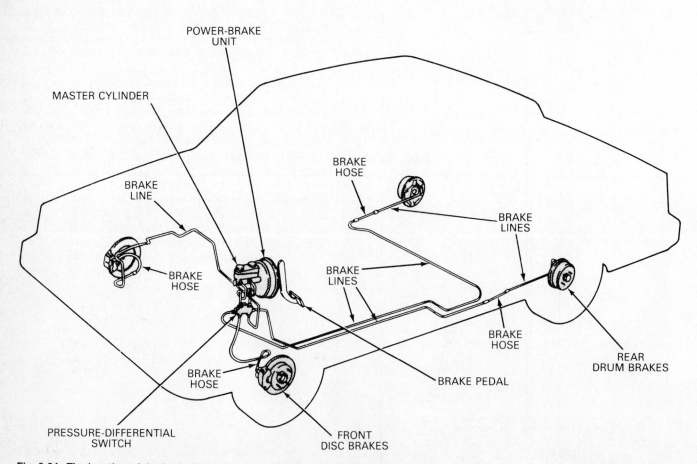

Fig. 3-34. The location of the brake lines on a front-wheel-drive vehicle. *(Chrysler Corporation)*

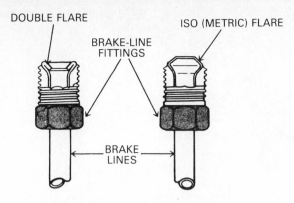

Fig. 3-35. Flared ends on steel brake lines. *(Bendix Aftermarket Brake Division)*

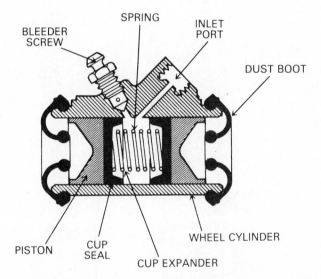

Fig. 3-36. The construction of a wheel cylinder. *(FMC Corporation)*

On a front-wheel-drive car, hoses are used at each rear wheel (Fig. 3-34).

Brake lines have flared ends that fit into a mating seat when they are connected, to provide a tight seal. Figure 3-35 shows two types of flared ends: the double flare and the International Standards Organization (ISO) flare, or metric flare.

WHEEL CYLINDERS

Wheel cylinders convert hydraulic pressure into a mechanical force (Fig. 3-36). Wheel cylinders are used with drum brakes to push the brake shoes into contact with the brake drum. An exploded view of a wheel cylinder is shown in Fig. 3-37. A brake line is attached to an *inlet port*, which is a threaded hole in the wheel cylinder. The brake line supplies brake fluid to the cylinder. The cylinder is filled with brake fluid. A bleeder screw is provided to *bleed*, or release, any air that enters the hydraulic system.

The holes for the brake line and the bleeder screw pass directly into the cylinder bore. Two pistons are located in the cylinder bore, and there are cup seals on the inside surfaces of the pistons. The lips of the cups face into the cylinder. A spring and metal cup expanders are used to hold the cups in position against the pistons (Figs. 3-37 and 3-38). The cup expanders help keep the lips of the cups held firmly against the cylinder bore. They help prevent brake-fluid leakage out of the wheel cylinder, and air leakage into the wheel cylinder, when the brakes are not applied. When cup expanders are used, residual-pressure check valves are not needed.

When the brake pedal is depressed, the master cylinder pressurizes the brake fluid in the hydraulic system and pushes brake fluid into the wheel cylinders. The lips of the cups are pushed against the cylinder bore to form a tight seal, and the pistons are pushed away from each

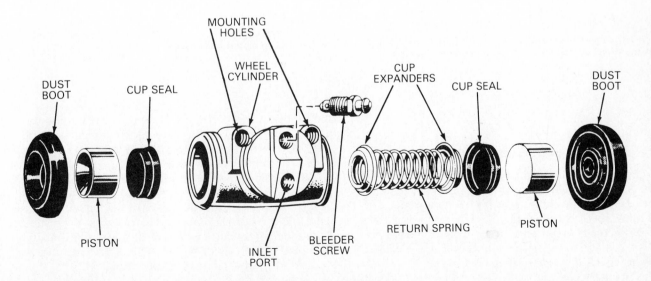

Fig. 3-37. An exploded view of a wheel cylinder. *(Ford Motor Company)*

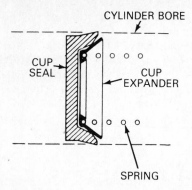

Fig. 3-38. A cup expander holding a cup seal against the cylinder bore. *(FMC Corporation)*

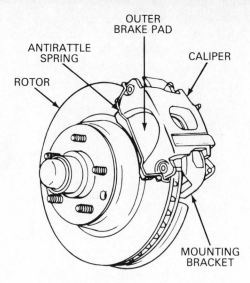

Fig. 3-40. A disc-brake caliper in position on its mounting bracket. *(FMC Corporation)*

other by hydraulic pressure. Small rods, called links, transmit the force of the pistons to the brake shoes (Fig. 3-17). On some cars the brake shoes have projections (Fig. 3-39) that fit into the cylinders and contact the pistons directly. Dust boots (Fig. 3-36) cover the ends of the cylinders to prevent dirt and moisture from contaminating the cylinder bore. The links, or brake-shoe projections, pass through openings in the dust boots.

When the brakes are released, retracting springs pull the brake shoes away from the drum. The brake shoes push against the links, which push the pistons in toward the center of the wheel cylinder. This action pushes some brake fluid out of the wheel cylinder, through the brake lines, and back to the master cylinder.

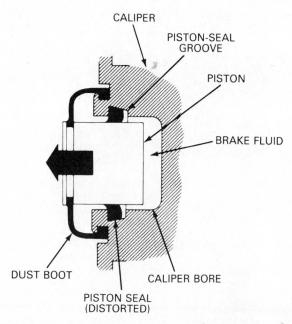

Fig. 3-41. A piston moving out of the caliper bore, causing the piston seal to distort. *(EIS Division of Parker Hannifin Corporation)*

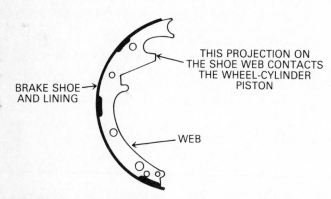

Fig. 3-39. A brake-shoe web, which has a projection that contacts the wheel-cylinder piston. *(Bendix Aftermarket Brake Division)*

CALIPERS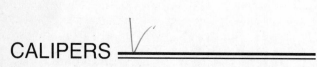

A caliper converts hydraulic pressure into a mechanical force. A caliper houses the piston (or pistons) and holds the brake pads in position near the friction surface of a disc-brake rotor. A caliper that has one piston is shown in position on its mounting bracket in Fig. 3-40. The piston is located in a drilled (or bored) hole in the caliper housing, called the *caliper bore* (Fig. 3-41).

A brake hose is attached to a threaded *inlet port* in the caliper (Fig. 3-18). The hose supplies brake fluid to

the caliper. A bleeder screw is also provided in the caliper to release any air that enters the hydraulic system. The inlet port and the hole for the bleeder screw pass directly into the caliper bore.

The caliper bore has a groove that holds a rubber seal (Fig. 3-41). The piston fits into the bore and is gripped tightly by the seal. The bore is filled with brake fluid, and the seal prevents fluid leakage past the piston. A dust boot fits into grooves in the piston and in the open end of the caliper bore. The boot prevents dirt or moisture from contaminating the caliper bore.

When the brake pedal is depressed, the master cylinder pressurizes the brake fluid in the hydraulic system and pushes brake fluid into the caliper. This forces the piston out of the bore, pushing the brake pad into contact with the rotor to apply the brakes. As the piston moves out of the bore, the piston seal distorts, or twists slightly (Fig. 3-41).

When the brake pedal is released, hydraulic pressure is removed from the piston. The seal returns to its original shape and pulls the piston back slightly (Fig. 3-42). This removes the braking force from the rotor, and brake fluid flows back to the master cylinder. Springs are not used to retract the pistons in most disc brakes. Various types of disc-brake calipers and their operation are described in Chap. 5.

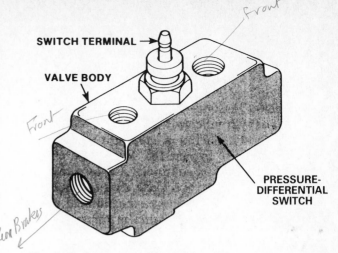

Fig. 3-43. A pressure-differential switch. (*Bendix Aftermarket Brake Division*)

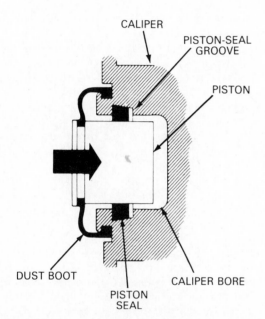

Fig. 3-42. A piston seal returning to its original shape, pulling the piston back a small distance. (*EIS Division of Parker Hannifin Corporation*)

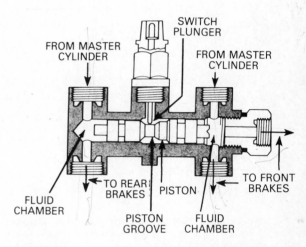

Fig. 3-44. The construction of a pressure-differential switch. (*Bendix Aftermarket Brake Division*)

PRESSURE-DIFFERENTIAL SWITCHES

The *pressure-differential switch* (Fig. 3-43) is also called a *pressure-differential valve* or a *brake warning-lamp switch*. It is an electric switch controlled by hydraulic pressure. The pressure-differential switch is connected between both sections of a dual hydraulic system (Fig. 3-44). The switch turns on a warning lamp on the instrument panel to signal a failure (leak) in one section of the hydraulic brake system. This alerts the driver that there is low pressure in one section of the hydraulic system.

There are threaded holes in the switch that lead to two internal chambers in the switch (Fig. 3-44). Brake lines thread into the holes and connect the switch to the hydraulic system. One chamber in the switch connects to the primary hydraulic system, and the other chamber connects to the secondary hydraulic system. A passage in the switch joins the two chambers. A piston

is located in the passage and is free to move in either direction toward either chamber.

An electric switch has a spring-loaded plunger that pushes against the piston. In the differential switch shown in Fig. 3-44, there is a groove in the center of the piston.

When the brake system is operating normally, there is equal hydraulic pressure in both sections of the hydraulic system. Therefore, the pressure in both chambers of the pressure-differential switch is equal. With equal pressure at both ends of the piston, the piston is centered in the switch. The switch plunger is extended and rests in the groove in the piston (Fig. 3-45a). With the plunger in this position, the switch contacts are apart, and the switch is off.

If a leak occurs in one section of the hydraulic system, the pressure in one chamber of the differential switch will drop. The difference in pressure from one chamber to the other will push the piston toward the low-pressure chamber. When the piston moves, the switch plunger is pushed out of the groove (Fig. 3-45b). This closes the switch contacts, which turns on the switch and lights the warning lamp.

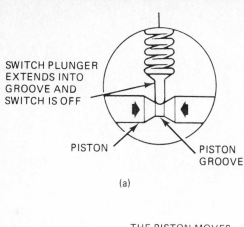

SWITCH PLUNGER
EXTENDS INTO
GROOVE AND
SWITCH IS OFF

PISTON   PISTON
                GROOVE

(a)

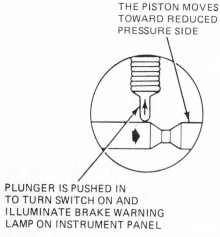

THE PISTON MOVES
TOWARD REDUCED
PRESSURE SIDE

PLUNGER IS PUSHED IN
TO TURN SWITCH ON AND
ILLUMINATE BRAKE WARNING
LAMP ON INSTRUMENT PANEL

(b)

Fig. 3-45. A pressure-differential-switch piston: *(a)* the piston in the normal (or center) position, with the switch plunger resting in the piston groove; *(b)* the piston moved toward the reduced-pressure side, with the switch plunger pushed out of the groove.

If the leak occurs in the other section of the system, the piston will be pushed in the opposite direction to turn on the switch. The pressure-differential switch is often part of the brake control valve, which is described in the following section of this chapter. Some pressure-differential switches are located in the master cylinder (Fig. 3-27).

Some vehicles have a brake-fluid-level switch in the master cylinder instead of a pressure-differential switch. On these vehicles, the brake warning lamp is turned on when the fluid level in the master cylinder drops too low.

HYDRAULIC-SYSTEM VALVES

A *valve* is a device that controls the pressure or the flow of a liquid or a gas either by opening or closing or by partially obstructing the flow. Valves, such as the metering valve and the proportioning valve, are used in the hydraulic system to control the pressure and flow of brake fluid.

Metering Valves

Metering valves (Fig. 3-46) are also called hold-off valves. They are used on cars that have both disc brakes and drum brakes so that the disc brakes and the drum brakes operate at approximately the same time. Without a metering valve, the disc brakes would operate first when the brakes were applied. This is because the disc-brake pads are in light contact with (or are very close to) the rotors, but the drum-brake shoes are pulled away from the drums by retracting springs. When the brake pedal is depressed, the pads do not have as far to move as the shoes, and the disc brakes would apply first.

The metering valve delays the operation of the disc brakes until a pressure of 75 to 135 psi [517.5 to 931.5 kPa] has built up in the hydraulic system. When the brake pedal is depressed, the initial buildup of hydraulic pressure moves the brake shoes outward, against retracting-spring tension. The metering valve is closed during this time. Then, after a slight delay, when the pressure in the hydraulic system reaches between 75 to 135 psi [517.5 to 931.5 kPa], the metering valve opens, allowing hydraulic pressure to reach the disc brakes. Therefore, all the brakes operate at approximately the same time.

One type of metering valve has a brake line from the master cylinder attached to a threaded hole in the valve; this hole is called the inlet port (Fig. 3-47). The brake line supplies brake fluid to the valve. There are two other threaded holes in the valve; these are the outlet ports. Brake lines connect from the outlet ports to the front-disc-brake calipers. The lines transmit fluid pressure from the valve to the calipers.

There is a small seal at the inlet of the valve. When the hydraulic pressure in the system is between 0 psi [0 kPa] (brakes released) and approximately 3 psi [20.7 kPa], the inlet seal is open. This allows movement of brake fluid through the valve. This movement is necessary to allow for expansion or contraction of the brake fluid with temperature.

When the brake pedal is depressed, the hydraulic pressure quickly goes above 3 psi [20.7 kPa]. This causes

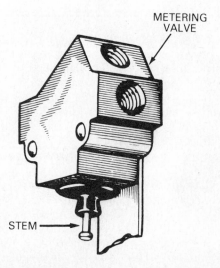

METERING
VALVE

STEM

Fig. 3-46. A metering valve. *(Chrysler Corporation)*

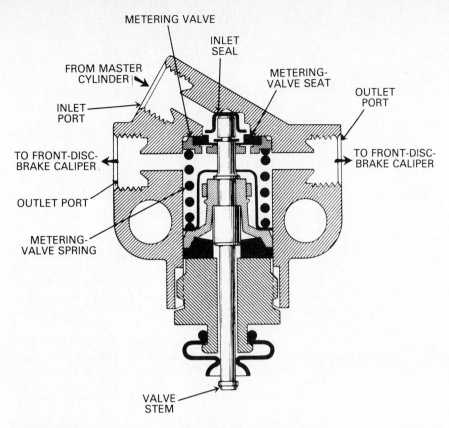

METERING VALVE
INLET SEAL
FROM MASTER CYLINDER
METERING-VALVE SEAT
INLET PORT
OUTLET PORT
TO FRONT-DISC-BRAKE CALIPER
TO FRONT-DISC-BRAKE CALIPER
OUTLET PORT
METERING-VALVE SPRING
VALVE STEM

Fig. 3-47. The construction of a metering valve. *(FMC Corporation)*

the inlet seal to be pushed into the valve, closing the inlet. Therefore, brake fluid can no longer flow through the valve.

A spring in the metering valve holds the valve closed against its seat. When the inlet pressure reaches approximately 75 to 135 psi [517.5 to 931.5 kPa], the fluid pressure overcomes the spring tension. This pushes the valve off its seat, opening the valve. Now brake fluid pressure is transmitted through the valve, and the front disc brakes operate.

Metering valves can be manually operated by pulling or pushing a valve stem (depending on the valve). This is done under certain conditions when bleeding the air from the hydraulic system. Metering valves are often part of the brake control valve (described later in this section under "Brake Control Valves").

Proportioning Valves

A proportioning valve, or pressure control valve, is used on some cars with front disc brakes and rear drum brakes (Fig. 3-48). Its purpose is to reduce hydraulic pressure to the rear-wheel cylinders during heavy braking. During a quick stop, most of the vehicle weight shifts to the front wheels. With little weight on the rear wheels, they would easily lock up and skid. By reducing hydraulic pressure to the rear brakes, there is less tendency for the wheels to lock. The proportioning valve does not reduce hydraulic pressure to the rear brakes during normal braking.

On many cars with a diagonally split hydraulic system, there are two proportioning valves. This is because each section of the hydraulic system controls one rear-wheel brake. On some cars the proportioning valves are located inside the master-cylinder housing or attach directly to the outlet fittings on the master cylinder (Fig. 3-49).

The proportioning valve has a passage that contains a piston (Fig. 3-50). The piston separates the passage into two chambers: an inlet chamber and an outlet chamber. A spring pushes the piston to the right in Fig. 3-50. The valve has two threaded holes called the inlet port and

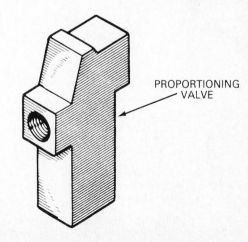

PROPORTIONING VALVE

Fig. 3-48. A proportioning valve. *(Chrysler Corporation)*

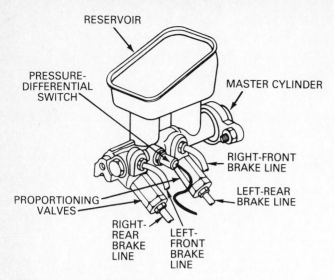

Fig. 3-49. Proportioning valves shown attached to a master cylinder. *(Bendix Aftermarket Brake Division)*

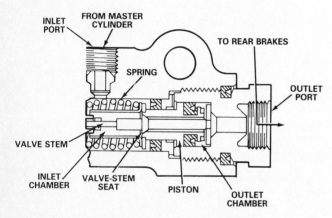

Fig. 3-50. The construction of a proportioning valve. *(Chevrolet Motor Division of General Motors Corporation)*

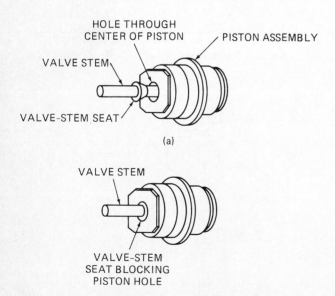

Fig. 3-51. A proportioning-valve piston and valve stem: *(a)* the hole in the piston open; *(b)* the hole in the piston blocked by the valve-stem seat.

the outlet port. The brake line from the master cylinder attaches to the inlet port and supplies brake fluid to the inlet chamber of the valve. A brake line attaches to the outlet port and transmits hydraulic pressure from the outlet chamber to the rear wheel cylinders.

The piston has a hole through its center and fits over a valve stem (Figs. 3-50 and 3-51*a*). One part of the valve stem is larger in diameter and is called the valve-stem seat. If the piston is moved against spring tension (to the left in Fig. 3-50), the end of the piston is pushed against the valve-stem seat (Fig. 3-51*b*). The seat blocks the opening of the hole through the center of the piston. When this occurs, brake fluid cannot flow through the valve, and the valve is closed. When the piston moves to the right in Fig. 3-50, the valve-stem seat does not block the hole in the piston, and the valve is open (Fig. 3-51*a*).

When the brakes are applied lightly, the hydraulic pressure in the proportioning valve is low. When the pressure is low, the spring holds the piston to the right in Fig. 3-50. In this position, the piston does not block fluid flow through the valve, and full hydraulic pressure is transmitted to the rear wheel cylinders.

The right end of the piston has a larger surface area than the left end (Fig. 3-52). When the brakes are applied harder, the hydraulic pressure in the valve increases. When a pressure called the *split point* is reached, hydraulic pressure acting on the larger (right) end of the piston overcomes the spring tension and pushes the piston to the left in Fig. 3-50. In this position, the piston restricts the flow of brake fluid through the valve and causes a pressure drop across the valve. Then less pressure is transmitted to the wheel cylinders than is applied to the inlet of the valve. As pressure increases on the inlet side of the valve, it also increases on the outlet side, but at a lesser amount. The split point for a typical proportioning valve is approximately 300 psi [2,070 kPa].

Proportioning-Valve Action
Figure 3-53 shows a graph of the pressure in the inlet chamber of the valve

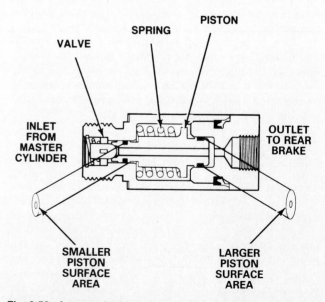

Fig. 3-52. A proportioning valve, showing the larger piston surface area at the outlet of the valve, and the smaller piston surface area at the inlet of the valve. *(General Motors Corporation)*

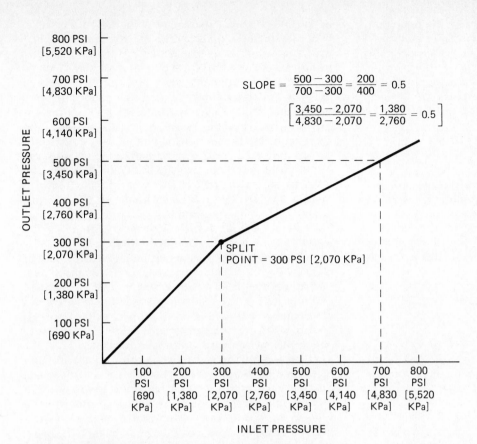

SLOPE $= \dfrac{500 - 300}{700 - 300} = \dfrac{200}{400} = 0.5$

$$\left[\dfrac{3,450 - 2,070}{4,830 - 2,070} = \dfrac{1,380}{2,760} = 0.5 \right]$$

SPLIT
POINT = 300 PSI [2,070 KPa]

Fig. 3-53. A graph of the hydraulic pressure in the inlet chamber of a proportioning valve compared to the pressure in the outlet chamber.

compared to the pressure in the outlet chamber. The horizontal direction on the graph shows the hydraulic-system pressure applied to the inlet of the proportioning valve. The vertical direction shows the outlet pressure from the valve.

The graph shows that on light brake applications, if the hydraulic-system pressure is below the split point (300 psi [2,070 kPa] in this example), the proportioning valve does not reduce the pressure to the rear wheel cylinders. Then, full pressure is transmitted to the wheel cylinders. But above 300 psi [2,070 kPa] the valve reduces the pressure. For example, when the hydraulic-system pressure applied to the valve is increased to 700 psi [4,830 kPa], the pressure to the rear wheels is only increased to 500 psi [3,450 kPa]. Therefore, for a 400-psi [2,760-kPa] increase in inlet pressure (700 psi - 300 psi [4,830 kPa - 2,070 kPa]), the outlet pressure increases by only 200 psi [1,380 kPa] (500 psi - 300 psi [3,450 kPa - 2,070 kPa]). The ratio of change in outlet pressure to the change in inlet pressure is called the *slope* of the proportioning valve:

$$\text{Slope} = \frac{\text{change in outlet pressure}}{\text{change in inlet pressure}}$$

In this example the slope is

$$\frac{200 \text{ psi}}{400 \text{ psi}} = 0.5$$

$$\left[\frac{1,380 \text{ kPa}}{2,760 \text{ kPa}} = 0.5 \right]$$

Load-Sensing Proportioning Valves Some vehicles have a load-sensing or height-sensing proportioning valve. Figure 3-54 shows a load-sensing proportioning valve, which has a lever and a rod that attaches to a rear-wheel control-arm bracket. The control arm is part of the vehicle suspension. When there is no load on the rear of the vehicle, the valve operates normally. When the rear end is heavily loaded, the rod moves the

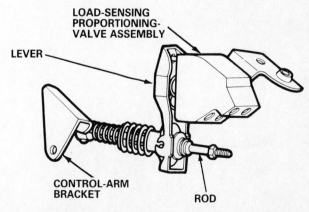

Fig. 3-54. A load-sensing proportioning valve. (*Ford Motor Company*)

43

lever and adjusts the proportioning valve. Then the valve does not reduce the hydraulic pressure to the rear wheel cylinders as much as when the vehicle is unloaded. This is done because there is less tendency to lock up the rear wheels when there is greater weight on the wheels. In addition, the added weight at the rear of the vehicle requires greater braking force to stop the vehicle.

Brake Control Valves

The pressure-differential switch, the metering valve, and the proportioning valve are often combined in a single unit called the combination valve, or brake control valve (Fig. 3-55). Because this valve has three functions, it is also called a three-function valve. Figure 3-56 shows a brake control valve used in a front/rear—split hydraulic system.

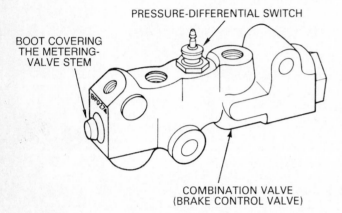

Fig. 3-55. A brake control valve. (*Bendix Aftermarket Brake Division*)

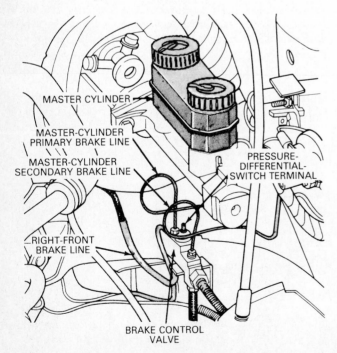

Fig. 3-56. The location of a brake control valve. (*Chrysler Corporation*)

44

Brake lines connect the master cylinder to the valve. Other brake lines connect the valve to the calipers and wheel cylinders. A diagram of a hydraulic system that includes a brake control valve is shown in Fig. 3-57.

The construction of a brake control valve is shown in Fig. 3-58. Dotted lines are used to separate the functional parts of the valve. The metering valve is the left part of the valve, the pressure-differential switch is the center part, and the proportioning valve is the right part.

In the brake control valve shown in Fig. 3-58, the piston that is part of the pressure-differential switch connects to the valve stem of the proportioning valve. If there is a failure in the front hydraulic system, the piston moves to the left to turn on the warning switch. This movement also pulls the proportioning-valve stem to the left and prevents proportioning to the rear brakes. This allows full hydraulic pressure to be applied to the rear brakes if there is a failure in the front hydraulic system.

Another type of brake control valve is the two-function valve (Fig. 3-59). It combines a pressure-differential switch with a proportioning valve. Figure 3-60 shows a two-function valve that combines a pressure-differential switch with a metering valve.

Figure 3-61 shows a brake control valve without a pressure-differential switch. This is because the valve is used on a car that has a brake-fluid-level switch in the master cylinder. The control valve has a proportioning valve and a shuttle valve. The shuttle valve is a piston that is located in a passage between two fluid chambers. The left chamber in Fig. 3-61 connects to the rear hydraulic system, and the right chamber connects to the front hydraulic system. The shuttle valve operates in a similar manner to the piston in a pressure-differential switch.

The function of the shuttle valve is to bypass the proportioning valve if there is a failure in the front hydraulic system. Low pressure in the front hydraulic system causes the shuttle valve to move to the right as in Fig. 3-61. This opens a bypass passage, allowing full hydraulic pressure to the rear brakes.

STOPLAMP SWITCHES

The stoplamp switch controls the stoplamps at the rear of the vehicle. When the brake pedal is depressed, the switch turns on (its contacts close) and lights the lamps. A stoplamp circuit diagram is shown in Fig. 3-62. When the switch contacts close, the switch connects battery voltage to the stoplamps. Stoplamp switches can either be hydraulic or mechanical.

A hydraulic switch is shown in Fig. 3-63. This switch threads into the end of the master cylinder. A metal disc is located near two electric contacts. The disc is held away from the contacts by a small spring. A rubber diaphragm, placed next to the metal disc, acts as a seal; it prevents brake fluid from reaching the switch contacts and leaking out of the switch assembly. When the brake pedal is depressed, hydraulic pressure builds up in the master cylinder. The pressure pushes against the diaphragm, which is pushed against the metal disc. When the force on the diaphragm is strong enough to over-

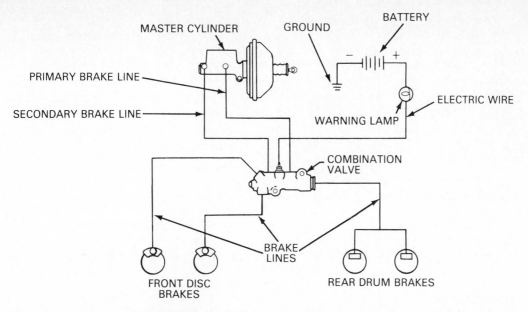

Fig. 3-57. A diagram of a hydraulic system that uses a brake control valve. (*Delco Moraine Division of General Motors Corporation*)

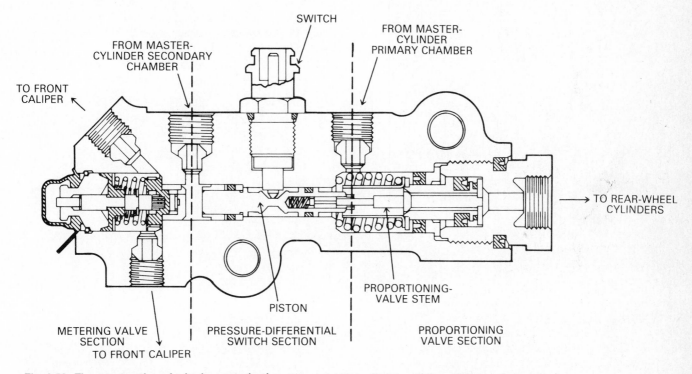

Fig. 3-58. The construction of a brake control valve. (*Chevrolet Motor Division of General Motors Corporation*)

come the spring tension, the metal disc is pushed against the electric contacts. This turns on the switch and lights the stoplamps. When the brake pedal is released, the spring pushes the disc away from the contacts and the switch is turned off.

A mechanical stoplamp switch is shown in Fig. 3-64. The switch is operated by the movement of the brake-pedal arm. When the brakes are not applied, the switch is off (its contacts are open). The switch is attached to the brake-pedal arm, and there is a small clearance between the pedal-arm pin and the brake-pedal-pushrod eye (Fig. 3-65). When the brakes are applied, the pedal arm moves the switch plunger against the brake-pedal

pushrod (Fig. 3-66). This closes the switch contacts, turning on the stoplamps.

Another type of mechanical stoplamp switch is shown in Fig. 3-67. This switch attaches with a clip to a bracket near the brake-pedal arm. The switch has a spring-loaded plunger. The spring pushes the plunger outward and keeps the switch in the ON position. When the brakes are not applied, the brake-pedal arm rests against the switch plunger. This pushes the plunger into the switch and holds the switch in the OFF position. When the switch is off, the stoplamps are off. When the brake pedal is depressed, the plunger is released. This turns the switch on and lights the stoplamps.

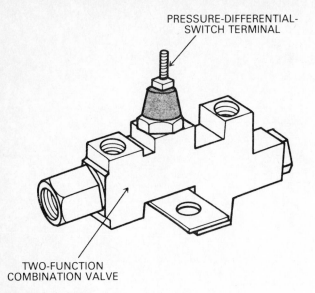

PRESSURE-DIFFERENTIAL-
SWITCH TERMINAL

TWO-FUNCTION
COMBINATION VALVE

Fig. 3-59. A two-function brake control valve that combines a pressure-differential switch with a proportioning valve. *(Bendix Aftermarket Brake Division)*

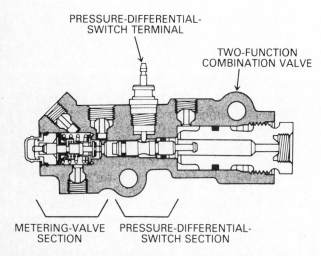

PRESSURE-DIFFERENTIAL-
SWITCH TERMINAL

TWO-FUNCTION
COMBINATION VALVE

METERING-VALVE
SECTION

PRESSURE-DIFFERENTIAL-
SWITCH SECTION

Fig. 3-60. A two-function brake control valve that combines a pressure-differential switch with a metering valve. *(Bendix Aftermarket Brake Division)*

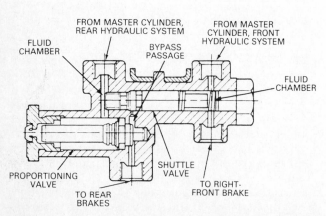

FROM MASTER CYLINDER,
REAR HYDRAULIC SYSTEM

FROM MASTER
CYLINDER, FRONT
HYDRAULIC SYSTEM

FLUID
CHAMBER

BYPASS
PASSAGE

FLUID
CHAMBER

PROPORTIONING
VALVE

SHUTTLE
VALVE

TO REAR
BRAKES

TO RIGHT-
FRONT BRAKE

Fig. 3-61. A brake control valve that contains a proportioning valve and a shuttle valve. *(Ford Motor Company)*

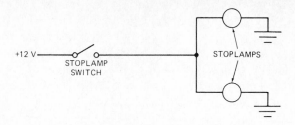

+12 V

STOPLAMP
SWITCH

STOPLAMPS

Fig. 3-62. A stoplamp circuit diagram.

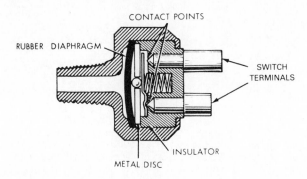

CONTACT POINTS

RUBBER DIAPHRAGM

SWITCH
TERMINALS

INSULATOR

METAL DISC

Fig. 3-63. A hydraulic stoplamp switch. *(FMC Corporation)*

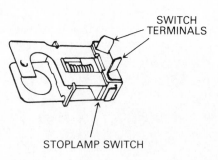

SWITCH
TERMINALS

STOPLAMP SWITCH

Fig. 3-64. A mechanical stoplamp switch. *(FMC Corporation)*

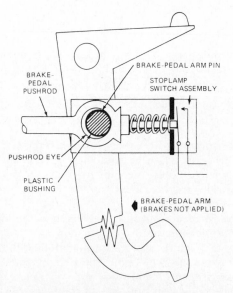

BRAKE-PEDAL ARM PIN

STOPLAMP
SWITCH ASSEMBLY

BRAKE-
PEDAL
PUSHROD

PUSHROD EYE

PLASTIC
BUSHING

BRAKE-PEDAL ARM
(BRAKES NOT APPLIED)

Fig. 3-65. A mechanical stoplamp switch mounted on the brake-pedal arm, shown when the brakes are not applied. *(Ford Motor Company)*

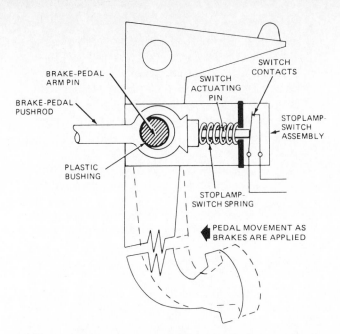

Fig. 3-66. A mechanical stoplamp switch mounted on the brake-pedal arm, shown when the brakes are applied. *(Ford Motor Company)*

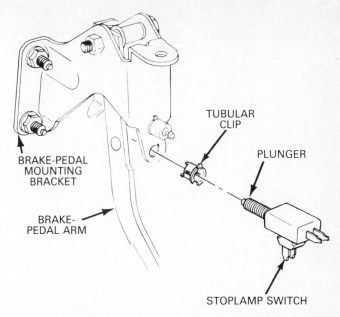

Fig. 3-67. A stoplamp switch that attaches to a bracket near the brake-pedal arm. *(Oldsmobile Division of General Motors Corporation)*

VOCABULARY REVIEW

Bleed To remove air from the hydraulic brake system.

Brake control valve A valve which controls hydraulic pressure to the wheel cylinders or calipers, which contains a metering valve and/or proportioning valve, and which usually includes a pressure-differential switch.

Combination valve Another name for a brake control valve.

Composite master cylinder A master cylinder in which the reservoirs attach to the master-cylinder housing and are made from a different material than the housing.

Cup seal A cup-shaped seal used in master cylinders and wheel cylinders.

Cylinder bore A drilled cylindrical passage in a hydraulic-system component in which a piston is located.

Fast-fill master cylinder A master cylinder which has a step bore and which moves a large quantity of brake fluid quickly with a relatively small brake-pedal travel.

Groove (of a master-cylinder piston) The small-diameter part of a spool-shaped piston.

High-pressure chamber The part of a master-cylinder bore ahead of a piston. The brake fluid is pressurized in this chamber.

Integral master cylinder A master cylinder in which the reservoir and cylinder bore are part of the same housing.

Land (of a master-cylinder piston) The large-diameter part of a spool-shaped piston.

Low-pressure chamber The part of a master-cylinder bore formed by the space around the piston groove. The brake fluid is usually not pressurized in this chamber.

Metering valve A brake control valve that momentarily holds off hydraulic pressure to the front disc brakes so that the disc brakes and drum brakes apply at approximately the same time. Also called a *hold-off valve*.

Port An opening or hole in a hydraulic-system component through which fluid flows.

Pressure-differential switch An electric switch controlled by hydraulic pressure, used to signal a low-pressure condition in one section of a hydraulic brake system. Also called a *pressure-differential valve* and a *brake warning-lamp switch*.

Primary cup The cup on the forward end of a master-cylinder piston.

Primary hydraulic system The section of the hydraulic brake system that is pressurized by the primary piston in the master cylinder.

Primary piston The rear piston in a master cylinder, acted on by the pushrod.

Proportioning valve A brake control valve that reduces hydraulic pressure to the rear brakes during a hard brake application to prevent rear-wheel lockup. Also called a *pressure control valve*.

Quick-takeup master cylinder Another name for a fast-fill master cylinder.

Replenishing port The larger rear port in the bottom of a master-cylinder reservoir.

Secondary cup The cup on the rear end of a master-cylinder piston.

Secondary hydraulic system The section of the hydraulic brake system that is pressurized by the secondary piston in the master cylinder.

Secondary piston The front piston in a master cylinder, acted on by hydraulic pressure produced by the primary piston.

Step bore A master-cylinder bore with two different diameters.

Tandem An arrangement of two or more parts placed one behind the other.

Translucent Partially transparent.

Valve A device that controls the flow of a liquid or a gas by opening or closing or by partially obstructing the flow.

Vent port The smaller front port in the bottom of a master-cylinder reservoir.

REVIEW QUESTIONS

Select the *one* correct, best, or most probable answer to each question.

1. The valve that holds off hydraulic pressure to the front-disc-brake calipers is the:
   a. pressure-differential switch.
   b. metering valve.
   c. proportioning valve.
   d. quick-takeup valve.

2. Technician A says that the replenishing port is larger than the vent port. Technician B says that the replenishing port allows for brake-fluid expansion with temperature. Who is right?
   a. A only
   b. B only
   c. Both A and B
   d. Neither A nor B

3. In a dual master cylinder, the cup seal farthest to the rear is the:
   a. primary-piston primary cup.
   b. primary-piston secondary cup.
   c. secondary-piston primary cup.
   d. secondary-piston secondary cup.

4. During brake application in a fast-fill master cylinder, from which chamber of the cylinder bore does brake fluid flow to the fluid control valve?
   a. The secondary high-pressure chamber
   b. The primary high-pressure chamber
   c. The secondary low-pressure chamber
   d. The primary low-pressure chamber

5. Technician A says that the master-cylinder cover seal has expandable sections to prevent a vacuum from forming in the master cylinder. Technician B says that the purpose of the seal is to prevent dirt and moisture from contaminating the brake fluid. Who is right?
   a. A only
   b. B only
   c. Both A and B
   d. Neither A nor B

6. What parts of a dual master cylinder allow pressure to build up in one half of the hydraulic system if there is a fluid leak in the other half of the system?
   a. The replenishing ports
   b. The piston return springs
   c. The vent ports
   d. The piston extensions

7. Pressure-differential switches are used to:
   a. turn on the brake warning lamp.
   b. maintain a difference in hydraulic pressure between the front and rear brakes.
   c. hold off pressure to the front brakes.
   d. reduce pressure to the rear brakes.

8. The proportioning valve is used to:
   a. allow the front brakes to operate first.
   b. reduce the tendency for rear-wheel skidding during a hard brake application.
   c. reduce pressure to the front-brake calipers.
   d. hold off pressure to the front-brake calipers.

9. Technician A says that a load-sensing proportioning valve provides normal proportioning when there is no load on the rear of the vehicle. Technician B says that the valve provides normal proportioning when the vehicle is heavily loaded. Who is right?
   a. A only
   b. B only
   c. Both A and B
   d. Neither A nor B

10. When the brakes are released after a brake application, what prevents a vacuum from forming in the high-pressure chambers in the master cylinder?
    a. The expandable cover seal
    b. The outlet ports
    c. The vent ports
    d. The replenishing ports

11. Technician A says that when the brakes are applied, the secondary piston is pushed by the primary return spring. Technician B says that the secondary piston is pushed by the brake fluid in the primary high-pressure chamber. Who is right?
    a. A only
    b. B only
    c. Both A and B
    d. Neither A nor B

12. Technician A says that when the brakes are not applied, the metering valve is open to allow for fluid expansion and contraction. Technician B says that the metering valve closes when the pressure in the hydraulic system exceeds 135 psi [931.5 kPa]. Who is right?
    a. A only
    b. B only
    c. Both A and B
    d. Neither A nor B

13. What causes the piston in a caliper to retract after the brake pedal is released?
    a. The retracting springs
    b. The dust boot
    c. The piston seal
    d. The vacuum in the caliper

14. All of the following are part of a wheel-cylinder assembly *except*:
    a. A cup expander
    b. A piston
    c. An O-ring seal
    d. A dust boot

15. A car has a front/rear—split hydraulic system. Technician A says that the reservoir chamber that supplies brake fluid to the drum brakes is larger than the chamber that supplies brake fluid to the disc brakes. Technician B says that the primary hydraulic system operates the front brakes on all cars. Who is right?
    a. A only
    b. B only
    c. Both A and B
    d. Neither A nor B

CHAPTER 4

DRUM BRAKES

OBJECTIVES

After you have studied this chapter, you should be able to:

1. Name the components of a drum brake.

2. Describe the operation of leading-trailing-shoe drum brakes.

3. Describe the operation of duo-servo drum brakes.

4. Describe the operation of self-adjusting brakes.

Drum brakes are used at the rear wheels of most cars. Older cars used drum brakes at all four wheels. Figure 4-1 shows a rear brake-and-drum assembly for a front-wheel-drive car. The brake components are attached to the *backing plate*. The backing plate is bolted to the trailing arm in the rear suspension. In the brake assembly shown in Fig. 4-1, a wheel *spindle* also bolts to the trailing arm. The spindle is a tapered shaft that is threaded at one end. On some cars the spindle is part of the *axle* (Fig. 4-2). An axle is a crossmember which supports the vehicle and on which the wheels turn.

The brake drum is supported on the spindle by two wheel bearings: an inner bearing and an outer bearing (Fig. 4-1). The inner bearing is the bearing closest to the center of the car; the outer bearing is farthest from the center of the car. The center part of the drum that houses the bearings is the *hub*. The drum spins on these bearings. A spindle nut threads onto the end of the spindle and holds the drum-and-bearing assembly on the spindle. A nut lock and cotter pin prevent the nut from loosening. When the drum is installed, the inner surface (friction surface) of the drum is positioned over the brake linings.

Some drums are hubless drums (Fig. 4-3). They fit over studs on an axle flange and are held in place by the wheel.

BASIC OPERATION OF A DRUM BRAKE

The basic operation of a drum brake is shown in Fig. 4-4. When the brake pedal is depressed, the wheel-cylinder pistons force the brake shoes and linings outward against the friction surface of the drum. The linings apply friction force to the drum, which slows the drum's rotation and stops the car.

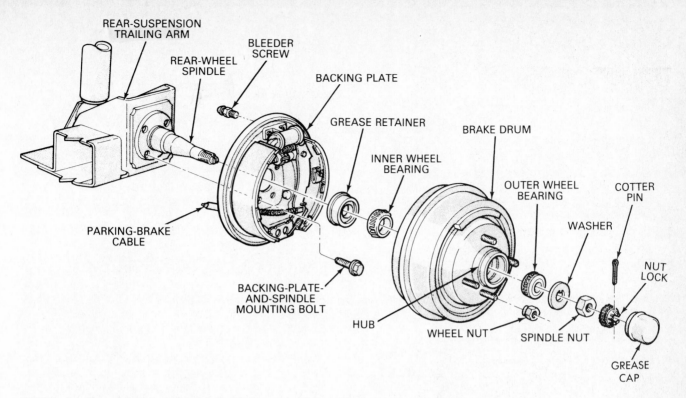

Fig. 4-1. **A left-rear brake-and-drum assembly for a front-wheel-drive car.** *(Chrysler Corporation)*

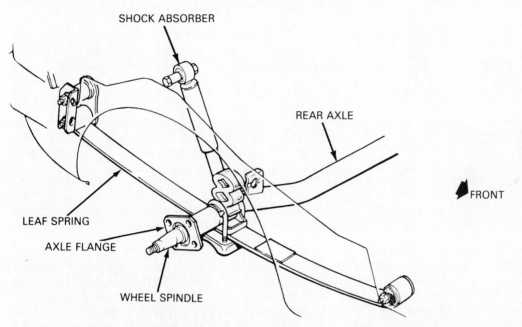

Fig. 4-2. **A rear-axle assembly for a front-wheel-drive car.** *Chevrolet Motor Division of General Motors Corporation)*

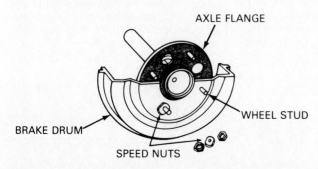

Fig. 4-3. **A hubless drum.** *(Bendix Aftermarket Brake Division)*

Self-Energizing Brake

Figure 4-5 shows a single brake shoe and lining pushed against a rotating drum. The wheel-cylinder force is applied to the upper end of the shoe. The shoe is held at its lower end by the *anchor pin*, which is attached to the backing plate. The shoe can pivot slightly around the anchor pin.

The drum shown in Fig. 4-5 is rotating in a clockwise direction. When the lining contacts the drum, the lining applies a friction force to the drum. The friction

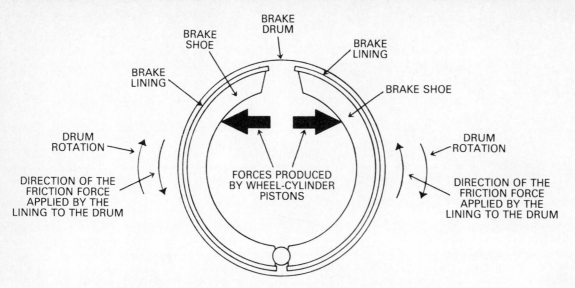

Fig. 4-4. The basic operation of a drum brake, showing the forces applied by the wheel-cylinder pistons pushing the shoes outward against the drum. *(EIS Division of Parker Hannifin Corporation)*

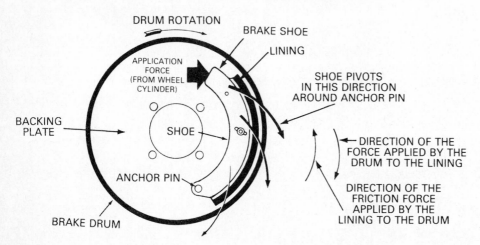

Fig. 4-5. A single brake shoe forced against a rotating drum. The force of the drum on the lining aids the force applied by the wheel cylinder. This is a self-energizing brake. *(FMC Corporation)*

force acts in a counterclockwise direction to oppose the motion of the drum.

For every action, there is an equal and opposite reaction. Therefore, when the lining is in contact with the drum, the drum also applies a force to the lining. The force applied by the drum to the lining is equal to and opposite to the friction force. The force applied by the drum tends to drag the lining along with the drum. But the lining cannot follow the drum, because the shoe is held by the anchor pin.

Instead, the motion of the drum causes the shoe to pivot slightly around the anchor pin in the clockwise direction, as shown in Fig. 4-5. The lining is dragged into, or pulled tighter against, the drum. This dragging action causes the lining to apply a greater friction force to the drum than that provided by the wheel cylinder alone. The type of brake that uses the increase in braking force caused by the rotation of the drum is called a *self-energizing brake*. With a self-energizing brake, the force that the drum applies to the lining acts in the same direction as the force that the wheel cylinder applies to the shoe.

Non-Self-Energizing Brake

In Fig. 4-6 the drum is shown rotating in the counterclockwise direction. When the wheel cylinder applies a force to the shoe, the lining applies a friction force to slow the rotation of the drum. Again, the drum applies to the lining a force that is equal to and opposite to the friction force. But now the force applied by the drum tends to push the shoe away from the drum. This force opposes the force applied by the wheel cylinder. This is called a *non-self-energizing brake*. With the same force applied by the wheel cylinder, a non-self-energizing brake provides less braking force than a self-energizing brake.

LEADING-TRAILING-SHOE DRUM BRAKES

The brake shown in Fig. 4-7 is a *leading-trailing-shoe* type of drum brake. The shoe that faces the front of the car is

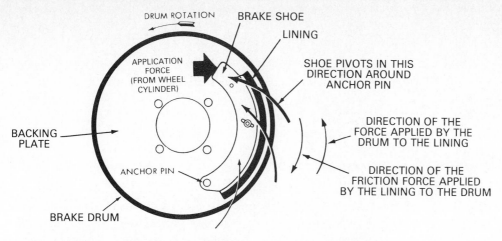

Fig. 4-6. A single brake shoe forced against a rotating drum. The force of the drum on the lining opposes the force applied by the wheel cylinder. This is a non-self-energizing brake. *(FMC Corporation)*

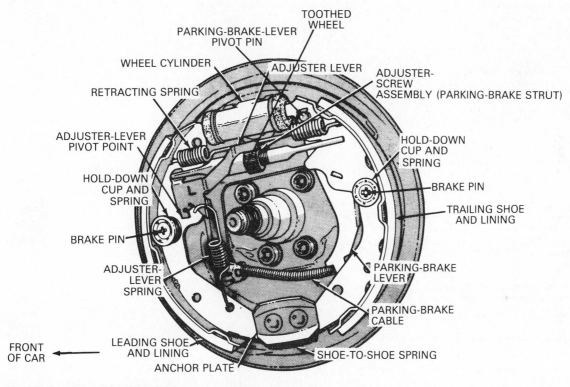

Fig. 4-7. Leading-trailing-shoe brake components. *(Chrysler Corporation)*

the *leading* shoe, and the shoe that faces the rear is the *trailing* shoe.

The shoes are held to the backing plate with a brake pin and with hold-down cups and springs. Several types of hold-down components are shown in Fig. 4-8. Hold-down components permit some movement of the brake shoes, while minimizing shoe vibration and noise.

The upper ends of the shoes contact the wheel cylinder (Fig. 4-7). A retracting spring (return spring) holds both shoes against the wheel cylinder.

Each shoe is anchored at its lower end. Instead of an anchor pin, most leading-trailing-shoe brakes have an anchor block (Fig. 4-9). The lower ends of the shoes rest against the sides of the anchor block. To prevent the lower ends of the shoes from moving away from the

backing plate, an anchor plate is attached to the anchor block (Fig. 4-7). The lower ends of the shoes fit behind the anchor plate. In Fig. 4-7 a shoe-to-shoe spring holds the shoes against the anchor block.

Other components shown in Fig. 4-7 are the parking-brake and self-adjuster components. These are described later in this chapter.

Figure 4-10 shows the operation of a leading-trailing-shoe brake. The brake shown is on the right side of the car. When the car moves forward, the drum rotates in the clockwise direction. Therefore, when the brakes are applied, the leading shoe is self-energizing and the trailing shoe is non-self-energizing. Because the leading shoe is self-energizing, it applies more braking force than the trailing shoe. Therefore, the leading shoe wears more than the trailing shoe.

53

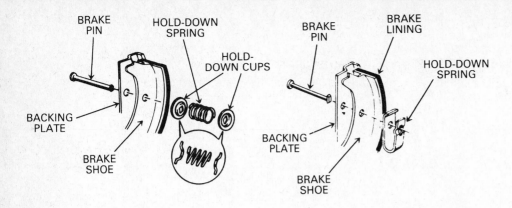

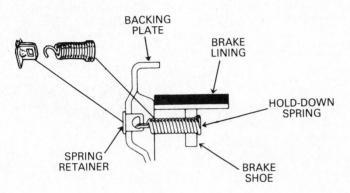

Fig. 4-8. Brake-shoe hold-down components. *(Wagner Division, Cooper Industries Inc.)*

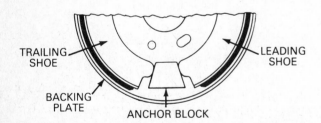

Fig. 4-9. A leading-trailing-shoe brake with an anchor block. *(FMC Corporation)*

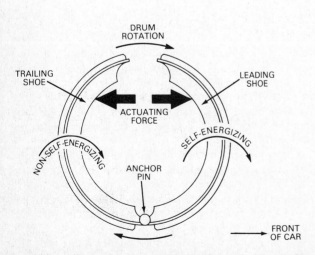

Fig. 4-10. The operation of a leading-trailing-shoe drum brake. *(EIS Division of Parker Hannifin Corporation)*

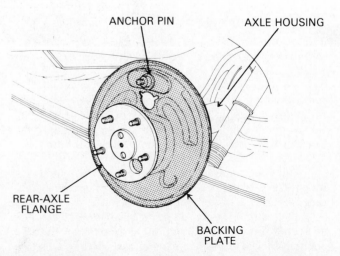

Fig. 4-11. The right-rear backing plate with the anchor pin attached to it. *(Ford Motor Company)*

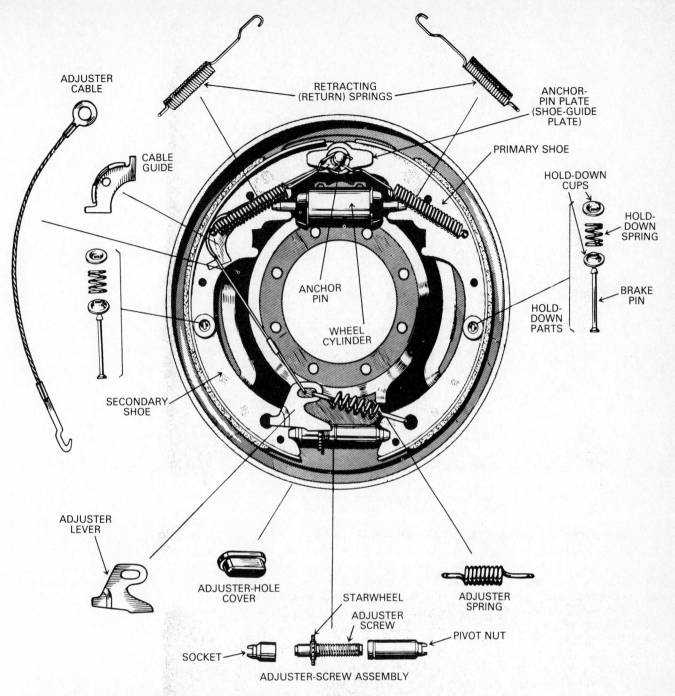

Fig. 4-12. The components of a duo-servo drum brake for a right-front wheel. (*Bendix Aftermarket Brake Division*)

When the car moves in reverse and the brakes are applied, the trailing shoe becomes self-energizing and the leading shoe becomes non-self-energizing.

DUO-SERVO DRUM BRAKES

Another type of drum brake has an anchor pin at the top of the backing plate (Figs. 4-11 and 4-12). The lower ends of the brake shoes are joined by a link, or adjuster-screw assembly. This is a *duo-servo* type of drum brake. The brake shown in Fig. 4-12 is a right-front brake. A

rear-wheel brake is similar, with additional parts for the parking brake (Fig. 4-13).

Hold-down cups and springs (Fig. 4-12) hold the shoes to the backing plate in a manner similar to that of leading-trailing-shoe brakes. Retracting (return) springs hold the upper ends of the shoes against the anchor pin when the brakes are not applied.

An *anchor-pin plate*, or *shoe-guide plate*, fits over the anchor pin and keeps the upper ends of the brake shoes in position (Fig. 4-12). It prevents movement of the upper ends of the shoes away from the backing plate.

The operation of a duo-servo brake is shown in Fig. 4-14. When the car moves forward, the drum rotates in

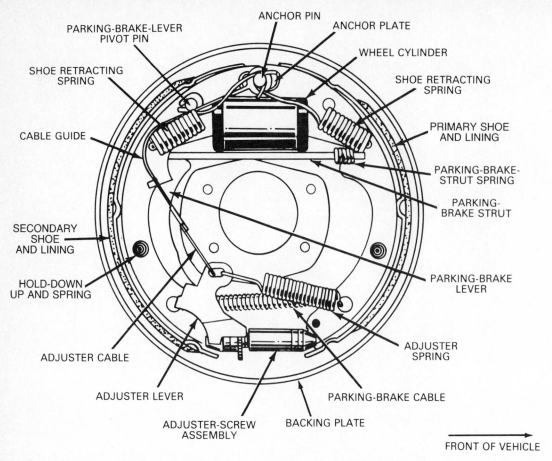

Fig. 4-13. **The components of a duo-servo drum brake for a right-rear wheel.** *(Ford Motor Company)*

the clockwise direction. When the brake pedal is depressed, the shoes and linings move outward. When the linings contact the drum, they apply a friction force to the drum. The drum applies an equal and opposite force to the linings.

Therefore, the shoes and linings tend to be dragged along with the drum in the clockwise direction. The shoe on the right in Fig. 4-14 is dragged downward against the link, and the shoe on the left is dragged upward against the anchor pin. The force of the right shoe against the link is applied through the link to the left shoe. When the right shoe pushes against the link and the left shoe stops against the anchor pin, both shoes become self-energizing shoes.

There are two forces acting on the left shoe to push it into the anchor pin: the force caused by the brake drum and the force caused by the right shoe (Fig. 4-15). The type of brake in which one shoe increases the force applied to the other shoe is called a *servo brake*. The brake shown in Fig. 4-10 is a *nonservo brake* because one shoe does not apply force to the other shoe. Servo brakes apply greater braking force than nonservo brakes for the same brake-pedal force.

The right shoe starts the servo action (Fig. 4-16) and for this reason is called the *primary shoe*. It faces the front of the car. The left shoe is called the *secondary shoe*, and it faces the rear of the car. Because there are greater forces acting on the secondary shoe, it applies a

greater braking force than the primary shoe. Therefore, the secondary shoe receives the greatest amount of wear. For this reason, the lining on the secondary shoe is longer than the lining on the primary shoe and has a greater surface area.

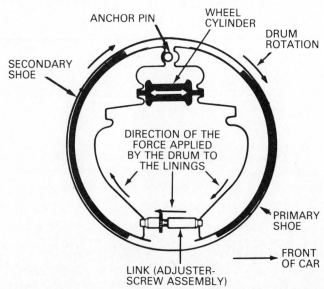

Fig. 4-14. **The operation of a duo-servo drum brake. The car is moving forward, and the drum is shown rotating in the clockwise direction.** *(Bendix Aftermarket Brake Division)*

56

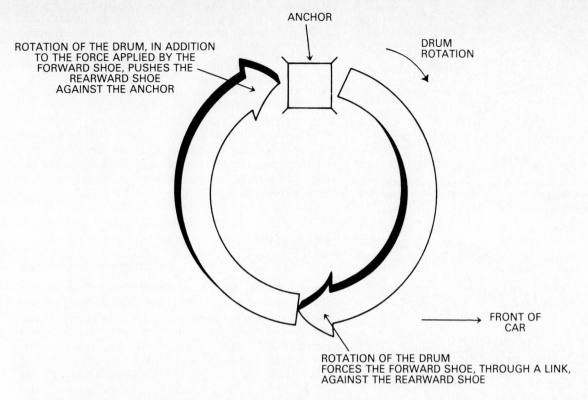

ANCHOR

DRUM ROTATION

ROTATION OF THE DRUM, IN ADDITION TO THE FORCE APPLIED BY THE FORWARD SHOE, PUSHES THE REARWARD SHOE AGAINST THE ANCHOR

FRONT OF CAR

ROTATION OF THE DRUM FORCES THE FORWARD SHOE, THROUGH A LINK, AGAINST THE REARWARD SHOE

Fig. 4-15. The forces acting in a servo brake. *(EIS Division of Parker Hannifin Corporation)*

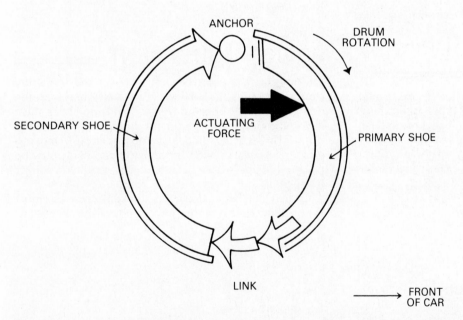

ANCHOR

DRUM ROTATION

SECONDARY SHOE

ACTUATING FORCE

PRIMARY SHOE

LINK

FRONT OF CAR

Fig. 4-16. A servo brake, showing the force of the primary shoe applied through the link to the secondary shoe. *(EIS Division of Parker Hannifin Corporation)*

On many vehicles the primary lining is made of a different material than the secondary lining. The primary lining has a high coefficient of friction so that, when the brakes are applied, a large force is applied by the drum to the primary shoe. Then the primary shoe pushes against the secondary shoe with a large force. This provides a greater self-energizing action than if the primary lining had a low coefficient of friction. The secondary lining has a lower coefficient of friction than the primary lining in order to minimize wear and provide a longer life.

When the car moves in reverse (Fig. 4-17), the servo action is reversed. The rear shoe acts as a primary shoe and applies servo action to the front shoe, which acts as a secondary shoe. Because the servo action takes place when the car is driven in either direction (forward or reverse), this type of brake is called a *duo-servo brake*. The prefix *duo* refers to operation in two directions.

57

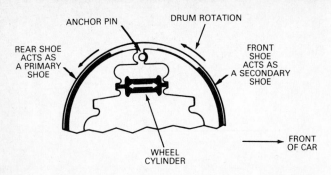

Fig. 4-17. A duo-servo brake. The car is moving in reverse, and the drum is shown rotating in the counterclockwise direction. *(Bendix Aftermarket Brake Division)*

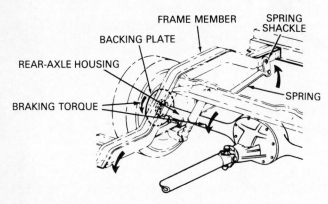

Fig. 4-18. Braking torque applied to a rear-axle housing. *(FMC Corporation)*

BRAKING TORQUE

When the brake pedal is depressed while the car is moving, the drum attempts to drag the brakes around with it. This movement is prevented by the anchor pin (Fig. 4-11) or the anchor block (Fig. 4-9), which is attached to the backing plate. The backing plate is bolted to the axle housing. The force of the shoe against the anchor pin or anchor block tends to twist the backing plate around the axle housing (Fig. 4-18). This twisting force is called the braking torque. A *torque* is a twisting or

turning force that may or may not result in motion. The braking torque is resisted by the suspension and frame or body of the car.

The backing plate must be strong enough to resist the braking torque without bending or deforming. Therefore, backing plates are usually made of heavy-gauge steel. However, this adds weight to the car.

To reduce weight, some cars have the anchor pin attached through the backing plate directly to a flange on the axle housing (Fig. 4-19). With this design, the backing plate can be made of light-weight material because the torque is applied directly to the axle housing. This is called a *direct-torque* drum bake.

PARKING-BRAKE COMPONENTS

A parking-brake lever is shown in Fig. 4-13 attached to the upper end of the secondary shoe with a pin (the parking-brake-lever pivot pin). The lever pivots around the pin. A parking-brake cable attaches to the lower end of the lever. A *parking-brake strut* is located between the primary and secondary shoes. One end of the strut also rests against the parking-brake lever. When the parking brake is applied, the cable pulls the lever and applies the brakes mechanically. Leading-trailing-shoe parking brakes operate in a similar manner. Parking-brake operation is covered in Chap. 6.

BRAKE ADJUSTMENT

The friction between the brake linings and the drum causes the lining material to wear away. Therefore, the linings gradually become thinner, and the shoes must move a greater distance for the linings to contact the drum. The wheel-cylinder pistons must also move a greater distance. Therefore, more brake fluid must be pumped to the wheel cylinders. This results in longer brake-pedal travel and a lower pedal.

On a duo-servo brake, an adjuster-screw assembly is positioned between the lower ends of the shoes (Fig.

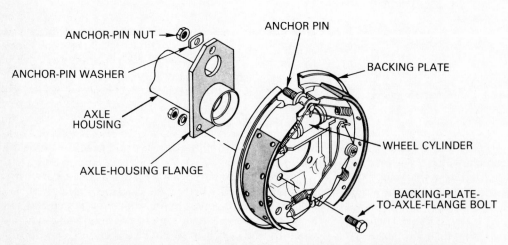

Fig. 4-19. A direct-torque drum brake, in which the anchor pin is attached directly to a flange on the axle housing. *(Bendix Aftermarket Brake Division)*

58

4-13). This assembly is the link that transmits the servo action from the primary shoe to the secondary shoe. The assembly includes the socket, the adjuster screw, and the pivot nut (Fig. 4-12). The adjuster screw has a wheel with teeth around its edge, called a *starwheel*. It is used to adjust the brakes to compensate for wear.

One end of the adjuster socket has a groove, as does one end of the pivot nut (Fig. 4-12). The lower end of the secondary shoe fits into the groove in the socket, and the lower end of the primary shoe fits into the groove in the pivot nut. When the starwheel is rotated, the pivot nut is held stationary by the primary brake shoe. If the starwheel is rotated in the proper direction, the adjuster-screw assembly lengthens. This pushes the shoes and linings closer to the drum, which adjusts the brakes. Then less brake-pedal travel is needed to apply the brakes.

On many leading-trailing-shoe brakes, the parking-brake strut also serves as the adjuster-screw assembly (Fig. 4-7). It operates in a manner similar to that of a duo-servo-brake adjuster-screw assembly.

The brakes on most cars are self-adjusting. During brake operation, a self-adjuster mechanism rotates the starwheel when the brakes need adjustment. The operation of self-adjusting brakes is covered in the next section of this chapter.

Self-adjusting brakes can also be manually adjusted if the brakes fail to self-adjust. A slot, or adjuster hole, is located in many backing plates. A cover is placed in the hole to prevent dirt and water from entering the brake assembly. To adjust the brakes, the adjuster-hole cover is removed from the backing plate. Then an adjuster tool is inserted in the hole and is used to rotate the starwheel to adjust the brakes (Fig. 4-20). On some cars the adjuster hole is located in the brake drum. The procedure for manually adjusting self-adjusting brakes is covered in Chap. 5 of the shop manual.

A type of manual brake adjuster used with a leading-trailing-shoe brake is shown in Fig. 4-21. This type of adjuster is not self-adjusting. Two links fit into a housing and rest against a tapered wedge. One end of the wedge is threaded, and it can be rotated by turning it with a wrench. The lower ends of the shoes contact the links, and the adjuster assembly acts as the anchor block.

The brakes are adjusted by rotating the wedge. This moves the tapered end of the wedge against the links, pushing them outward. The links then push the brake shoes closer to the drum to adjust them.

SELF-ADJUSTING BRAKES

Self-adjusting brakes automatically adjust the clearance between the brake linings and the drum. There are several different types of self-adjusting mechanisms. On cars with duo-servo brakes, the brakes self-adjust when the brakes are applied and released while the car is moving in reverse. Some leading-trailing-shoe brakes self-adjust when the parking brake is applied and released. Others adjust when the service brakes are applied and released. The car can be moving or standing still.

Duo-servo brakes use cable- or lever-type self-adjusters. Leading-trailing-shoe brakes use cams, ratchet-

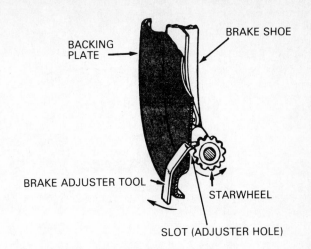

Fig. 4-20. Manual brake adjustment. An adjuster tool is inserted through a slot in the backing plate to rotate the starwheel. *(Bendix Aftermarket Brake Division)*

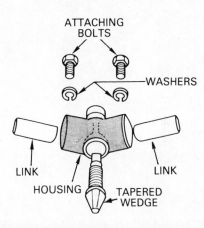

Fig. 4-21. A manual brake adjuster used with a leading-trailing-shoe brake. *(Bendix Aftermarket Brake Division)*

ing arms, adjustable parking-brake struts, or tapered wedges.

Cable Type

Figure 4-22 shows a cable-type self-adjuster on a duo-servo brake. The cable has a washerlike part at one end called the *cable eye*. The other end of the cable has a hook. The cable eye attaches to the anchor pin, and the cable fits over a cable guide. A projection on the guide fits into the same hole in the secondary shoe that the retracting spring fits into. The guide is held in position by the retracting spring. The other end of the cable hooks into an adjuster lever. The adjuster lever hooks into a hole in the lower end of the secondary shoe. An adjuster-lever spring is positioned between the lower edge of the primary shoe and the adjuster lever. This spring pulls the cable and holds it under tension. Part of the lever rests against the teeth of the starwheel.

Figure 4-23 shows a right-rear brake. When the car is moving in reverse, the brake drum rotates in a counterclockwise direction. When the brakes are applied, the secondary shoe moves outward and the lining contacts

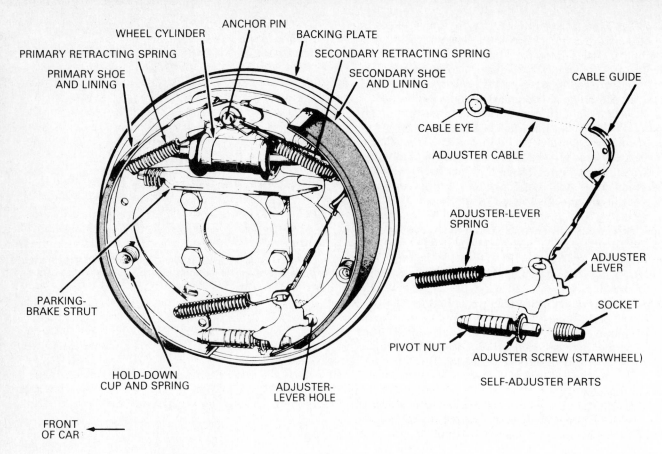

PRIMARY RETRACTING SPRING
WHEEL CYLINDER
ANCHOR PIN
BACKING PLATE
PRIMARY SHOE AND LINING
SECONDARY RETRACTING SPRING
SECONDARY SHOE AND LINING
CABLE GUIDE
CABLE EYE
ADJUSTER CABLE
ADJUSTER-LEVER SPRING
ADJUSTER LEVER
SOCKET
PIVOT NUT
ADJUSTER SCREW (STARWHEEL)
SELF-ADJUSTER PARTS
PARKING-BRAKE STRUT
HOLD-DOWN CUP AND SPRING
ADJUSTER-LEVER HOLE
FRONT OF CAR

Fig. 4-22. A cable-type self-adjusting brake. *(Bendix Aftermarket Brake Division)*

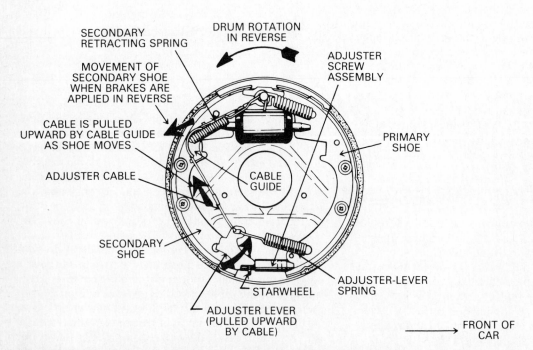

SECONDARY RETRACTING SPRING
DRUM ROTATION IN REVERSE
ADJUSTER SCREW ASSEMBLY
MOVEMENT OF SECONDARY SHOE WHEN BRAKES ARE APPLIED IN REVERSE
CABLE IS PULLED UPWARD BY CABLE GUIDE AS SHOE MOVES
PRIMARY SHOE
ADJUSTER CABLE
CABLE GUIDE
SECONDARY SHOE
STARWHEEL
ADJUSTER-LEVER SPRING
ADJUSTER LEVER (PULLED UPWARD BY CABLE)
FRONT OF CAR

Fig. 4-23. The operation of a cable-type self-adjuster when the car is moving in reverse and the brakes are applied. *(Delco Moraine Division of General Motors Corporation)*

the drum. When this occurs, the drum drags the secondary shoe downward. As the shoe moves outward and downward, the cable guide pulls the cable. The cable lifts the adjuster lever, and the lever engages one of the teeth of the starwheel.

When the brakes are released, the shoe is pulled against the anchor pin by the retracting spring. This releases tension from the cable, and the lever is pulled downward by the adjuster-lever spring (Fig. 4-24). When this occurs, the lever rotates the starwheel one tooth. This turns the adjuster screw and adjusts the brakes. Therefore, an adjustment takes place when the brakes are released, after they have been applied. This is a *release-actuated adjuster*.

Each time the brakes are applied and released when the shoes need adjusting, the starwheel is rotated one tooth. This requires the brakes to be applied in reverse often enough to keep them adjusted. If the car is not driven in reverse enough, the brakes will not completely adjust. Then they will either have to be manually adjusted or the brakes will have to be applied in reverse repeatedly to adjust them.

When the brakes are correctly adjusted, there is little outward movement of the secondary shoe when the brakes are applied. As a result, the cable guide does not pull the cable far enough for the lever to engage a starwheel tooth. This prevents overadjustment of the brakes.

When the car is moving forward and the brakes are applied, the secondary shoe moves upward toward the anchor pin. When this happens, the cable is not pulled and the brakes do not adjust.

Figure 4-25 shows another cable-type self-adjuster. The self-adjuster lever is positioned below the center of the starwheel. When the car is moving in reverse and the brakes are applied, the movement of the secondary shoe causes the cable to lift the adjuster lever. The upward movement of the lever rotates the starwheel to adjust the brake.

When the brake pedal is released, the secondary shoe is pulled back against the anchor pin by the retracting spring. This releases the cable, and the adjuster lever moves downward and engages another tooth on the starwheel. Now the adjuster is in position for the next brake application. With this design, the brakes adjust when they are applied in reverse (*not* when they are released). This is an *apply-actuated adjuster*.

The self-adjusting brake shown in Fig. 4-25 has an overload spring on the end of the cable. When the brakes are applied in reverse and the shoes are correctly adjusted, the lever is not pulled upward far enough to rotate the starwheel. Therefore, the brakes cannot overadjust.

However, on a hard brake application the drum may distort. This could cause the brakes to move farther outward than normal and overadjust. The overload spring prevents this from happening. On a hard brake application, the starwheel does not turn easily because the servo action produces a large force between the threads of the adjuster screw and the pivot nut. If the starwheel cannot turn easily, the overload spring stretches and the lever is not forced upward. Therefore, the brakes will not overadjust on a hard brake application.

Lever Type

A lever-type self-adjusting brake is shown in Fig. 4-26. An adjuster link attaches to the anchor pin. The other end of the link hooks over the upper end of the adjuster lever. A lever pivot sleeve fits through a hole in the le-

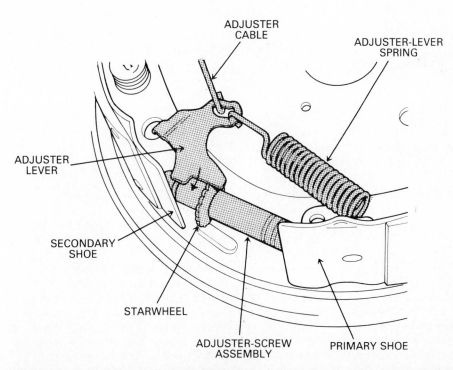

Fig. 4-24. A cable-type self-adjusting brake. When the lever moves downward, it rotates the starwheel and adjusts the brake. This is a release-actuated self-adjuster. *(Ford Motor Company)*

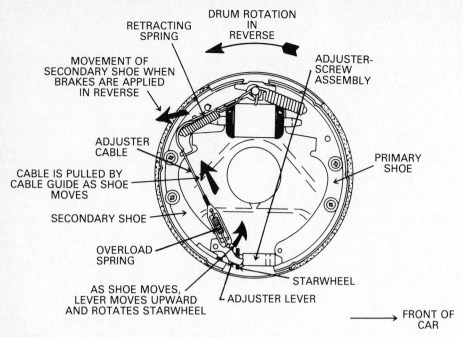

Fig. 4-25. A cable-type self-adjusting brake with an overload spring. This is an apply-actuated self-adjuster. *(Delco Moraine Division of General Motors Corporation)*

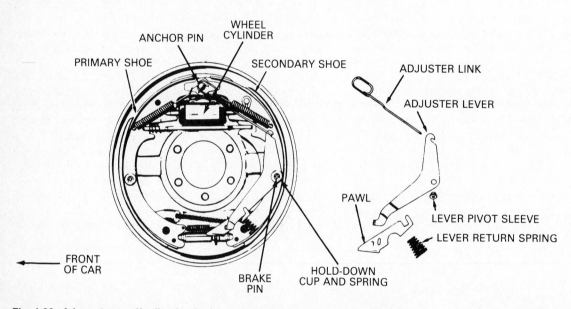

Fig. 4-26. A lever-type self-adjusting brake. *(Bendix Aftermarket Brake Division)*

ver and into a hole in the secondary shoe. The brake pin fits through the sleeve, and the lever is held against the secondary shoe by the brake pin and hold-down cup and spring. The lever can rotate around the sleeve. A pawl, which fits into the lower end of the lever, rests against a starwheel tooth. A *pawl* is a pivoted part, one end of which can drop into a notch or groove in another part to permit motion in one direction only.

When the car is moving in reverse and the brakes are applied, the secondary shoe moves outward and downward (Fig. 4-27). Because the top of the adjuster lever is held by the adjuster link, when the shoe moves outward the end of the lever is pushed downward. The pawl engages a tooth on the starwheel, which rotates it

to adjust the brake. This mechanism is an apply-actuated adjuster.

The pawl pivots slightly around its point of attachment to the lever. This prevents the brakes from over-adjusting because of drum distortion during a hard brake application. On a hard brake application, the starwheel does not turn easily because of the large force between the threads of the adjuster screw and the pivot nut. If this occurs, as the lever moves downward the pawl will contact the starwheel and pivot upward. Then the lever can continue its downward motion without forcing the starwheel to turn. This prevents overadjustment.

When the brakes are released, the secondary shoe is pulled back against the anchor pin by the retracting

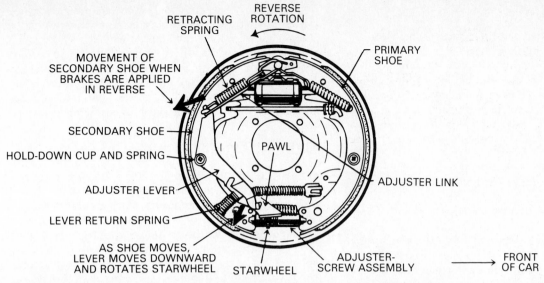

Fig. 4-27. The operation of a lever-type self-adjuster when the car is moving in reverse and the brakes are applied. *(Delco Moraine Division of General Motors Corporation)*

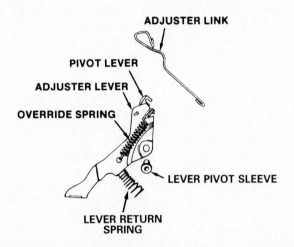

Fig. 4-28. A self-adjusting brake lever with an override spring. *(Bendix Aftermarket Brake Division)*

spring. This releases the lever. The lever return spring pushes the pawl and lever upward and engages another tooth of the starwheel. Now the pawl is in position for the next brake application.

Some self-adjusting brakes use an adjuster lever with an override spring (Fig. 4-28). The adjuster link is attached to a small pivot lever. The pivot lever is held to the adjuster lever by the override spring. The brakes adjust in the same way as with the lever-and-pawl type. On a hard brake application, the override spring stretches and the adjuster lever pivots upward around the pivot lever. This prevents overadjustment.

Figure 4-29*a* shows a lever-type self-adjuster that is release-actuated. When applying the brakes in reverse, the adjuster lever moves downward and engages a tooth in the starwheel (Fig. 4-29*b*). When the brakes are released, the lever return spring pushes the lever upward. This rotates the starwheel one tooth, adjusting the brakes.

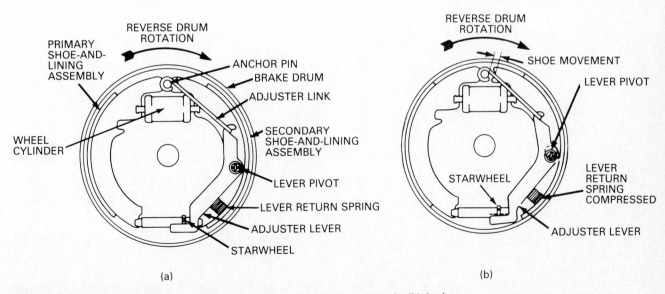

Fig. 4-29. A release-actuated lever-type self-adjuster: *(a)* brakes released; *(b)* brakes applied in reverse. *(General Motors Corporation)*

Cam Type

Figure 4-30 shows a self-adjusting brake that has two cam adjusters. A *cam* is a circular-shaped part with a projection or lobe that, when rotated, pushes against another part to change rotary motion into reciprocating motion. The cams in this brake differ from many cams, because they do not make a complete revolution. Instead, they only rotate through a small angle. Therefore, these cams change rotary motion into a short-distance straight-line motion.

The cam adjusters are located on the backing plate. Each cam has an adjuster pin that fits into a slot in a shoe (Fig. 4-31). The pin has a smaller diameter than the width of the slot. This type of adjuster is used on a leading-trailing-shoe brake.

When the brakes are applied, the shoes contact the adjuster pins (Fig. 4-31a). If the brakes need adjusting, the shoes push the adjuster pins and rotate the cam adjusters to a new position. Now the adjuster pins are closer to the drum. When the brakes are released, the cam adjusters remain in their new positions. The adjuster-pin diameters are smaller than the slots in the shoes. This allows the shoes to move away from the drum until the edge of the slot contacts the adjuster pin (Fig. 4-31b).

Therefore, the shoes are prevented from moving any farther away from the drum than the distance between the pin and the slot. This adjusts the clearance between the brake lining and drum. Brake adjustment occurs whenever the brakes are applied, with the car moving or stopped. The brakes completely adjust with one application of the brake pedal. For this reason, this type of adjuster is sometimes called a one-shot adjuster.

Ratchet Type

Figure 4-32 shows a leading-trailing-shoe brake that includes a ratchet-type self-adjuster. A *ratchet* is a wheel or lever with teeth that engages another component and allows movement in one direction only. Two ratchets are located behind the trailing shoe (Fig. 4-33). One ratchet is large, and the other is small. Both ratchets are attached to the trailing shoe with a pin, and each ratchet can pivot around the pin. Each ratchet has teeth on the opposite end from the pin.

The ratchets are positioned so that the teeth on one interlock with the teeth on the other. If the large ratchet is moved inward (to the right in Fig. 4-33), the teeth disengage and the ratchet can move. If the large ratchet is pushed outward (to the left in Fig. 4-33), its teeth lock into the teeth of the small ratchet. Then the large ratchet cannot move.

A spacer strut is located between the leading and trailing shoes. The spacer strut serves as the parking-brake strut. The parking-brake actuating lever is attached to the strut and pivots on it (Fig. 4-34). A shoulder on the end of the strut fits into a slot in the large ratchet. The shoulder is smaller than the slot. There is a small gap between the right edge of the strut shoulder (in Fig. 4-33) and the right edge of the slot in the large ratchet.

When the brakes are applied, the wheel-cylinder pistons push the shoes outward. The trailing shoe moves to the left in Fig. 4-33, and the leading shoe moves to the right. The strut is held against the leading shoe by the parking-brake-lever return spring; therefore, the strut moves to the right with the leading shoe. As the strut moves to the right and the trailing shoe moves to the

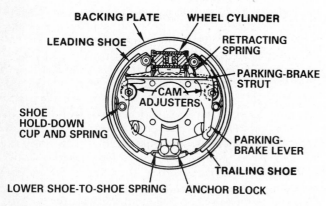

Fig. 4-30. A self-adjusting brake that has two cam adjusters. *(Bendix Aftermarket Brake Division)*

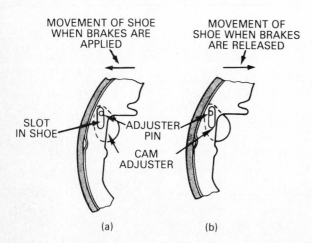

Fig. 4-31. The operation of the cam adjuster. *(a)* The cam adjuster is rotated outward when the brakes are applied; *(b)* the cam adjuster remains in its new position when the brakes are released, and the pin limits the inward movement of the shoe. *(Bendix Aftermarket Brake Division)*

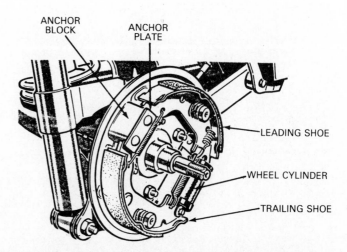

Fig. 4-32. A leading-trailing-shoe brake assembly for a right-rear brake. This assembly uses a ratchet-type self-adjuster. *(Ford Motor Company)*

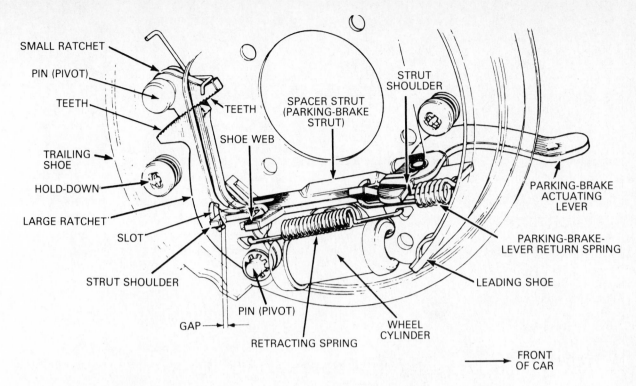

Fig. 4-33. The components of a ratchet-type self-adjuster. *(Wagner Division, Cooper Industries Inc.)*

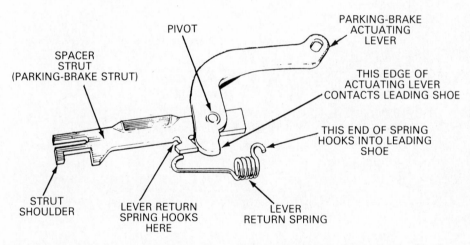

Fig. 4-34. The parking-brake actuating lever and strut used with the ratchet-type self-adjuster. *(Ford Motor Company)*

left, the gap between the strut shoulder and the edge of the slot in the large ratchet is closed. Then, the right edge of the shoulder touches the right edge of the slot. Now the gap is between the left edge of the shoulder and the left edge of the slot in the large ratchet.

If the brakes need adjusting, the shoes continue to move outward. Further movement causes the strut shoulder to pull the large ratchet, which pivots inward (to the right in Fig. 4-33). The ratchet teeth disengage, and the large ratchet pivots to a new position against the small ratchet.

When the brakes are released, the retracting spring pulls the shoes inward. The trailing shoe moves to the right in Fig. 4-33, and the leading shoe and strut move to the left. The movement stops when the strut shoulder contacts the left edge of the slot in the large ratchet.

The strut pushes against the large ratchet. However, the ratchet cannot move to the left because its teeth are locked into the teeth of the small ratchet. Therefore, the shoes are prevented from moving any farther away from the drum than a distance equal to the width of the gap between the strut shoulder and the slot in the ratchet. Now the shoes are adjusted. The brakes completely adjust with one application of the brakes.

Another type of ratchet adjuster is shown in Fig. 4-35. A parking-brake strut has a knurled pin. A *knurl* is a series of ridges on a surface. A small ratchet, called an adjuster quadrant, has a curved part that is also knurled (Fig. 4-36). The knurled part functions like the teeth of the ratchet. The quadrant has a pivot pin that fits between two prongs in the end of the parking-brake strut. The quadrant can rotate around the pivot pin. Part of

65

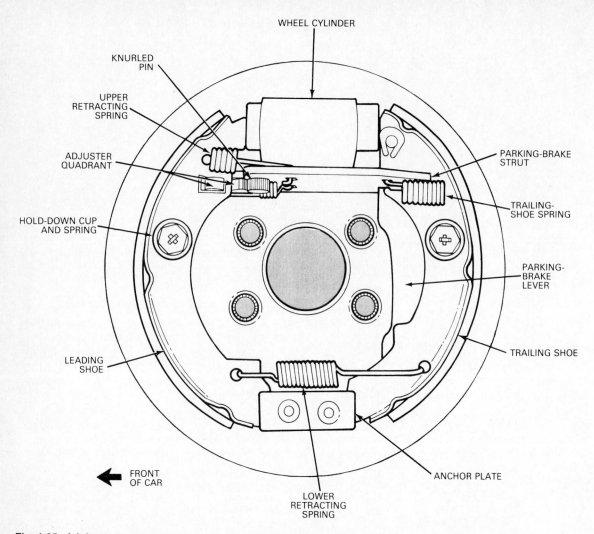

WHEEL CYLINDER

KNURLED PIN

UPPER RETRACTING SPRING

ADJUSTER QUADRANT

HOLD-DOWN CUP AND SPRING

LEADING SHOE

FRONT OF CAR

LOWER RETRACTING SPRING

ANCHOR PLATE

PARKING-BRAKE STRUT

TRAILING-SHOE SPRING

PARKING-BRAKE LEVER

TRAILING SHOE

Fig. 4-35. A left-rear brake that uses a ratchet-type self-adjuster with a knurled pin. *(Ford Motor Company)*

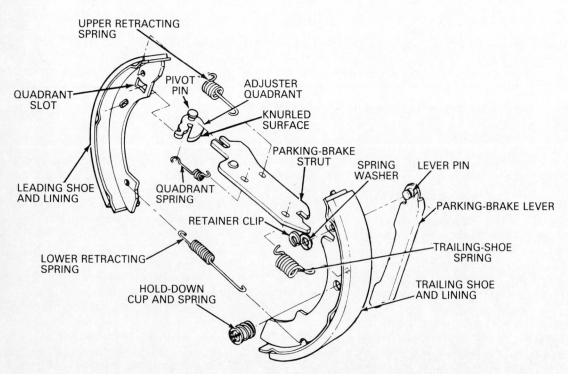

UPPER RETRACTING SPRING

QUADRANT SLOT

PIVOT PIN

ADJUSTER QUADRANT

KNURLED SURFACE

PARKING-BRAKE STRUT

SPRING WASHER

LEVER PIN

PARKING-BRAKE LEVER

LEADING SHOE AND LINING

QUADRANT SPRING

RETAINER CLIP

LOWER RETRACTING SPRING

HOLD-DOWN CUP AND SPRING

TRAILING-SHOE SPRING

TRAILING SHOE AND LINING

Fig. 4-36. The components of a ratchet-type self-adjuster with a knurled pin. *(Ford Motor Company)*

the quadrant fits into a slot in the leading shoe of a leading-trailing-shoe brake (Fig. 4-37). The quadrant contacts the knurled pin, and the knurled surface of the quadrant grips the knurled surface of the pin. A *quadrant spring* is connected between the quadrant and the strut. The spring holds the quadrant against the knurled pin.

When the brakes are applied, the wheel-cylinder pistons push the shoes outward. If the brakes need adjusting, the edge of the slot in the leading shoe pushes against the quadrant. This pivots the quadrant in the direction shown in Fig. 4-37. The quadrant is shaped like a cam. As the quadrant pivots, its knurled surface moves past the pin and remains in light contact with the pin. When the brakes are released, the shoes move away from the drum until the other edge of the slot in the leading

shoe contacts the quadrant. The knurled surface of the quadrant grips the knurled surface of the pin. This holds the quadrant in its new position. Because the quadrant has pivoted to a new position, the shoes remain closer to the drum. The brakes completely adjust with one brake application. The car can be moving or stopped.

Adjustable Parking-Brake-Strut Type

Figure 4-7 shows a leading-trailing-shoe brake that has an adjustable-length parking-brake strut. The strut fits between the leading shoe and the parking-brake lever and trailing shoe (Fig. 4-38). Part of the strut is an adjuster screw that has a toothed wheel (or adjuster nut). As the wheel rotates, the strut lengthens.

A projection on the adjuster lever fits into a hole in the leading shoe and pivots around this hole (Figs. 4-7 and 4-38). One end of the lever is positioned against the toothed wheel. An adjuster-lever spring is placed between the lever and the lower part of the leading shoe.

When the brake pedal is depressed, the wheel-cylinder pistons push the shoes outward. The spring pulls the adjuster lever downward, and the end of the lever rotates the toothed wheel one tooth. When the brake pedal is released, the retracting spring pulls the shoes inward. The lever pivots upward and engages another tooth on the wheel. Therefore, if the brakes need adjustment, several brake applications may be required in order to adjust the brakes completely.

Another type of adjustable parking-brake strut is shown in Fig. 4-39. The strut assembly fits between the leading and trailing shoes (Fig. 4-40). A rod (shown in Fig. 4-39) hooks into a hole in the trailing shoe. The leading shoe fits into a groove in the other end of the strut assembly. When the parking brake is applied, the trailing shoe is moved outward against the drum. This pulls the rod, which is free to move out of the strut assembly. Movement of the rod lengthens the strut assembly and adjusts the brake. Because of a spring-operated latch, or lock, the rod cannot move back into the strut assembly. If the brakes need adjustment, they are completely adjusted with one application of the parking brake.

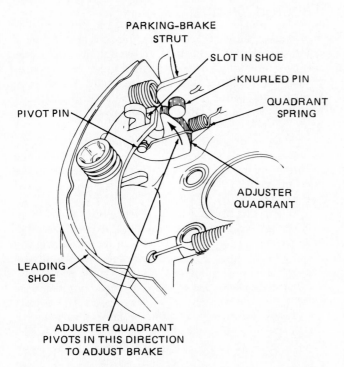

Fig. 4-37. The operation of a ratchet-type self-adjuster with a knurled pin. *(Ford Motor Company)*

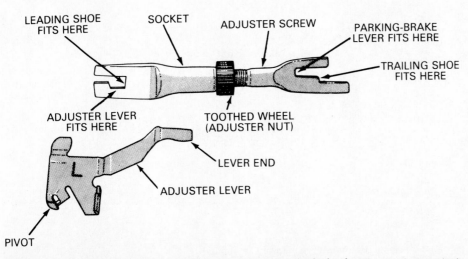

Fig. 4-38. An adjustable parking-brake strut that has a toothed wheel. *(Chrysler Corporation)*

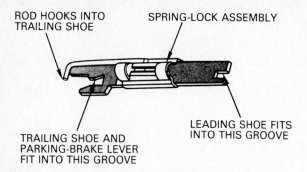

Fig. 4-39. An adjustable parking-brake strut that uses a rod and a spring lock. *(Bendix Aftermarket Brake Division)*

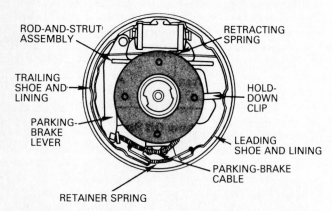

Fig. 4-40. The location of the rod-and-strut assembly between the leading and the trailing shoes. *(Bendix Aftermarket Brake Division)*

Figure 4-41 shows a leading-trailing-shoe brake with an adjustable-length parking-brake strut. Part of the parking-brake strut is an adjuster screw, which has a toothed wheel. An adjuster lever is attached to the parking-brake lever, and a spring is connected between the adjuster lever and the trailing shoe. An arm on the adjuster lever contacts the toothed wheel.

When the parking brake is applied, the parking-brake lever is pulled to the left in Fig. 4-41. This causes the adjuster lever to pivot, and the arm on the lever moves upward and engages a tooth on the toothed wheel. This action stretches the adjuster-lever spring. When the parking brake is released, the adjuster-lever spring pulls the adjuster lever, and the arm on the lever moves downward. This rotates the toothed wheel one tooth, lengthening the parking-brake strut to adjust the brakes.

If the brakes need adjustment, the toothed wheel is rotated one tooth each time that the parking brake is applied and released. Therefore, if the brakes need adjustment, several parking-brake applications may be required in order to adjust the brakes completely.

Tapered-Wedge Type

Figure 4-42 shows a leading-trailing-shoe brake with a tapered-wedge self-adjuster. The wedge fits between a slot in the parking-brake strut and a guide block that is riveted to the leading shoe. The narrow end of the wedge attaches to a spring, which, in turn, attaches to the leading shoe. The spring applies a downward force to the wedge in Fig. 4-42.

When the brakes are not applied, the retracting springs pull the shoes together. This clamps the wedge between the leading shoe and the edge of the slot in the parking-brake strut and prevents the wedge from moving downward.

When the brake pedal is depressed, the wheel-cylinder pistons push the shoes outward. If sufficient lining wear has taken place, the shoes move away from the parking-brake strut. This removes the force from the wedge, and the spring pulls the wedge downward. Now the wedge holds the shoes closer to the drum than they were before the brake pedal was depressed. This adjusts the brakes completely with one brake application.

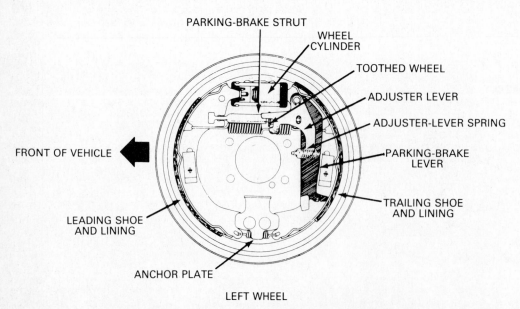

Fig. 4-41. A leading-trailing-shoe brake that self-adjusts when the parking brake is applied and released. *(Toyota Motor Sales, U.S.A., Inc.)*

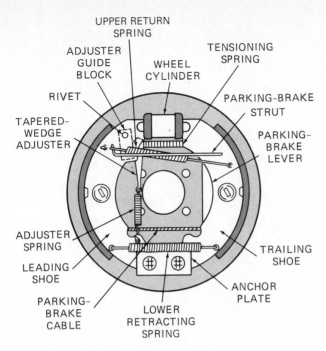

Fig. 4-42. A leading-trailing-shoe brake that uses a tapered-wedge-type self-adjuster.

VOCABULARY REVIEW

Anchor The pin or block in a drum brake that prevents the brake shoes from being dragged around by the brake drum.

Apply-actuated self-adjuster A self-adjusting mechanism that adjusts the brakes when the brake pedal is depressed to apply the brakes.

Axle A crossmember which supports the vehicle and on which the wheels turn.

Backing plate The plate on which the brake shoes are mounted.

Cam A circular-shaped part with a projection or lobe that, when rotated, pushes against another part to change rotary motion into reciprocating motion.

Direct-torque drum brake A drum brake in which the braking torque is applied directly to the axle housing, not to the backing plate.

Duo-servo brake A servo brake in which the servo action takes place when the vehicle is moving forward or in reverse.

Knurl A series of ridges on a surface.

Leading-trailing-shoe brake A brake in which one shoe is self-energizing and the other shoe is not self-energizing.

Manually adjusted brake A brake that must be adjusted by hand.

Non-self-energizing brake A brake in which the force applied by the brake drum to the shoe opposes the force applied by the wheel cylinder.

Nonservo brake The type of brake in which one shoe does not apply force to the other shoe.

Pawl A pivoted part, one end of which can drop into a notch or groove in another part in order to permit motion in one direction only.

Primary shoe The shoe that faces forward in a duo-servo brake. It starts the servo action.

Ratchet A wheel or lever with teeth that engages another component and allows movement in one direction only.

Release-actuated self-adjuster A self-adjusting mechanism that adjusts the brakes when the brake pedal is released.

Secondary shoe The shoe that faces rearward in a duo-servo brake.

Self-adjusting brake A brake that adjusts automatically.

Self-energizing brake A brake in which the rotation of the brake drum increases the braking force of the lining against the drum. The force applied by the drum to the shoe aids the force applied by the wheel cylinder.

Servo brake A brake in which one shoe increases the braking force of the other shoe.

Starwheel The toothed wheel that is part of the adjuster-screw assembly.

Torque A twisting or turning force that may or may not result in motion.

Select the *one* correct, best, or most probable answer to each question.

1. On a cable-type self-adjusting brake, the brakes adjust when the:
   a. brake is applied while the car is moving forward.
   b. brake is applied and released while the car is moving in reverse.
   c. parking brake is applied.
   d. car is moving in reverse.

2. On the lever-type self-adjusting brake shown in Fig. 4-26, the brakes adjust when the:
   a. brake is applied in reverse.
   b. brake is released after being applied in reverse.
   c. parking brake is applied.
   d. car is driven in reverse.

3. Which shoe lining receives the greatest wear on a duo-servo brake?
   a. The leading shoe
   b. The training shoe
   c. The primary shoe
   d. The secondary shoe

4. Technician A says that the leading-shoe lining receives the greatest wear on a leading-trailing-shoe brake. Technician B says that leading-trailing-shoe brakes are nonservo brakes. Who is right?
   a. A only
   b. B only
   c. Both A and B
   d. Neither A nor B

5. Technician A says that for the same brake-pedal force, duo-servo brakes apply greater braking force than leading-trailing-shoe brakes. Technician B says that the servo action of duo-servo brakes only takes place when the car is moving forward. Who is right?
   a. A only
   b. B only
   c. Both A and B
   d. Neither A nor B

6. Technician A says that on a self-energizing brake, the force applied by the drum to the lining aids the force applied by the wheel cylinder. Technician B says that on a non-self-energizing brake, the force applied by the drum to the lining opposes the force applied by the wheel cylinder. Who is right?
   a. A only
   b. B only
   c. Both A and B
   d. Neither A nor B

7. Technician A says that some leading-trailing-shoe brakes with an adjustable parking-brake strut self-adjust when the service brakes are applied. Technician B says that some brakes with an adjustable parking-brake strut self-adjust when the parking brake is applied. Who is right?
   a. A only
   b. B only
   c. Both A and B
   d. Neither A nor B

8. In a duo-servo brake, the servo action is applied from the primary shoe to the secondary shoe through the:
   a. anchor pin.
   b. wheel cylinder.
   c. parking-brake strut.
   d. adjuster-screw assembly.

9. On a cable-type self-adjusting brake, the cable guide is held to the brake shoe by the:
   a. primary retracting spring.
   b. brake pin and hold-down cup and spring.
   c. secondary retracting spring.
   d. adjuster-lever spring.

10. On a lever-type self-adjusting brake, the adjuster lever is held to the brake shoe by the:
    a. brake pin and hold-down cup and spring.
    b. secondary retracting spring.
    c. lever return spring.
    d. adjuster link.

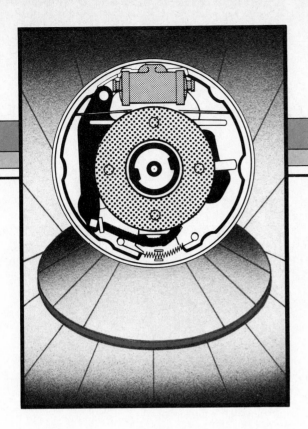

CHAPTER 5

DISC BRAKES

OBJECTIVES

After you have studied this chapter, you should be able to:

1. Name the components of a disc brake.

2. Describe the operation of disc brakes.

3. Explain the difference between fixed, floating, and sliding calipers.

4. Describe disc-brake wear indicators.

Disc brakes have a greater ability to dissipate heat than drum brakes do. With drum brakes, the heat is trapped inside the drum. The heat must then be transferred through the drum and dissipated to the surrounding air. Disc-brake rotors and calipers are exposed to the air; therefore, the heat is dissipated directly to the air.

DISC-BRAKE COMPONENTS

Disc brakes are used at the front wheels of most cars and also at the rear wheels of some cars. A front-wheel disc-brake-and-rotor assembly for a rear-wheel-drive car is shown in Fig. 5-1. The rotor mounts on a spindle and

is supported on wheel bearings. There are two wheel bearings: an inner bearing and an outer bearing. The inner bearing is the bearing closest to the center of the car; the outer bearing is farthest from the center of the car. The center part of the rotor that houses the bearings is the *hub*.

The spindle is part of the *steering knuckle*. The steering knuckle attaches to the front suspension of the car, and it pivots to allow the wheels to move in and out for steering. A spindle nut threads onto the end of the spindle and holds the rotor-and-bearing assembly on the spindle. A nut lock and cotter pin prevent the nut from loosening. A splash shield (Fig. 5-1) protects the rotor from water splashes and road debris.

A front-wheel disc-brake-and-rotor assembly for a front-wheel-drive car is shown in Fig. 5-2. The bearings are part of the hub-and-bearing assembly, which attaches to the steering knuckle. The rotor fits over studs in the hub-and-bearing assembly and is held in place by the wheel. The caliper is attached to the steering knuckle (Fig. 5-3). The function of the caliper is to push the brake pads against both sides of the rotor.

A brake hose supplies brake fluid from the master cylinder to the caliper (Fig. 5-3). On some calipers, the brake hose threads into the caliper inlet port (Fig. 5-4). On other calipers, the hose is attached with a special bolt, sometimes called a *banjo bolt* (Figs. 5-3 and 5-5). The bolt has a drilled passage. Brake fluid flows from the brake hose, through the passage in the bolt, and into the caliper. A bleeder screw (Fig. 5-2) threads into another

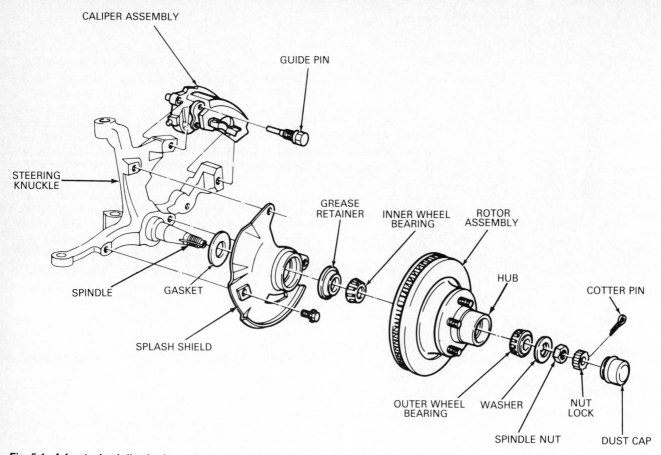

Fig. 5-1. A front-wheel disc-brake-and-rotor assembly for a rear-wheel-drive car. *(Ford Motor Company)*

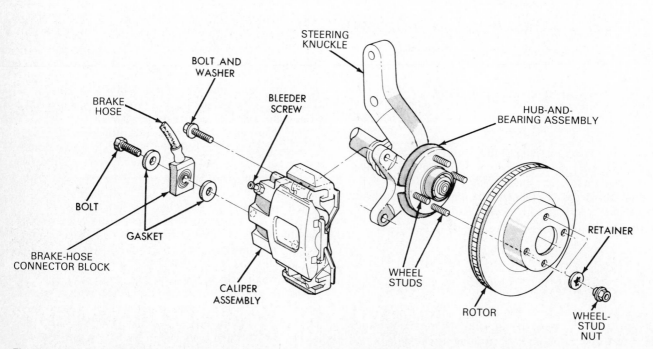

Fig. 5-2. A front-wheel disc-brake-and-rotor assembly for a front-wheel-drive car. *(Chrysler Corporation)*

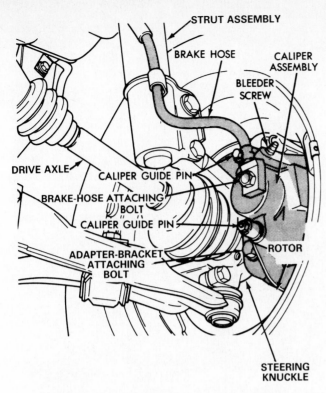

Fig. 5-3. A disc-brake caliper shown attached to the steering knuckle on a front-wheel-drive car. *(Chrysler Corporation)*

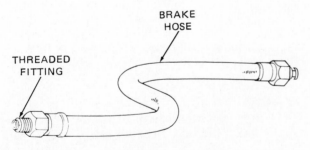

Fig. 5-4. A brake hose that threads into a caliper. *(EIS Division of Parker Hannifin Corporation)*

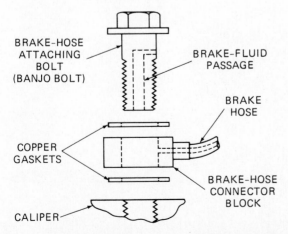

Fig. 5-5. The bolt that attaches the brake hose to the caliper.

hole in the caliper and permits air to be bled from the hydraulic system.

In the brake assembly shown in Fig. 5-1, the steering knuckle is the mounting bracket for the brake caliper. Some calipers do not attach directly to the steering knuckle. Instead, they are attached to an adapter, or *mounting bracket* (Fig. 5-6), and the bracket bolts to the steering knuckle.

When the brakes are applied, the brake pads apply friction force to the rotor to slow its rotation (Fig. 5-7). The rotor applies an equal and opposite force to the pads. This force is transferred through the pads to the caliper and tends to drag the caliper around with the rotor. This twisting or rotating force on the caliper is the braking torque. The caliper mounting bracket and steering knuckle resist the braking torque. For this reason, the caliper mounting bracket is also called the *anchor plate*.

There are two basic types of calipers: *fixed calipers* and *moving calipers*.

FIXED CALIPERS

When disc brakes were first introduced on cars, fixed calipers were used at the front wheels. They are now used only at the rear wheels of some cars that have four-wheel disc brakes. The fixed caliper is bolted to the mounting bracket and remains in a fixed position. Pistons on both sides of the caliper move to push the brake pads into contact with the rotor (Fig. 5-8). Some fixed calipers use four pistons, two on each side of the rotor. A four-piston caliper is shown in Figs. 5-9 and 5-10. The caliper body is made in two halves. Each half has two pistons. The caliper halves are bolted together with bolts called *bridge bolts*.

The brake hose attaches to the inlet port, which is located in the inner half of the caliper. The caliper shown in Figs. 5-9 and 5-10 has a transfer tube. This tube transfers brake fluid from the inner half of the caliper to the outer half. Some fixed calipers have internal transfer passages (Fig. 5-11). The caliper in Fig. 5-11 has springs that help keep the brake pads in light contact with the rotor.

A piston seal is used to prevent brake-fluid leakage past the pistons. The seal is square in cross section (Fig. 5-12). The piston seal on some fixed calipers is located in a groove in the piston. As the piston moves, the seal slides in the caliper bore. This type of seal is called a *stroking seal*. On most calipers, the piston seal is located in a groove in the caliper bore. As the piston moves, it slides through the seal. This type of seal is called a *fixed seal*.

A dust boot is used to prevent dirt or moisture from contaminating the caliper bore (Fig. 5-13). The dust boot fits into a groove near the outer end of the piston. The outer diameter of the boot fits into a groove in the caliper. In the caliper shown in Fig. 5-14, the outer diameter of the dust boot fits into a groove in the open end of the caliper bore.

Some fixed calipers have three pistons, two in one half of the caliper and one in the other half. Other fixed calipers have two pistons, one in each half of the caliper.

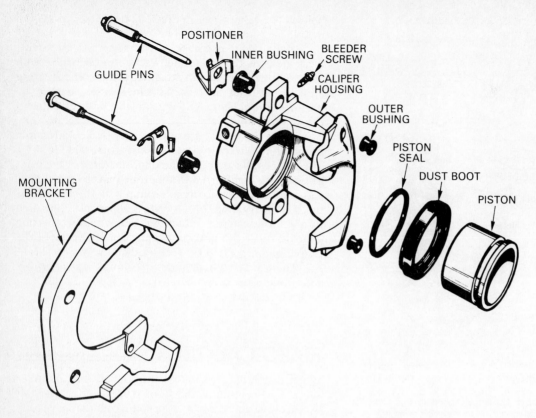

Fig. 5-6. A mounting bracket used to attach a caliper to a steering knuckle. *(Bendix After-market Brake Division)*

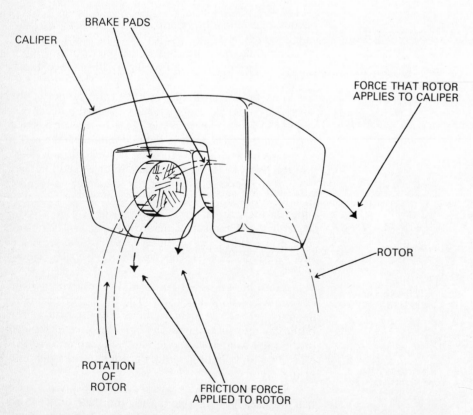

Fig. 5-7. The forces acting in a disc-brake caliper and rotor when the brakes are applied.
(EIS Division of Parker Hannifin Corporation)

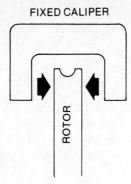

Fig. 5-8. The operation of a fixed caliper. *(EIS Division of Parker Hannifin Corporation)*

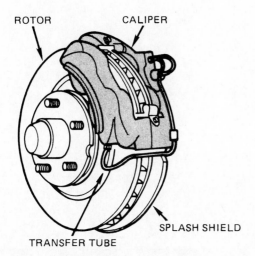

Fig. 5-9. A four-piston disc-brake caliper and rotor. *(Bendix Aftermarket Brake Division)*

MOVING CALIPERS

Most moving calipers are made in one piece and have only one piston (Fig. 5-15). However, some have two pistons located in the same part of the caliper (Fig. 5-16). A moving caliper is mounted so that it is free to move on the mounting bracket (Fig. 5-17). The piston is located in the inner part of the caliper. The inner brake pad is located between the piston and the rotor. The outer pad is located between the outer part of the caliper and the other side of the rotor.

The piston seal in a moving caliper is a fixed seal. It is located in a groove in the caliper bore (Fig. 5-18). When the brake pedal is depressed, the brake fluid in the caliper is pressurized. This pushes the piston toward the rotor. The movement of the piston distorts the seal (Fig. 5-19). The piston forces the inner brake pad against the rotor. When the pad is pressed against the rotor, the piston cannot move farther and stops (Fig. 5-20).

Hydraulic pressure acts equally in all directions. This means that hydraulic pressure also pushes against the inside surface of the caliper. This pressure pushes the caliper inward toward the center of the car (Fig. 5-21). The movement of the caliper forces the outer brake pad against the other side of the rotor. Therefore, both brake pads apply friction force to the rotor, slowing its rotation.

When the brake pedal is released, hydraulic pressure is removed from the piston. The piston seal returns to its original shape (Fig. 5-18) and pulls the piston slightly back into the caliper bore. At the same time, the caliper moves outward slightly, which removes the force from the outer pad. Now the brake pads no longer apply friction force to the rotor, and the rotor can spin. Because the piston-and-caliper movement is so small, the brake pads are not pulled completely away from the rotor. Instead, they remain in light contact with the rotor.

Because the pads remain in light contact with the rotor when the brakes are released, there is a slight drag

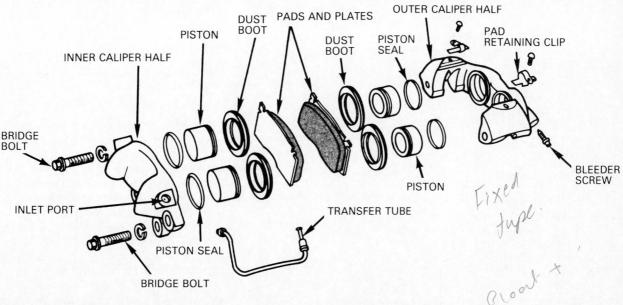

Fig. 5-10. An exploded view of a four-piston caliper with a transfer tube. *(Bendix Aftermarket Brake Division)*

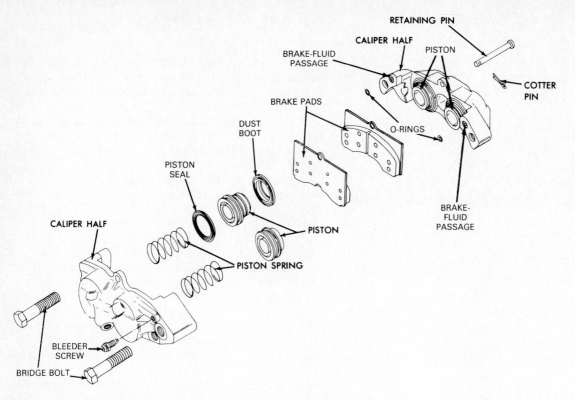

Fig. 5-11. An exploded view of a four-piston caliper with an internal transfer passage. *(Chevrolet Motor Division of General Motors Corporation)*

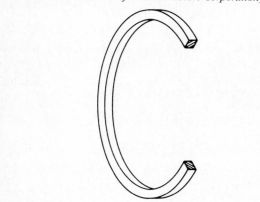

Fig. 5-12. A piston seal.

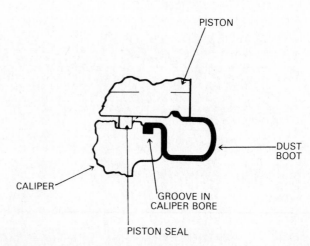

Fig. 5-14. A dust boot that fits into a groove in the open end of the caliper bore. *(Ford Motor Company)*

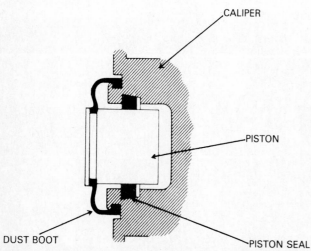

Fig. 5-13. The location of the dust boot, which prevents dirt or water from contaminating the caliper bore. *(EIS Division of Parker Hannifin Corporation)*

on the rotor. Therefore, the engine must work harder to overcome this drag. The result is a slightly reduced fuel economy.

Some calipers are called *zero-drag calipers*. In a zero-drag caliper, the groove that the piston seal fits into is a different shape than the groove in other calipers (Fig. 5-22). When the brakes are applied, the seal distorts by a greater amount than do the seals in other calipers. Then, when the brakes are released, the seal pulls the piston back farther from the rotor. Therefore, the brake pads are pulled completely away from the rotor. Zero-drag calipers provide greater fuel economy.

There are two common mounting arrangements of moving calipers. These are called *floating calipers* and *sliding calipers*.

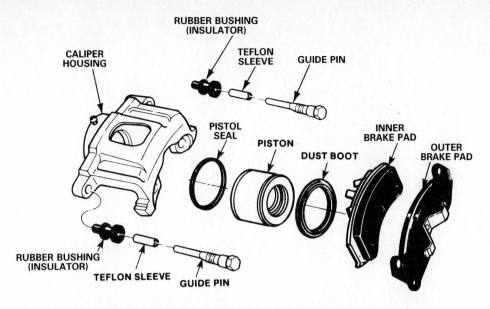

Fig. 5-15. A moving caliper with one piston. *(Bendix Aftermarket Brake Division)*

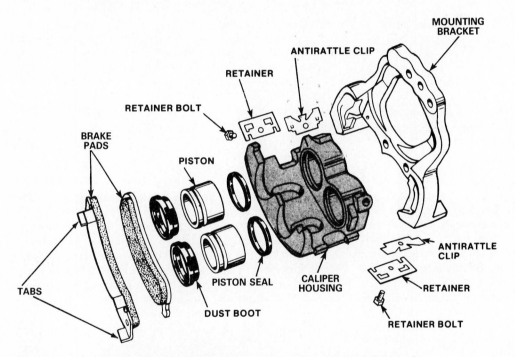

Fig. 5-16. A moving caliper with two pistons. *(Bendix Aftermarket Brake Division)*

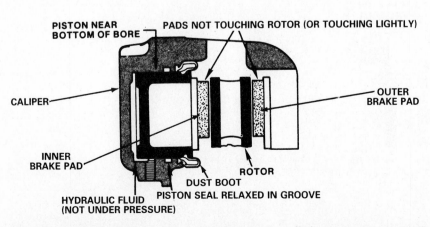

Fig. 5-17. A moving caliper, when the brakes are not applied. *(Bendix Aftermarket Brake Division)*

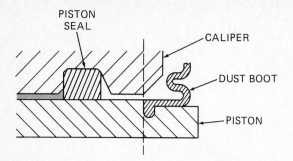

Fig. 5-18. The piston seal shown in its relaxed position, with the brakes not applied. *(General Motors Corporation)*

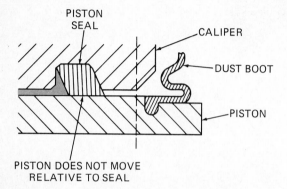

Fig. 5-19. When the brakes are applied, the piston moves out of the caliper bore and distorts the piston seal. *(General Motors Corporation)*

Floating Calipers

Figure 5-23 shows a caliper assembly attached to the mounting bracket. It is attached to the bracket with two mounting bolts, or *guide pins*. The bolts are called guide pins because the caliper can move on the pins, and the pins guide the inward and outward movement of the caliper.

Sleeves are provided in the caliper to allow it to move on the pins (Fig. 5-15). The sleeves are held by rubber bushings, or *insulators*, which fit in grooves in the guide-pin holes. When the brakes are applied, the

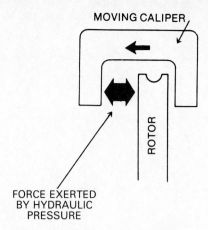

Fig. 5-21. The operation of a moving caliper. *(EIS Division of Parker Hannifin Corporation)*

bushings allow a slight sideward movement of the caliper with respect to the guide pins. The name "floating" is given because of the ability of the caliper to move inward, outward, and sideward.

Figure 5-24 shows a floating-caliper assembly that attaches to the steering knuckle with mounting bolts. These mounting bolts are *not* guide pins, because the caliper does not slide on them. The caliper guide pins are part of the mounting bracket (Fig. 5-25), and the mounting bracket is part of the caliper assembly (Fig. 5-26).

Sliding Calipers

The principle of operation of a sliding caliper (Fig. 5-27) is the same as that of a floating caliper. The difference is in the method of attaching the caliper to the mounting bracket (Fig. 5-28). Machined grooves in the caliper slide on the mounting bracket. The grooves (or sliding surfaces) in the caliper and mounting bracket are called *ways*. The caliper is held in the ways by a retaining key, a spring, and a lock screw. There is no sideward motion of the caliper when the brakes are applied.

Figure 5-29 shows a sliding caliper that is made up of a frame (called a *yoke*) and a cylinder housing. The

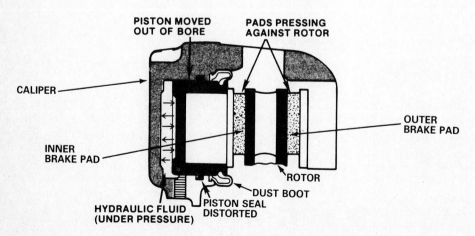

Fig. 5-20. A moving caliper, with the brakes applied. *(Bendix Aftermarket Brake Division)*

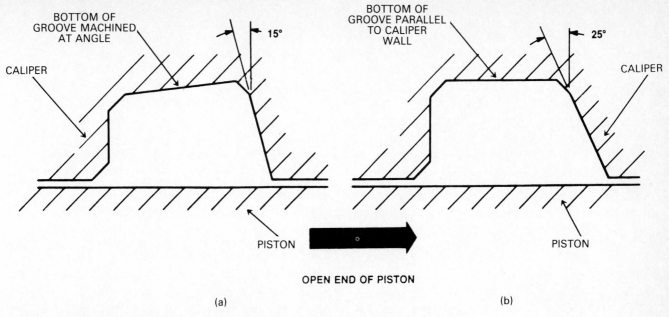

Fig. 5-22. Piston seal grooves in disc-brake-caliper bores: *(a)* non-zero-drag caliper; *(b)* zero-drag caliper. *(General Motors Corporation)*

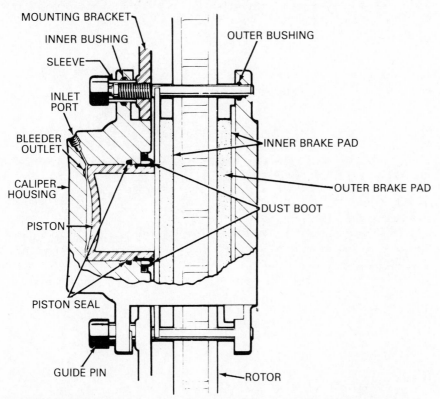

Fig. 5-23. A floating caliper. *(Delco Moraine Division of General Motors Corporation)*

cylinder housing is only part of a caliper because the piston in the housing can apply force to a brake pad only on one side of the rotor. The yoke is needed to apply force to the pad on the other side of the rotor.

The mounting bracket is bolted to the steering knuckle. The brake pads are held in the bracket with two retaining pins. The cylinder housing is attached to the yoke, and the yoke is free to slide on the mounting bracket. When the brakes are applied, hydraulic pressure pushes against the piston in the cylinder housing. The

piston pushes the inner brake pad against the inner side of the rotor. Hydraulic pressure also pushes the cylinder housing inward toward the center of the car. Because the yoke is attached to the cylinder housing, the yoke moves with the housing. This pushes the outer brake pad against the other side of the rotor.

Figure 5-30 shows a sliding-yoke caliper that has two pistons. Both pistons are in the same cylinder bore. When the brakes are applied, hydraulic pressure pushes the pistons away from each other (Fig. 5-31). The operation is

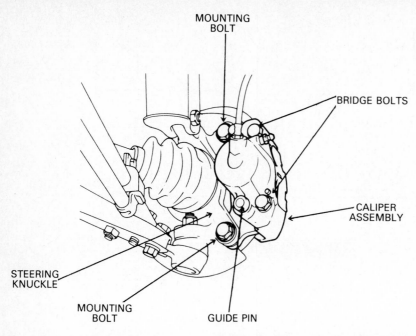

MOUNTING
BOLT

BRIDGE BOLTS

CALIPER
ASSEMBLY

STEERING
KNUCKLE

MOUNTING
BOLT

GUIDE PIN

Fig. 5-24. A floating-caliper assembly that attaches to the steering knuckle with mounting bolts. *(Chrysler Corporation)*

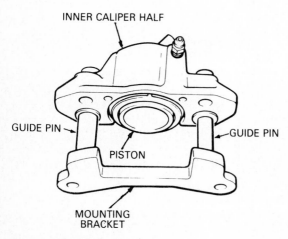

INNER CALIPER HALF

GUIDE PIN

PISTON

GUIDE PIN

MOUNTING
BRACKET

Fig. 5-25. A mounting bracket with guide pins, which is part of a caliper assembly. *(Chrysler Corporation)*

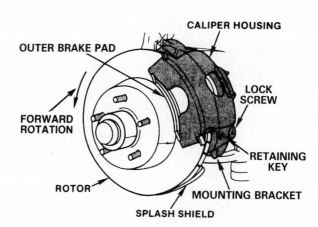

OUTER BRAKE PAD

CALIPER HOUSING

LOCK
SCREW

FORWARD
ROTATION

RETAINING
KEY

ROTOR

MOUNTING BRACKET

SPLASH SHIELD

Fig. 5-27. A sliding caliper. *(Bendix Aftermarket Brake Division)*

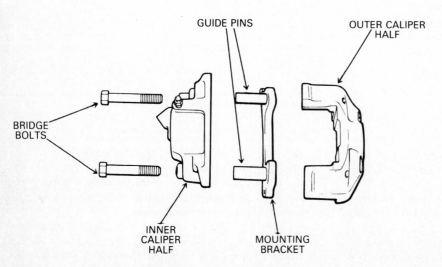

GUIDE PINS

OUTER CALIPER
HALF

BRIDGE
BOLTS

INNER
CALIPER
HALF

MOUNTING
BRACKET

Fig. 5-26. A caliper assembly that includes a mounting bracket. *(Chrysler Corporation)*

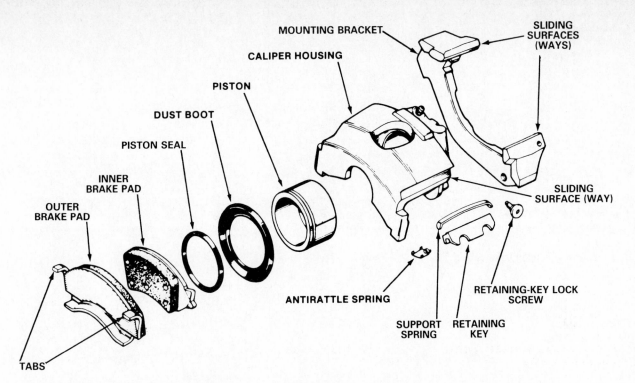

Fig. 5-28. An exploded view of a sliding caliper. *(Bendix Aftermarket Brake Division)*

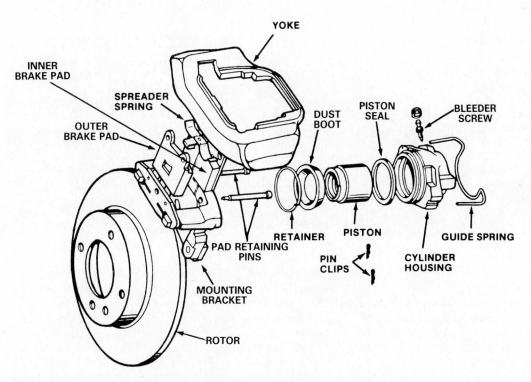

Fig. 5-29. A single-piston sliding-yoke caliper. *(Bendix Aftermarket Brake Division)*

similar to that of a wheel cylinder used with a drum brake.

The pistons are called the *direct piston* and the *indirect piston*. Hydraulic pressure causes the direct piston to push the inner brake pad against the inner side of the rotor. The pressure also causes the indirect piston to push the yoke inward toward the center of the car. The movement of the yoke pushes the outer pad against the other side of the rotor.

BRAKE-PAD WEAR

Figure 5-32 shows the position of the piston in the caliper bore with new brake pads. As the brake pads wear, the piston gradually moves farther and farther out through the seal. Figure 5-33 shows the position of the piston when the pads are worn. More brake fluid is needed to fill the space between the piston and the end of the caliper when the pads are worn. This fluid is grad-

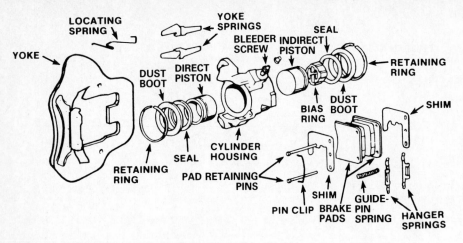

Fig. 5-30. A dual-piston sliding-yoke caliper. *(Bendix Aftermarket Brake Division)*

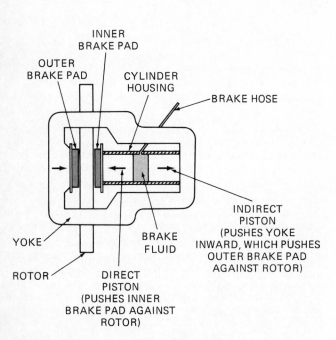

Fig. 5-31. The operation of a dual-piston sliding-yoke caliper.

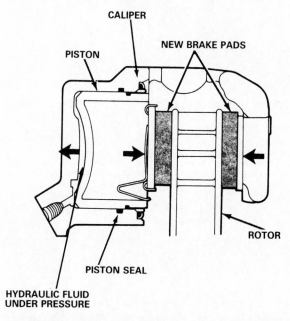

Fig. 5-32. The position of the piston in a moving caliper with new brake pads. *(Chevrolet Motor Division of General Motors Corporation)*

ually transferred from the master cylinder to the calipers as the pads wear.

Some floating-caliper brake pads wear in a tapered pattern (Fig. 5-34). This is because of the sideward or twisting movement of the caliper when the brakes are applied. This wear pattern is considered normal, unless the linings are excessively tapered.

BRAKE-PAD WEAR INDICATORS

As the brake pads wear, the friction material becomes thinner. This causes the rivets, on riveted linings, to move gradually closer to the rotor. When enough wear has taken place, the rivets contact the rotor. This metal-to-metal contact causes a squealing or scraping sound when the rotor spins, and it damages the rotor. On bonded

linings, if enough wear has taken place, the metal shoe contacts the rotor. Again, noise and damage result.

Some cars have a wear indicator on the inner brake pad of each caliper assembly (Fig. 5-35a). A spring clip is attached to the shoe with a rivet. When a certain amount of wear has taken place, the end of the clip contacts the rotor. As the rotor spins and rubs against the clip (Fig. 5-35b), a scraping or squealing noise is produced. This alerts the driver that the brakes require service.

ELECTRICAL WEAR SENSORS

Some brake pads have an electrical wear sensor located inside the lining material (Fig. 5-36). Two wires attach to the brake pad shown in Fig. 5-36. The wires form a loop, and a part of the loop is imbedded in the lining material. When the pad wears to a predetermined thick-

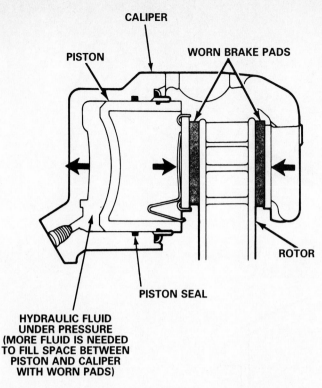

Fig. 5-33. The position of the piston in a moving caliper with worn brake pads. *(Chevrolet Motor Division of General Motors Corporation)*

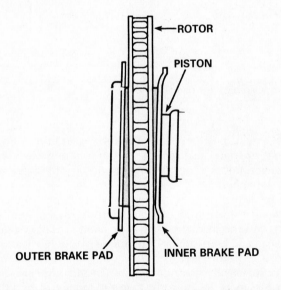

Fig. 5-34. The tapered wear pattern sometimes found on brake pads used with floating calipers. *(Bendix Aftermarket Brake Division)*

ness, the loop breaks, and an electronic circuit lights the warning lamp. The lamp will also light if the sensor is unplugged.

Other brake pads with wear sensors have a single wire. The wire connects to the sensor in the lining material. When a certain amount of wear has taken place, the sensor is exposed and touches the rotor. When this occurs, an electric circuit is grounded through the rotor, and the warning lamp is turned on.

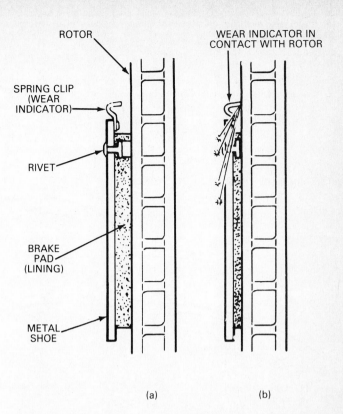

Fig. 5-35. A wear indicator attached to an inner brake pad. *(a)* With new brake pads, the wear indicator does not touch the rotor; *(b)* with worn brake pads, the wear indicator touches the rotor and makes a scraping or squealing sound when the rotor turns. *(Delco Moraine Division of General Motors Corporation)*

Figure 5-37 shows a brake pad that uses a plug-in sensor, which is part of the vehicle wiring. The sensor is plugged into a mounting hole in the metal shoe when the pad is installed in the caliper. When a certain amount of wear has taken place, the sensor touches the rotor. This grounds the warning-lamp circuit and lights the lamp.

PISTON MATERIALS

A fixed piston seal grips the piston tightly so that fluid cannot pass between the seal and the piston. For the seal to work, the piston surface must be smooth; otherwise, the caliper will leak. In addition, the piston must be smooth so that it can slide through the seal as the brake pads wear. If the piston surface is corroded, the piston will not slide properly through the seal.

For this reason, pistons are usually made of nickel-chrome-plated steel. The plating is smooth and tends to resist corrosion. However, most metal pistons may corrode eventually.

Some cars use plastic pistons made of *phenolic*. This material is not as strong as steel, but it remains smooth and does not corrode. In addition, plastic pistons are lighter in weight than steel pistons. Phenolic does not conduct heat as well as steel. Therefore, when phenolic pistons are used, less heat is transferred to the brake fluid during braking.

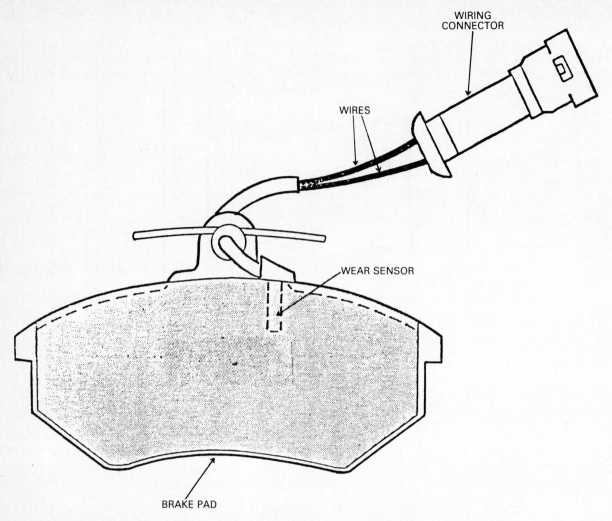

Fig. 5-36. An electrical wear sensor in the lining of a disc-brake pad. *(Vera Imported Parts Corporation)*

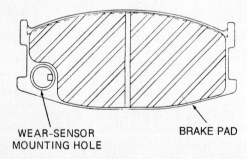

Fig. 5-37. A disc-brake pad with a mounting hole for an electrical wear sensor. *(Vera Imported Parts Corporation)*

BRAKE-PAD MATERIALS

Disc brakes may use either semimetallic or organic linings. At high temperatures, semimetallic linings provide better braking. At lower temperatures, organic linings are better. The lining material chosen by the vehicle manufacturer depends on the temperature at which the brakes will operate.

In theory, moving calipers apply an equal braking force to each brake pad. The piston pushes the inner brake pad against one side of the rotor, and the caliper pushes the outer pad against the other side of the rotor. However, under actual driving conditions this does not always happen.

For equal force to be applied to each pad, the calipers must move freely. The guide pins on floating calipers, and the machined ways on sliding calipers, must be clean and lubricated. Sometimes a lack of lubrication, corrosion from water, or road contamination prevents the caliper from moving freely. Then the outer pad applies less force to the rotor than the inner pad, and the inner pad does most of the braking. The result is that the inner pad becomes hotter and wears more than the outer pad.

For this reason, some cars use a semimetallic lining on the inner pad and an organic lining on the outer pad. When two different lining materials are used for the inner and outer pads, they are called *hybrid brake pads*.

DISC-BRAKE COOLING

One of the most important factors that determine the effectiveness of brakes is how effectively the brake parts can dissipate heat to the surrounding air. If this is not done effectively, the temperature of the brake parts can become too high. This can result in heat fade and can cause the brake fluid to boil. The underbody of the car and the splash shield on the brake assembly are designed to direct cooling air past the brake parts.

Some calipers have cooling fins to help dissipate heat (Fig. 5-38). Most of the heat generated during braking is produced in the rotor; therefore, the rotor must effectively dissipate heat. Some rotors are solid, and some are ventilated (Fig. 5-39). Ventilated rotors have two friction surfaces that are joined by cooling fins (louvers).

Heat flows faster through metal than it does from metal to air. In solid rotors, the heat flows quickly from the friction surfaces of the rotor to its interior; then the heat is gradually dissipated from the rotor to the surrounding air. The advantage of a solid rotor over a ventilated rotor is fast removal of heat from the friction surfaces. The disadvantage is that if the brakes are applied for long periods of time, the heat will build up in the rotor and will cause its temperature to become excessive. For this reason, solid rotors are usually used on light-weight cars.

Heavier cars use ventilated rotors that have fins, or louvers, between the two friction surfaces. With ventilated rotors, cooling air flows between the friction surfaces (Fig. 5-40). The louvers increase the surface area of the rotor so that more heat can be dissipated to the surrounding air. These rotors do not have a solid interior to absorb heat quickly, but their greater surface area provides better cooling than does a solid rotor.

Some rotors have curved louvers, which scoop the air so that more air flows through the rotor for greater

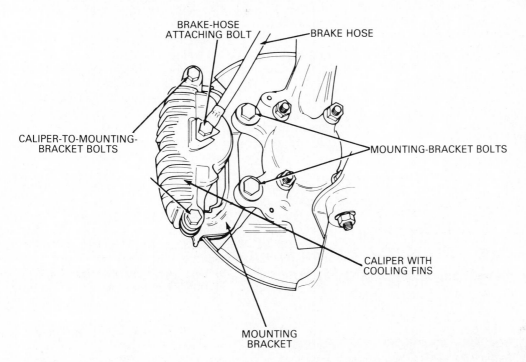

Fig. 5-38. A disc-brake caliper with cooling fins. *(Delco Moraine Division of General Motors Corporation)*

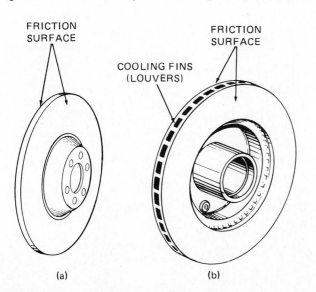

Fig. 5-39. Disc-brake rotors: *(a)* solid; *(b)* ventilated. *(FMC Corporation)*

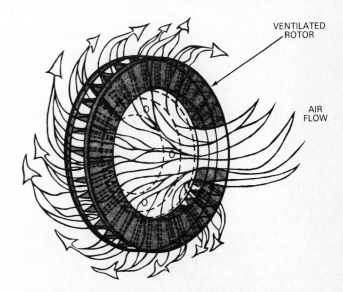

Fig. 5-40. The flow of air through a ventilated rotor. *(General Motors Corporation)*

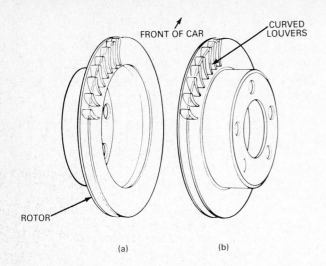

Fig. 5-41. Disc-brake rotors with curved louvers: *(a)* **left-rear brake;** *(b)* **right-rear brake.** *(Ford Motor Company)*

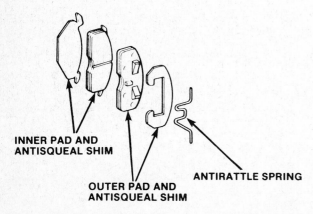

Fig. 5-42. Shims used with disc-brake pads to prevent squeal. *(Bendix Aftermarket Brake Division)*

cooling (Fig. 5-41). Because the louvers are curved, air flows through the rotor only when it is spinning in the proper direction. If the rotor spins in the opposite direction, air does not flow through it. Therefore, these rotors cannot be interchanged from one side of the car to the other. They are marked for the side of the car on which they should be installed.

DISC-BRAKE NOISE

Disc-brake noise, or squeal, can be caused by metal-to-metal contact when the brake pads are worn. But squeal can also be produced with new brake pads. When the brakes are applied, the brake pads contact the spinning rotor. Sometimes the friction between the pad and the rotor produces a vibration in the pad. The metal shoes then vibrate against the piston or the caliper, which causes a high-pitched sound.

Several methods are used to prevent squeal. Some brakes have a thin *shim*, or *insulator*, between the shoe and the piston (Fig. 5-42). The shim acts as a cushion, minimizing pad vibration and squeal. Other disc brakes have antirattle clips (Fig. 5-16) or springs (Fig. 5-28) to help minimize pad vibration. Sometimes a thin coating of antisqueal compound is applied to the backs of the shoes. *Antisqueal compound* is a heat-resistant material in the form of a paste or spray that minimizes pad vibration.

Some rotors are manufactured with a single groove in the center of the friction surface (Fig. 5-43). The brake pad wears into this groove, and the groove holds the pad to help minimize pad noise and vibration.

On some brakes a clicking sound is heard each time the brakes are applied. This is caused by a slight shift in

Fig. 5-43. A rotor with a groove in the center of the friction surface. The groove holds the pad to help minimize pad vibration and squeal. *(Oldsmobile Division of General Motors Corporation)*

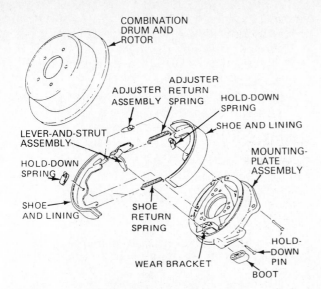

Fig. 5-44. A cable-operated drum brake, which functions as a parking brake on a vehicle with rear disc brakes. *(Wagner Division, Cooper Industries Inc.)*

the brake-pad position. Many brake pads have tabs on the outer shoe that are bent to grip the caliper when the pads are installed (Figs. 5-16 and 5-28). This usually prevents clicking noises.

REAR-DISC-BRAKE PARKING BRAKES

Two types of parking brakes are used with rear disc brakes. One type has a small cable-operated drum brake that functions only as a parking brake (Fig. 5-44). The drum is part of a combination disc-brake rotor and brake drum. The caliper and rotor are the service brake.

Another type of parking brake is a disc-brake caliper with a built-in parking brake (Fig. 5-45). When the brakes are applied, the brake pads are applied mechanically.

Both types of parking brakes are described in Chap. 6.

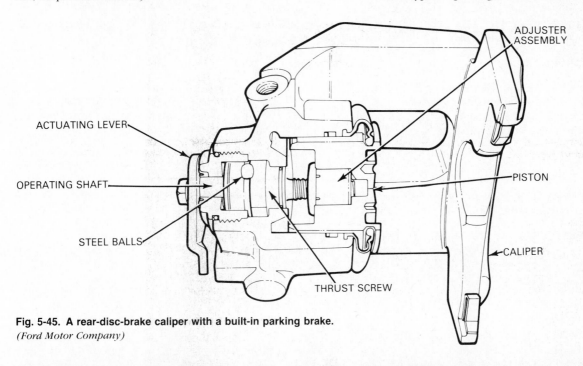

Fig. 5-45. A rear-disc-brake caliper with a built-in parking brake. *(Ford Motor Company)*

Hybrid brake pads Two brake pads, used on the same wheel, that have different lining materials.

Indirect piston That piston in a dual-piston sliding-yoke caliper which pushes the yoke and causes the outer brake pad to be pushed against the outer side of the rotor.

Mounting bracket The bracket which attaches to a steering knuckle and to which the caliper is bolted.

Phenolic A plastic material.

Shim A thin material used as a spacer.

Sliding caliper A moving caliper that slides on machined ways.

Spindle A tapered shaft, threaded at one end, on which a rotor is mounted on bearings.

Steering knuckle The part of a car which attaches to the front suspension and which pivots to allow the wheels to move in and out for steering.

Stroking seal A piston seal that fits into a groove in a caliper piston. The seal slides over the surface of the caliper bore.

Ways The machined grooves or sliding surfaces on a caliper or mounting bracket on which the caliper slides.

Yoke The metal frame that is used with a cylinder housing to form a disc-brake caliper.

Zero-drag caliper A caliper in which the brake pads do not produce a drag on the rotor when the brakes are not applied.

REVIEW QUESTIONS

Select the *one* correct, best, or most probable answer to each question.

1. Technician A says that hybrid brake pads are used only on some moving calipers. Technician B says that with hybrid pads, the semimetallic lining is used on the outside of the rotor. Who is right?
   a. A only
   b. B only
   c. Both A and B
   d. Neither A nor B

2. Disc-brake pads are most likely to wear in a tapered pattern on:
   a. rear calipers.
   b. fixed calipers.
   c. floating calipers.
   d. sliding calipers.

3. All of the following are true of phenolic pistons *except*:
   a. Phenolic does not corrode
   b. Phenolic is lighter than steel
   c. Phenolic transfers heat better than steel does
   d. Phenolic remains smooth

4. Which of the following dissipates the greatest amount of heat?
   a. A brake drum
   b. A solid rotor
   c. A ventilated rotor
   d. A ventilated rotor with curved louvers

5. Technician A says that moving calipers provide equal braking force at each brake pad. Technician B says that the inner brake pad often wears more than the outer pad. Who is right?
   a. A only
   b. B only
   c. Both A and B
   d. Neither A nor B

6. All of the following are true of single-piston sliding-yoke calipers *except*:
   a. The yoke forces the outer brake pad against the rotor
   b. Hydraulic pressure causes the yoke to move
   c. The yoke slides on the mounting bracket
   d. The direct piston applies force directly to the yoke

7. All of the following can cause disc-brake noise *except*:
   a. Brake-pad vibration
   b. A worn piston seal
   c. Loose brake pads
   d. Metal-to-metal contact

8. Zero-drag calipers have:
   a. hybrid brake pads.
   b. four pistons.
   c. a piston-seal groove that is shaped differently than the groove in a non-zero-drag caliper.
   d. larger-diameter pistons than a non-zero-drag caliper.

9. Guide pins are used with:
   a. sliding yoke calipers.
   b. sliding calipers.
   c. fixed calipers.
   d. floating calipers.

10. Which type of caliper moves in machined ways in the mounting bracket?
    a. A sliding caliper
    b. A caliper with hybrid brake pads
    c. A floating caliper
    d. A fixed caliper

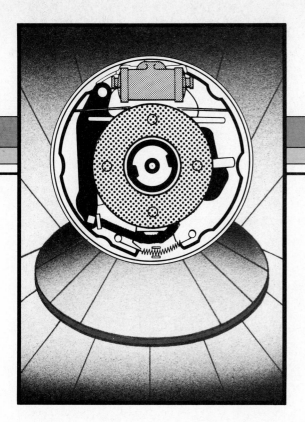

CHAPTER 6

PARKING BRAKES

OBJECTIVES

After you have studied this chapter, you should be able to:

1. Name the components of the various types of parking brakes.

2. Describe the operation of drum-brake parking brakes.

3. Describe the operation of caliper-type parking brakes.

Parking brakes are used to prevent the car from moving while it is parked. They can also be used in an emergency if the service brakes fail. However, parking brakes are not as effective in stopping a moving car as are the service brakes. Parking brakes operate on two wheels only. On most cars they operate on the rear wheels, but on some front-wheel-drive cars they operate on the front wheels.

Because parking brakes must be able to stop a car if the service brakes fail, parking brakes must operate independently of the service brakes. For this reason, parking brakes are mechanical brakes. On most cars the parking brakes use the same brake shoes as the service brakes. These are called *integral parking brakes*. Those which use a different set of shoes are called *independent parking brakes*.

There are two methods used to apply parking brakes. Some parking brakes are applied by hand, and others are applied by foot. Figure 6-1 shows a hand-operated lever. Most hand-operated levers are located either in the center console or in the floor between the driver's seat and the passenger's seat. When the lever is pulled upward, the brake is applied. A ratchet and pawl hold the lever in the applied position. A push button is located at the end of the lever. Pressing the button lifts the pawl and unlocks the ratchet so that the brake can be released.

Some hand-operated parking brakes have a T-shaped handle located beneath the instrument panel. When the handle is pulled toward the driver, the brake is applied. To release the brake, the handle is twisted and then returned to its released position. The mechanism that is used to apply and release the parking brake is the *control unit*.

Figure 6-2 shows a control unit with a foot-operated pedal. A ratchet (sometimes in the form of a wheel) and pawl are used to hold the brake in the applied position. A release handle and rod attach to a ratchet release lever. When the handle is pulled, the pawl is lifted from the ratchet and releases the brake. On some vehicles the release handle is connected to the control unit with a cable.

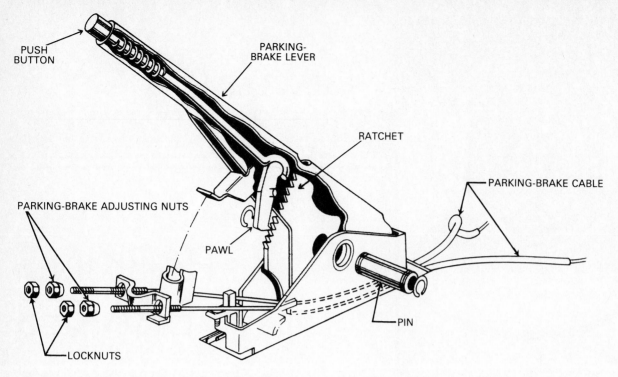

PUSH BUTTON

PARKING-BRAKE LEVER

RATCHET

PARKING-BRAKE CABLE

PARKING-BRAKE ADJUSTING NUTS

PAWL

PIN

LOCKNUTS

Fig. 6-1. A hand-operated parking-brake control unit. *(Audi of America, Inc.)*

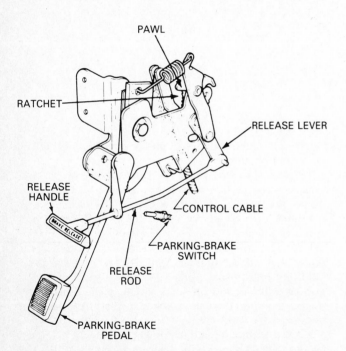

PAWL

RATCHET

RELEASE LEVER

RELEASE HANDLE

CONTROL CABLE

PARKING-BRAKE SWITCH

RELEASE ROD

PARKING-BRAKE PEDAL

BRAKE RELEASE

Fig. 6-2. A foot-operated parking-brake control unit. *(Chrysler Corporation)*

VACUUM-RELEASE PARKING-BRAKE SYSTEMS

On some cars the brake is automatically released when the transmission selector lever is placed in DRIVE or REVERSE. On other cars the parking brake automatically releases only when the selector lever is placed in DRIVE.

Figure 6-3 shows a *vacuum motor* connected to the parking-brake control unit. A vacuum motor has two chambers separated by a *diaphragm* (Fig 6-4). The diaphragm is flexible, and has a rod attached to it. The rod extends out through one of the chambers and attaches to the parking-brake release lever (Fig. 6-3). This chamber of the vacuum motor is open to the atmosphere.

The other chamber has a small tube that connects to an opening in the chamber (Fig. 6-4). A vacuum hose connects to that tube. The other end of the hose connects through a vacuum valve to the engine intake manifold (Fig. 6-5). The intake manifold is used as the source of vacuum (the engine must be running to build up vacuum). The vacuum valve is operated by the transmission selector lever, and the valve controls the vacuum that is applied to the vacuum motor.

When the parking brake is applied and the transmission selector lever is in PARK or NEUTRAL, no vacuum is applied to the diaphragm (Fig. 6-4a). When the transmission selector lever is moved to DRIVE or REVERSE, the vacuum valve applies vacuum to the diaphragm. Now, with vacuum on one side of the diaphragm and atmospheric pressure on the other side, the diaphragm moves downward (Fig. 6-4b). This movement pulls the rod and releases the parking brake. The parking-brake release lever can be manually operated if there is a failure in the vacuum system.

Vacuum and atmospheric pressure are described in Chap. 7.

PARKING-BRAKE CABLES

Cables connect the parking-brake pedal or lever to the brake assemblies (Fig. 6-6). A *cable* is a bundle of wire strands that are twisted together. A *front cable*, or *con-*

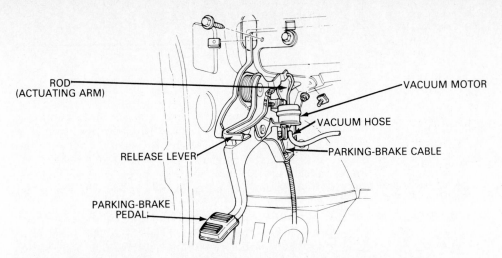

Fig. 6-3. A vacuum motor connected to the release lever of a parking-brake control unit.
(Cadillac Motor Car Division of General Motors Corporation)

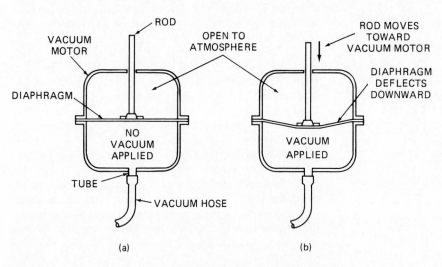

Fig. 6-4. A vacuum motor: (a) no vacuum applied; (b) vacuum applied.

trol cable, connects from the parking-brake control unit to an *equalizer*. The equalizer provides equal braking force to each wheel.

A *rear cable* passes through a guide in the equalizer. Each end of the cable connects to a rear-brake assembly. The equalizer provides equal braking because the rear cable can slip through the guide in the equalizer. If there is greater tension in either part of the cable, the cable slips through the guide until the tension in both parts of the cable is equal (Fig. 6-7).

Hooks, or *cable retainers*, are often used to hold the cables in position along the frame or underbody of the car (Fig. 6-8). The cable retainers pivot at their point of attachment to the frame or underbody. The movement of the cable retainer also serves to equalize the braking force at each rear wheel.

The control cable and the rear cables are partially covered with a flexible metal housing (Fig. 6-9). The cable slides in the housing, and the housing prevents the cable from rubbing against the body or frame of the car. One end of the housing is usually held to a bracket on the underbody of the car with a clip (Fig. 6-10). The part of the front cable enclosed by the housing passes through the underbody of the car and attaches to the parking-brake control unit. The housing usually attaches to the unit with a clip. On a car with drum brakes, the part of the rear cable enclosed by the housing passes through the backing plate. On most cars the housing is held to the backing plate with retaining prongs, which are part of the housing (Figs. 6-9 and 6-11). On disc brakes with an integral parking brake, the housing attaches to a bracket on the axle assembly (Fig. 6-12) or to the caliper.

Some parking-brake cables are plastic-coated. Plastic-coated cables slide more easily through their housings and are less affected by corrosion. Because the cables slide more easily, less force is required to apply the brakes.

Many cars have a three-part rear cable (Fig. 6-8). An *intermediate cable* passes through the guide on the equalizer. Two short rear cables attach to the ends of the intermediate cable. In the parking-brake system shown in Fig. 6-8, one rear cable is connected to the intermediate cable with a cable connector (Fig. 6-13). The other rear cable is connected to the intermediate cable with the cable adjuster.

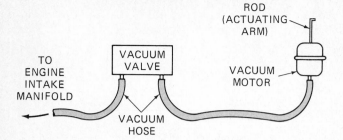

Fig. 6-5. A vacuum-release parking-brake system.

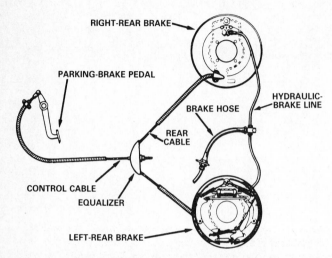

Fig. 6-6. A parking-brake-cable arrangement for a typical vehicle. *(Bendix Aftermarket Brake Division)*

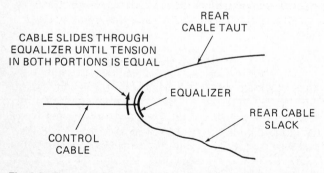

Fig. 6-7. The operation of an equalizer that provides equal braking force to each wheel.

Some cars with a hand-operated lever have two cables (Fig. 6-1). Each cable runs from the lever directly to a rear wheel.

Other cars with a foot-operated parking brake have two rear cables and no intermediate cable (Fig. 6-14). A control cable connects from the control unit to the equalizer. Each rear cable also connects to the equalizer. When the parking brakes are applied, the control cable pulls the equalizer. Then the equalizer pivots at the control-cable connection to apply an equal pull to each rear cable.

DRUM-TYPE PARKING BRAKES

Duo-Servo Type

Figure 6-15 shows a duo-servo drum-brake assembly that has a parking-brake lever and parking-brake strut. This is an integral parking brake. The strut fits between the primary and secondary shoes. The parking-brake cable attaches to the lower end of the lever. The lever attaches to the upper end of the secondary shoe with a pin (Fig. 6-16). The lever can pivot on the pin.

When the parking brake is applied, the cable pulls the lower end of the lever (Fig. 6-17). This pushes the strut against the primary shoe, forcing the shoe and lining against the drum. When the primary shoe and lining contact the drum, the strut cannot move farther. Additional movement of the cable causes the lever to pivot around the end of the strut. The lever pin then forces the upper end of the secondary shoe and lining against the drum.

A simplified diagram of the parking-brake-lever operation is shown in Fig. 6-18. Figure 18*a* shows the motion of the lever when the parking brake is first applied. The fulcrum of the lever is the lever pin. Figure 6-18*b* shows the motion of the lever after the primary shoe has contacted the drum. Now the fulcrum of the lever is the parking-brake strut.

With the parking brakes applied, the car is prevented from rolling by the static friction between the brake linings and the drum. If the parking brake is applied and the car tries to roll forward, the drum drags the primary brake shoe against the adjuster-screw assembly (Fig. 6-15). This assembly transfers the force to the secondary shoe, pushing the secondary shoe into the anchor pin.

If the car tries to roll rearward, the drum drags the secondary brake shoe against the adjuster-screw assembly. This assembly transfers the force to the primary shoe, and the primary shoe is pushed into the anchor pin. Therefore, the parking brakes are self-energizing in either direction. This is the same as the self-energizing action of the service brakes described in Chap. 4.

However, if the brakes are only partially applied, the self-energizing effect only takes place if the car tries to roll in the forward direction. This is because a partial application of the parking brake forces only the primary shoe and lining against the drum. It requires a full application of the parking brake to force the secondary shoe and lining against the drum.

If the car tries to roll forward, the self-energizing effect takes place as described previously. The force of the primary shoe is transferred to the secondary shoe, which pushes the secondary shoe and lining against the drum. Therefore, both shoes and linings are forced against the drum. If the car tries to roll rearward, the secondary shoe is not dragged into the adjuster-screw assembly by the drum, because the shoe is not in contact with the drum. When this occurs, the primary shoe alone provides the braking force. The braking force is then greater in the forward direction than in the rearward direction. Therefore, if the parking brake is only

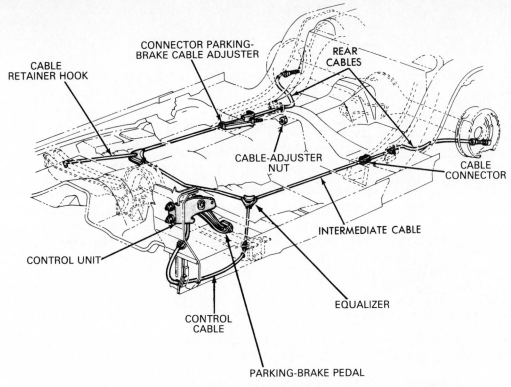

Fig. 6-8. A three-part rear-cable system: an intermediate cable and two short rear cables. *(Chrysler Corporation)*

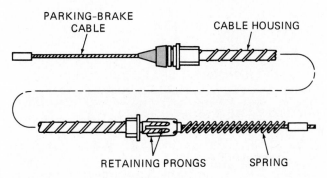

Fig. 6-9. A rear parking-brake cable.

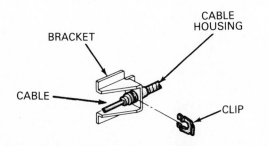

Fig. 6-10. The attachment of a parking-brake-cable housing to an underbody bracket. *(Chrysler Corporation)*

partially applied, the car will not roll forward, but it will roll in reverse.

Figure 6-19 shows a parking-brake-cable arrangement in which the equalizer is located near the left-rear wheel. The control cable is attached to the equalizer and also passes through it. Then the cable passes through the backing plate and attaches to the left-rear parking-brake

lever. The parking-brake lever is attached to the secondary brake shoe. One end of the right-rear cable attaches to the equalizer. The other end passes through the rear of the backing plate and attaches to the parking-brake lever. But on this wheel the lever attaches to the primary brake shoe. The braking effect is the same in either direction with a partial brake application. When the parking brake is released, the primary and secondary retracting springs return the shoes to their nonapplied positions.

Leading-Trailing-Shoe Type

Figure 6-20 shows a leading-trailing-shoe brake. A parking-brake strut is placed between the leading shoe and the trailing shoe. When the parking brake is applied, the leading and trailing shoes are pushed against the drum in the same manner as the primary and secondary shoes of a duo-servo brake. Figure 6-21 shows an adjustable-length parking-brake strut. This strut functions with the automatic brake adjuster, as described in Chap. 4.

Another type of parking-brake lever is shown in Fig. 6-22. This lever passes through the backing plate and is attached to the parking-brake strut with a pin. When the parking brakes are applied, the cable pulls the lever, and the lever pivots on the parking-brake strut. As the lever pivots, it pushes the strut against the trailing shoe, which pushes the shoe and lining against the brake drum (Fig. 6-23). The lever has a projection that also pushes the leading shoe and lining against the brake drum. Leading-trailing-shoe brakes are not self-energizing when either the service brakes or the parking brakes are applied.

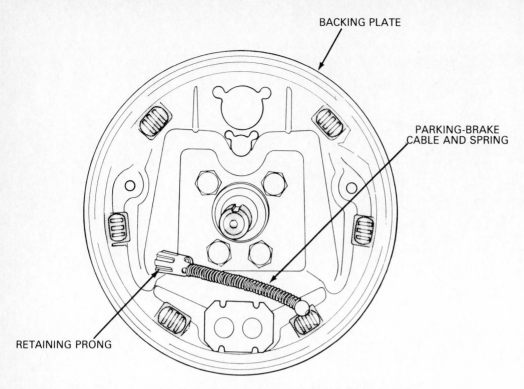

Fig. 6-11. A rear parking-brake cable held to the backing plate with retaining prongs. *(Chrysler Corporation)*

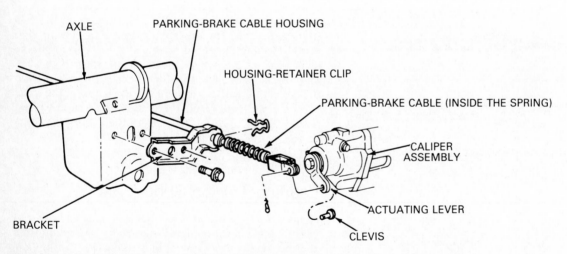

Fig. 6-12. A parking-brake-cable housing attached to a bracket on the axle of a car with rear disc brakes. *(Ford Motor Company)*

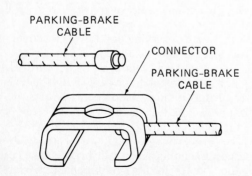

Fig. 6-13. A parking-brake-cable connector.

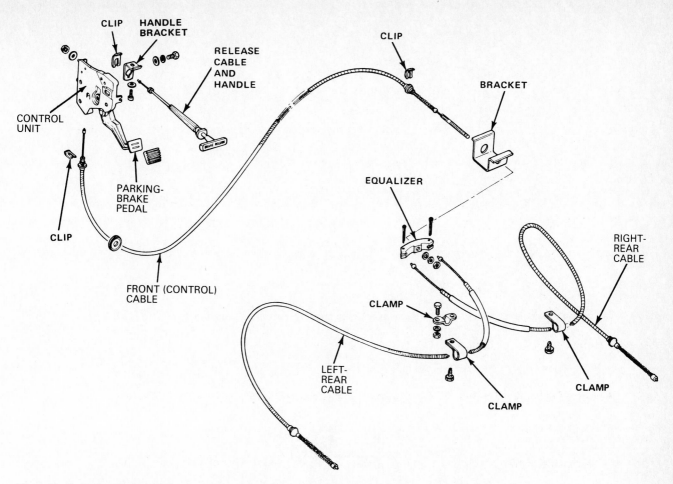

Fig. 6-14. A parking-brake-cable arrangement, using two rear cables that attach to the equalizer. *(American Motors Corporation)*

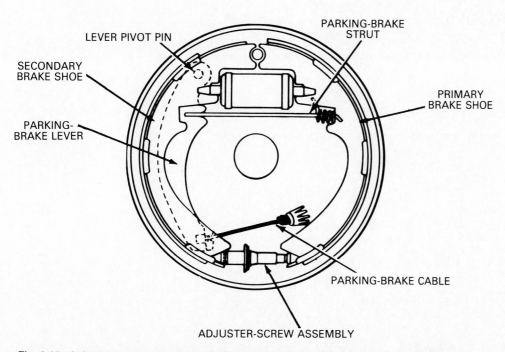

Fig. 6-15. A duo-servo drum-brake assembly showing the parking-brake lever and strut. *(Chrysler Corporation)*

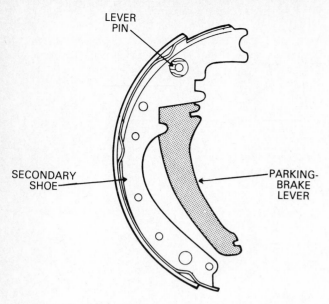

LEVER PIN

SECONDARY SHOE

PARKING-BRAKE LEVER

Fig. 6-16. The parking-brake lever attached to the secondary brake shoe. *(Ford Motor Company)*

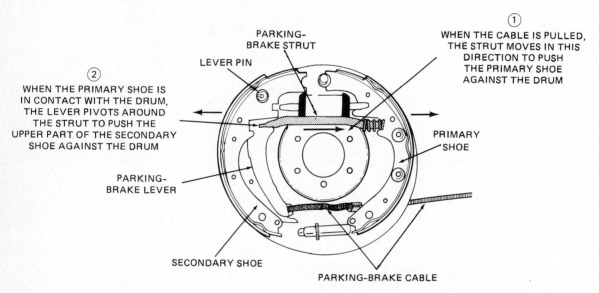

PARKING-BRAKE STRUT

LEVER PIN

① WHEN THE CABLE IS PULLED, THE STRUT MOVES IN THIS DIRECTION TO PUSH THE PRIMARY SHOE AGAINST THE DRUM

② WHEN THE PRIMARY SHOE IS IN CONTACT WITH THE DRUM, THE LEVER PIVOTS AROUND THE STRUT TO PUSH THE UPPER PART OF THE SECONDARY SHOE AGAINST THE DRUM

PARKING-BRAKE LEVER

PRIMARY SHOE

SECONDARY SHOE

PARKING-BRAKE CABLE

Fig. 6-17. The movement of the brake shoes when the parking brake is applied. *(Ford Motor Company)*

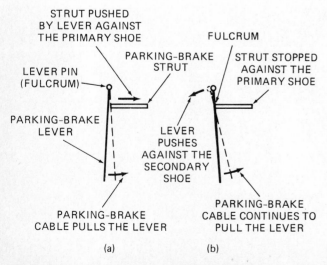

STRUT PUSHED BY LEVER AGAINST THE PRIMARY SHOE

PARKING-BRAKE STRUT

FULCRUM

STRUT STOPPED AGAINST THE PRIMARY SHOE

LEVER PIN (FULCRUM)

PARKING-BRAKE LEVER

LEVER PUSHES AGAINST THE SECONDARY SHOE

PARKING-BRAKE CABLE PULLS THE LEVER

PARKING-BRAKE CABLE CONTINUES TO PULL THE LEVER

(a)   (b)

Fig. 6-18. A simplified diagram of the movement of the parking-brake lever: (a) initial (partial) application of the parking brake; (b) full application of the parking brake.

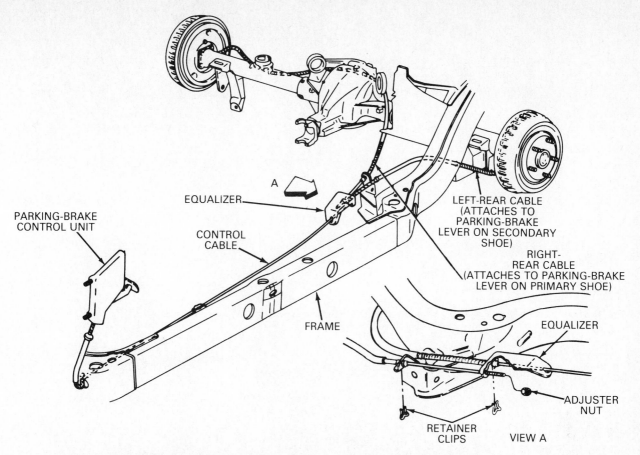

Fig. 6-19. A parking-brake-cable arrangement in which one rear cable attaches to a parking-brake lever on the secondary shoe, and the other rear cable attaches to a parking-brake lever on the primary shoe. *(Delco Moraine Division of General Motors Corporation)*

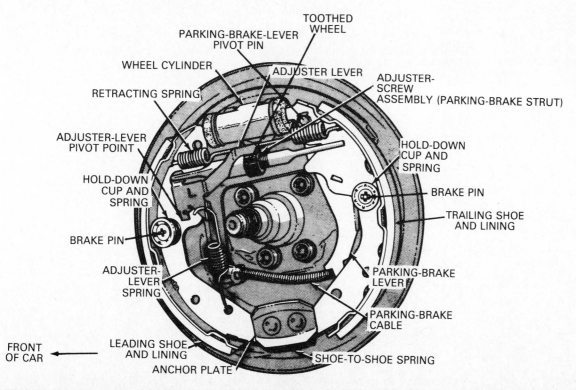

Fig. 6-20. A leading-trailing-shoe brake, showing the parking-brake lever and strut. *(Chrysler Corporation)*

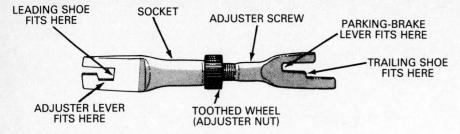

Fig. 6-21. An adjustable-length parking-brake strut. *(Chrysler Corporation)*

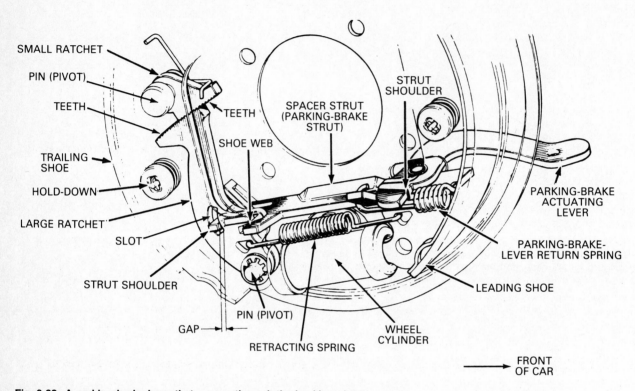

Fig. 6-22. A parking-brake lever that passes through the backing plate.
(Wagner Division, Cooper Industries Inc.)

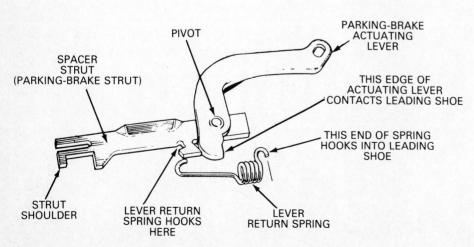

Fig. 6-23. A parking-brake lever and strut. *(Ford Motor Company)*

98

PARKING-BRAKE ADJUSTMENT

When the parking brakes are applied, the movement of the foot pedal or hand lever must first remove the slack in the cable system. Further movement then forces the brake shoes and linings against the drum. As the linings wear, the amount of slack in the system gradually increases. Then a greater lever or pedal movement is needed to apply the parking brakes. Eventually, there will be so much slack that the brakes will not fully apply.

For this reason, parking brakes must be adjusted as the brake linings wear. Most drum-type parking brakes are adjusted by changing the length of the control cable (Fig. 6-24). When the adjusting nut is turned, the cable is shortened to remove the slack. On other parking brakes, the length of the intermediate cable is changed (Fig. 6-25). Figure 6-26 shows another type of adjuster assembly used on a rear or intermediate cable. In the parking brake shown in Fig. 6-1, each cable is adjusted separately. Parking-brake adjustment procedures are covered in the shop manual.

A self-adjusting parking brake is shown in Fig. 6-27. A spring-loaded ratchet wheel is part of the parking-brake control unit. If there is slack in the cable, the spring causes the ratchet wheel to rotate. As the wheel rotates, it pulls the cable and removes the slack. This automatically adjusts the parking brake for wear.

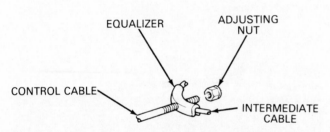

Fig. 6-24. A parking-brake-cable arrangement. The parking-brake adjustment is made by shortening the length of the control cable. *(Chrysler Corporation)*

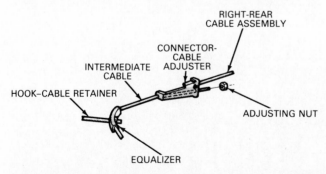

Fig. 6-25. A parking-brake-cable arrangement. The parking-brake adjustment is made by shortening the length of the intermediate cable. *(Chrysler Corporation)*

CALIPER-TYPE PARKING BRAKES

Several different calipers include an integral parking brake. The Delco Moraine, Ford, and Nissan calipers are described on the pages that follow.

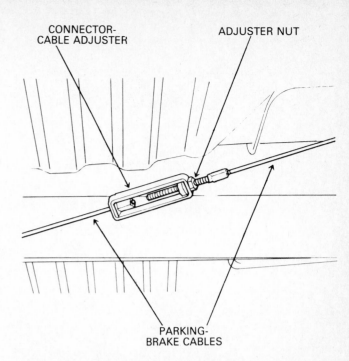

Fig. 6-26. A parking-brake-cable adjuster used on an intermediate cable or a rear cable. *(Chrysler Corporation)*

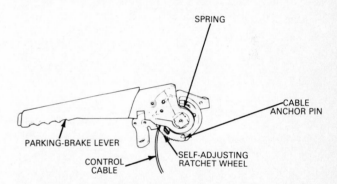

Fig. 6-27. A hand-operated parking-brake control unit with an automatic parking-brake adjuster. *(Ford Motor Company)*

Delco Moraine Type

Figure 6-28 shows an exploded view of a Delco Moraine caliper that includes a parking brake. An assembled, cutaway view of this caliper is shown in Fig. 6-29. An exploded view of the piston assembly is shown in Fig. 6-30. Located inside the piston are the cone, adjuster nut, adjuster spring, and three washers. One of the washers is a *thrust bearing*. This is a washer with roller bearings or ball bearings that allows a part in contact with it to rotate. These components are held inside the piston by a retainer.

Service-Brake Operation The cone has a seal around its outer diameter that prevents brake fluid from leaking between the cone and the piston. When the service brakes are applied, hydraulic pressure pushes against the cone. The cone, in turn, pushes against the piston. Then, the cone and piston move together to push the inner brake pad against the rotor. The piston moves through the piston seal (Fig. 6-29) and distorts it. Hy-

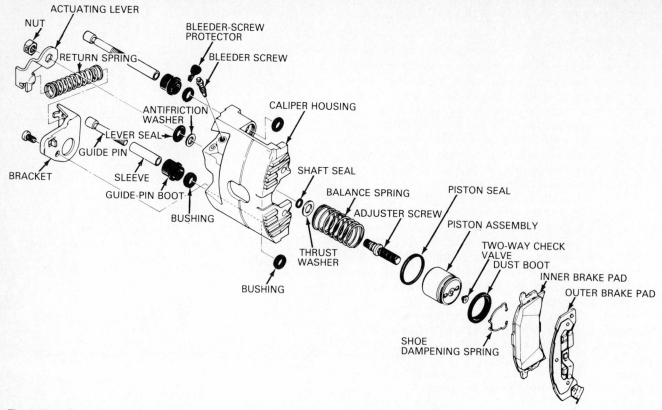

Fig. 6-28. A Delco Moraine rear caliper. *(Delco Moraine Division of General Motors Corporation)*

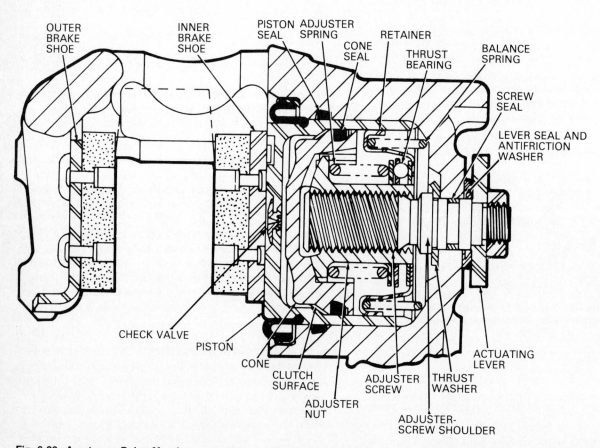

Fig. 6-29. A cutaway Delco Moraine rear caliper. *(Delco Moraine Division of General Motors Corporation)*

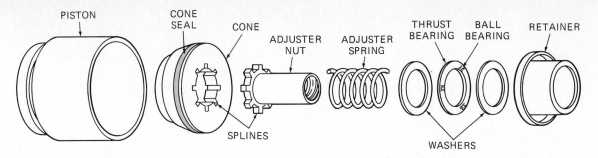

Fig. 6-30. A Delco Moraine piston assembly.

draulic pressure also forces the caliper inward, which pushes the outer pad against the other side of the rotor.

When the service brakes are released, the piston seal returns to its original shape. This pulls the piston back a small distance into the caliper bore, which removes the braking force from the inner pad. In addition, the caliper moves a small distance, which removes the force from the outer pad. The hydraulic part of the operation is the same as that of the moving calipers described in Chap. 5.

Parking-Brake Operation
The parking-brake actuating lever is attached to an adjuster screw (Fig. 6-29). The adjuster screw is threaded into the adjuster nut located inside the piston assembly. The adjuster nut is *splined* (Fig. 6-30) and fits into a matching splined opening in the cone. *Splines* are a series of grooves or keyways cut around a hole or a shaft. The splined opening does not pass completely through the cone. The adjuster nut can slide into and out of the cone along the splines.

When the parking brake is applied, the parking-brake cable pulls the actuating lever (Fig. 6-31). This causes the lever to rotate and turn the adjuster screw through the adjuster nut. This causes the nut to move along the screw. The nut slides along the splines of the cone until the nut bottoms against the inside surface of the cone. Then the nut pushes the cone and the piston against the inner brake pad. This presses the inner brake pad against the rotor.

The piston is prevented from rotating by the inner brake pad. This is because a projection on the pad (a D-shaped tab) fits into a D-shaped hole in the piston (Fig. 6-32). The nut and cone do not rotate, because a part of the cone contacts a seat in the inside of the piston. This seat is called the *clutch surface* (Fig. 6-29). The friction between the cone and the clutch surface prevents the cone from rotating.

There is a shoulder on the adjuster screw, and a washer fits between the shoulder and the caliper housing. When the parking brakes are applied, the screw turns and pushes the nut and cone against the piston. At the same time, the shoulder of the screw pushes back against the washer and the caliper housing. This moves the caliper housing inward and forces the outer brake pad against the other side of the rotor. In this way, when the parking brakes are applied, both brake pads are mechanically forced against the rotor.

When the parking brake is released, the adjuster screw rotates in the opposite direction. The adjuster nut

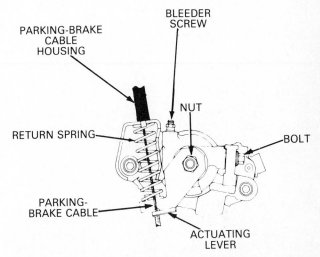

Fig. 6-31. A parking-brake cable attached to a Delco Moraine rear caliper. (Delco Moraine Division of General Motors Corportation)

moves back, which removes the force from the inner brake pad. In addition, the caliper moves back to remove the force from the outer brake pad.

The adjuster screw is called a *high-lead screw. Lead* is the distance a screw thread advances when the screw is rotated one turn. *High lead* means that the nut moves a relatively large distance when the screw turns.

Parking-Brake Adjustment
As the brake pads wear, the cone and piston gradually move away from the adjuster nut. This leaves a small gap between the end of the nut and the inside surface of the cone. Then, when the parking brakes are applied, the nut will have to move a greater distance before it bottoms against the inside surface of the cone. Eventually, the gap between the nut and the cone will become so large that the parking brakes will not work. To prevent this failure, the parking brake adjusts automatically as the brake pads wear.

An adjuster spring pushes against the adjuster nut (Figs. 6-29 and 6-30). If there is a gap between the nut and the cone, the spring causes the nut to rotate and move along the high-lead screw. The cone rotates along with the nut. The cone is free to rotate because it is not being pushed against the clutch surface. The cone and nut stop rotating when the cone contacts the clutch surface. As the nut rotates along the screw, the gap between the nut and the cone is closed. This automatically adjusts the parking brake for wear.

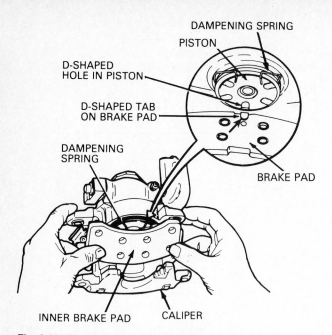

DAMPENING SPRING
PISTON
D-SHAPED
HOLE IN PISTON
D-SHAPED TAB
ON BRAKE PAD
DAMPENING
SPRING
BRAKE PAD
INNER BRAKE PAD
CALIPER

Fig. 6-32. The D-shaped tab on the inner brake pad that aligns with the D-shaped hole in the piston to prevent the piston from rotating. (*Cadillac Motor Car Division of General Motors Corporation*)

An automatic adjustment should take place anytime the brakes are not applied and there is a gap between the nut and the cone. The adjustment cannot take place if either the service brake or the parking brake is applied. With either brake applied, the cone is forced against the clutch surface of the piston and cannot rotate. Then the cone prevents the nut from rotating.

Functions of Other Brake Components

A balance spring is located between the caliper and the retainer in the piston (Fig. 6-29). The balance spring is needed to counteract the force produced by the adjuster spring. Without a balance spring, the adjuster spring would retract the piston back into the caliper bore each time the service brakes are released. This is because the adjuster spring is located between the adjuster nut and the retainer in the piston. The adjuster nut is held in position by the threads of the adjuster screw; therefore, the adjuster nut cannot move. The retainer is a press fit in the piston and cannot move out of the piston. Because the adjuster spring pushes against the retainer, the spring tends to move the piston into the caliper bore. The balance spring pushes against the retainer in the opposite direction and prevents this from happening. The balance spring "balances" the force produced by the adjuster spring.

A check valve is located in the end of the piston. This valve releases any moisture or air pressure that builds up between the cone and the piston.

A dampening spring hooks on the end of the piston. This spring holds the inner pad against the piston and minimizes pad vibration and squeal.

Ford Type

A Ford disc-brake caliper that includes a parking brake is shown in Fig. 6-33. It is a single-piston sliding-type caliper. In this caliper, a parking-brake thrust screw fits through a hole in the end of the caliper and threads into an adjuster assembly in the piston (Fig. 6-34). An O-ring seal prevents brake fluid from leaking out of the caliper housing past the thrust screw. A parking-brake operating shaft is positioned near the thrust screw and is held away from the thrust screw by three steel balls. The balls fit into indentations in the faces of the thrust screw and the operating shaft.

An actuating lever is bolted to the operating shaft. An outer seal, parking-brake end retainer, inner seal, and thrust bearing are located between the actuating lever and the operating shaft.

The end retainer threads into the caliper housing. The outer seal prevents water and road contaminants from entering the caliper through the opening in the end retainer. The inner seal prevents water and road contaminants from entering the caliper past the threads of the end retainer.

When the parking brake is applied, the parking-brake cable pulls the actuating lever. Because the actuating lever is bolted to the operating shaft, the shaft rotates. The thrust bearing allows the operating shaft to rotate against the end retainer.

The thrust screw is prevented from rotating by an antirotation pin, which fits into grooves in the thrust screw and caliper housing. Therefore, when the operating shaft rotates, the indentations in the operating-shaft and thrust-screw faces no longer align. This forces the three steel balls to move up ramps in the indentations, and this pushes the thrust screw away from the operating shaft. Then the thrust screw pushes against the piston, and the piston pushes the brake pad against the rotor and applies the brakes.

As the brake pads wear, the piston gradually moves out of the caliper bore. The thrust screw moves with the piston, and the gap between the thrust screw and the operating shaft widens. This results in a greater parking-brake-cable movement to apply the parking brakes. The adjuster assembly in the piston automatically adjusts the parking brake for wear.

When the service brake is applied, the piston and thrust screw move outward. The large end of the thrust screw bottoms on a step in the caliper bore. Then the thrust screw is held by the step, and the piston moves away from the thrust screw (Fig. 6-35).

When this happens, an adjuster nut in the adjuster assembly rotates and moves along the threads of the thrust screw.

When the service brakes are released, the adjuster nut remains stationary and a drive ring in the adjuster assembly rotates (Fig. 6-36).

This causes the adjuster nut to remain in its new position on the thrust screw. When this occurs, the thrust screw remains in its extended position out of the piston. Therefore, the gap between the operating shaft and thrust screw is prevented from widening and the parking brakes remain adjusted.

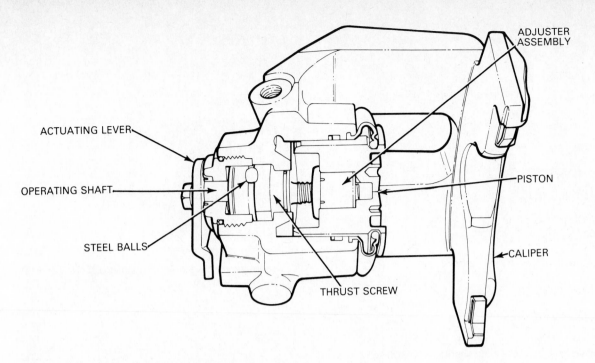

Fig. 6-33. A Ford rear caliper. *(Ford Motor Company)*

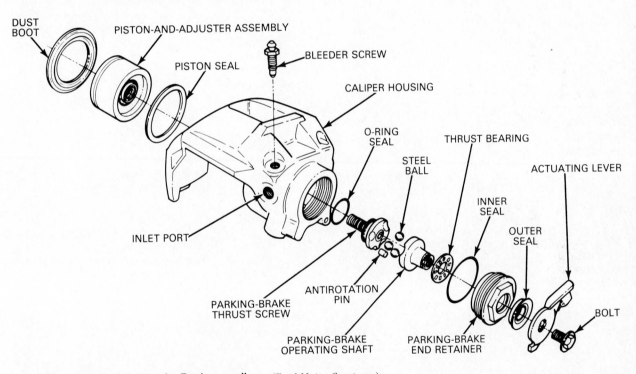

Fig. 6-34. An exploded view of a Ford rear caliper. *(Ford Motor Company)*

Nissan Type

Figure 6-37 shows a Nissan rear caliper. The parking-brake lever is attached to an adjusting cam. The cam fits into an opening in the caliper housing. A small rod fits in a hole in the closed end of the caliper bore and contacts the cam. The other end of the rod contacts a pushrod, which has a high-lead-screw thread. The pushrod threads into an adjuster nut in the piston assembly. The nut rests against the inside surface of the piston.

When the parking brake is applied, the cable pulls the parking-brake lever. This causes the adjusting cam to rotate. As the cam rotates, it pushes the small rod against the pushrod. The pushrod forces the adjuster nut against the inside surface of the piston to apply the brake.

As the brake pads wear, the piston gradually moves out of the caliper bore. To maintain parking-brake adjustment, the adjuster nut gradually rotates and moves outward on the pushrod. Therefore, the parking brake is automatically adjusted for brake-pad wear.

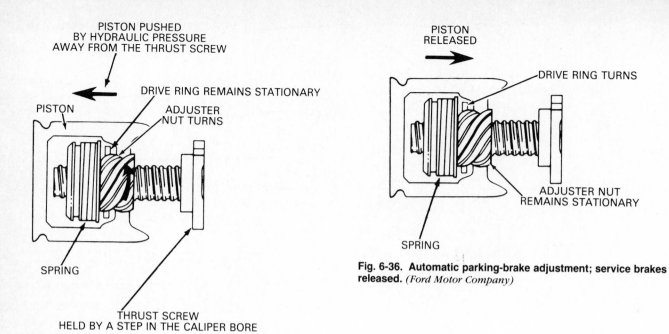

**PISTON PUSHED
BY HYDRAULIC PRESSURE
AWAY FROM THE THRUST SCREW**

DRIVE RING REMAINS STATIONARY

PISTON

ADJUSTER
NUT TURNS

SPRING

THRUST SCREW
HELD BY A STEP IN THE CALIPER BORE

Fig. 6-35. Automatic parking-brake adjustment; service brakes applied. *(Ford Motor Company)*

**PISTON
RELEASED**

DRIVE RING TURNS

ADJUSTER NUT
REMAINS STATIONARY

SPRING

Fig. 6-36. Automatic parking-brake adjustment; service brakes released. *(Ford Motor Company)*

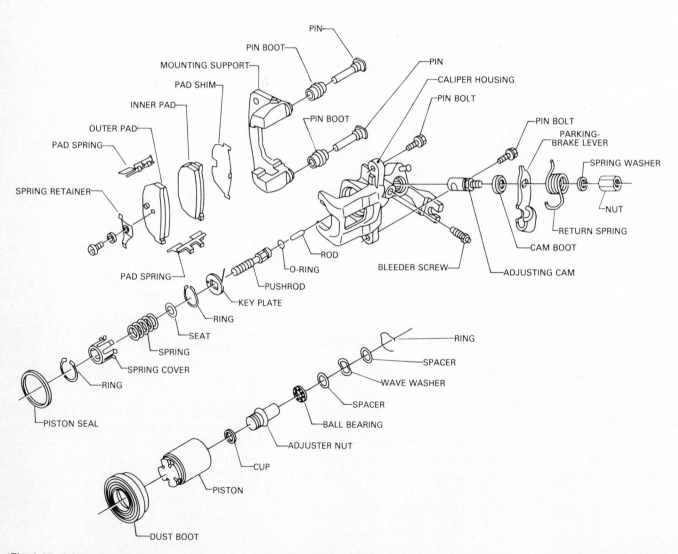

PIN

PIN BOOT

MOUNTING SUPPORT

PAD SHIM

INNER PAD

OUTER PAD

PAD SPRING

SPRING RETAINER

PAD SPRING

PIN BOOT

PIN

CALIPER HOUSING

PIN BOLT

PIN BOLT

PARKING-
BRAKE LEVER

SPRING WASHER

NUT

RETURN SPRING

CAM BOOT

ADJUSTING CAM

ROD

O-RING

BLEEDER SCREW

PUSHROD

KEY PLATE

RING

SEAT

SPRING

SPRING COVER

RING

PISTON SEAL

RING

SPACER

WAVE WASHER

SPACER

BALL BEARING

ADJUSTER NUT

CUP

PISTON

DUST BOOT

Fig. 6-37. A Nissan rear caliper. *(Nissan Motor Corporation in U.S.A.)*

AUXILIARY-DRUM PARKING BRAKES

An auxiliary-drum parking brake is an independent-type parking brake. A combination disc-brake rotor and brake drum is shown in Fig. 6-38. The drum is called an *auxiliary brake drum*. A set of drum-brake components, and the auxiliary brake drum, function as the parking brake (Fig. 6-39). The rotor and caliper function as the service brake.

The parking-brake cable is attached to the parking-brake lever-and-strut assembly. This assembly fits between the two shoes. When the parking brake is applied, the lever pivots, and the strut and lever push the brake shoes outward. This forces the brake linings against the brake drum and prevents the combination drum-and-rotor from turning.

An adjuster assembly is positioned between the brake shoes. The adjuster assembly consists of the adjuster screw, adjuster nut, and adjuster socket (Fig. 6-40). When the adjuster nut is rotated, the adjuster assembly lengthens, pushing the shoes closer to the drum. This adjusts the shoe-to-drum clearance and adjusts the parking brake. The adjustment is made by inserting a screwdriver through a hole in the rotor and rotating the adjusting nut (Fig. 6-41).

DRIVE-SHAFT PARKING BRAKES

Some vehicles use parking brakes that prevent the drive shaft from rotating. These are called *drive-shaft*, or *transmission, parking brakes*. There are two types of drive-shaft parking brakes: the external-contracting type and the internal-expanding type. Both types are independent parking brakes.

External-Contracting Type

Figure 6-42 shows an external-contracting drive-shaft parking brake. A steel band lined with a brake lining is placed around a brake drum. The drum is usually attached to the drive shaft. When the parking brake is applied, the band is tightened around the brake drum, and the lining prevents the drum and drive shaft from turning.

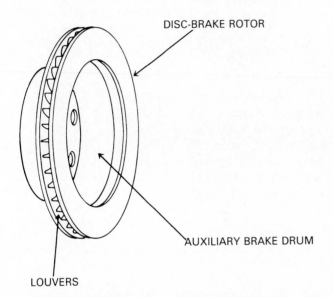

Fig. 6-38. A combination disc-brake rotor and brake drum. *(EIS Division of Parker Hannifin Corporation)*

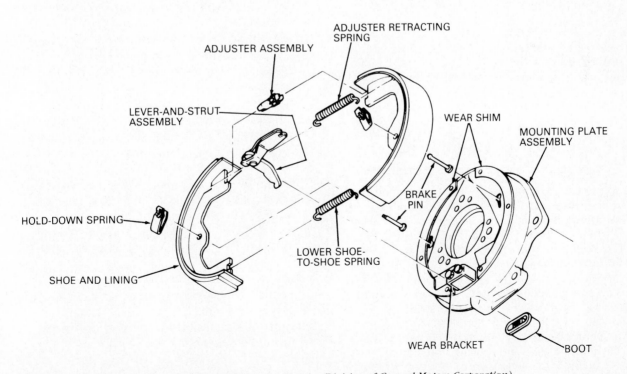

Fig. 6-39. Auxiliary-drum brake components. *(Delco Moraine Division of General Motors Corporation)*

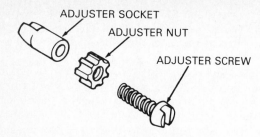

Fig. 6-40. An auxiliary-drum brake adjuster assembly. (Delco Moraine Division of General Motors Corporation)

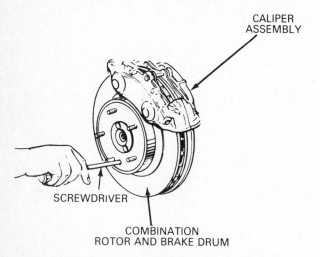

Fig. 6-41. The method of adjusting an auxiliary-drum parking brake. (Wagner Division, Cooper Industries Inc.)

Internal-Expanding Type

Figure 6-43 shows an internal-expanding drive-shaft parking brake. The brake assembly is usually attached to the rear of the transmission. The drum is attached to the drive shaft.

When the parking brake is applied, an operating lever pivots to apply the brake mechanically. The shoes move outward, forcing the linings against the brake drum. This prevents the drum and drive shaft from turning.

PARKING-BRAKE WARNING LAMPS

The parking-brake warning lamp is usually located on the instrument panel. The lamp is on when the parking brakes are applied (with the ignition switch on) and is off when the parking brakes are released. The lamp is controlled by the parking-brake switch. This switch is usually located in the parking-brake control unit (Fig. 6-2).

A diagram of a parking-brake warning-lamp circuit is shown in Fig. 6-44. When the ignition switch is on, battery voltage is applied to one terminal of the lamp. The parking-brake switch is connected between the other terminal of the lamp and ground. When the parking brake is applied, the switch contacts close, which grounds the lamp. When the lamp is grounded, it lights.

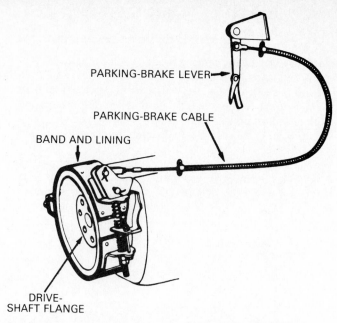

Fig. 6-42. An external-contracting drive-shaft parking brake. (Wagner Division, Cooper Industries Inc.)

When the parking brake is released, the switch contacts open and the lamp goes off.

On some cars the parking-brake warning lamp is the same lamp used to indicate a failure in the hydraulic brake system. The pressure-differential switch (brake-warning-lamp switch) is shown in Fig. 6-44. A failure in one section of the hydraulic system will close the switch contacts. This will also ground the warning lamp and turn it on.

VOCABULARY REVIEW

Cable   A bundle of wire strands that are twisted together.

Control cable   The parking-brake cable connected from the parking-brake control unit to the equalizer or to a guide on the intermediate cable.

Control unit   The mechanism used to apply and release a parking brake.

Diaphragm   A thin flexible sheet or layer that separates chambers in a component such as a vacuum motor.

Equalizer   A parking-brake-cable guide that allows the cable to slip so that equal force will be applied to each parking-brake assembly.

High-lead screw   A screw on which the thread advances a relatively large distance when the screw is rotated one turn.

Independent parking brake   A parking brake that uses a different set of brake shoes than the service brakes do.

Integral parking brake   A parking brake that uses the same set of brake shoes that the service brakes do.

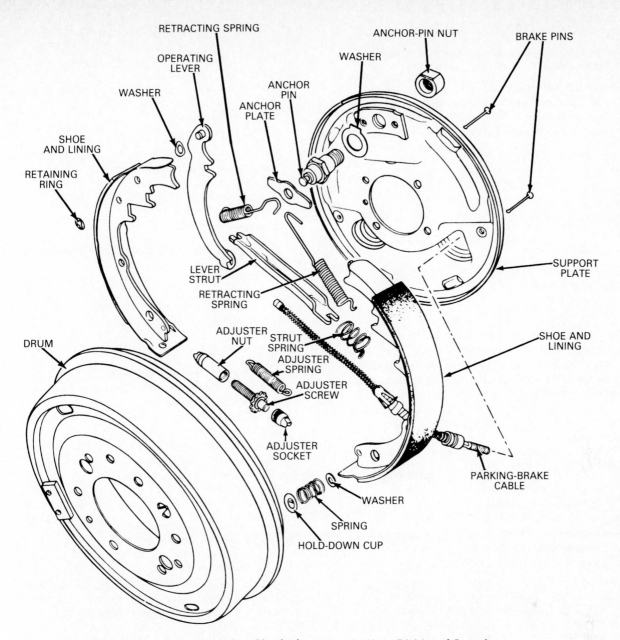

RETRACTING SPRING

OPERATING LEVER

WASHER

ANCHOR-PIN NUT

WASHER

BRAKE PINS

ANCHOR PIN

ANCHOR PLATE

SHOE AND LINING

RETAINING RING

SUPPORT PLATE

LEVER STRUT

RETRACTING SPRING

DRUM

ADJUSTER NUT

STRUT SPRING

ADJUSTER SPRING

ADJUSTER SCREW

ADJUSTER SOCKET

SHOE AND LINING

PARKING-BRAKE CABLE

WASHER

SPRING

HOLD-DOWN CUP

Fig. 6-43. An internal-expanding drive-shaft parking brake. (*Chevrolet Motor Division of General Motors Corporation*)

Intermediate cable   The cable on a three-cable parking-brake system that passes through the equalizer and connects to the rear cables.

Lead   The distance that a screw thread advances when the screw is rotated one turn.

Splines   A series of grooves or keyways cut around a hole or a shaft.

Thrust bearing   A washer with ball or roller bearings that allows another part in contact with it to rotate.

Vacuum motor   A device with two chambers separated by a diaphragm, used to produce motion and apply a force when a vacuum is applied to one of the chambers.

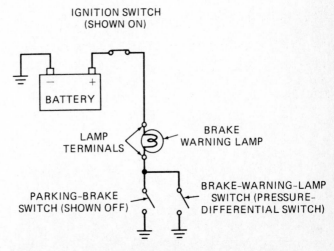

IGNITION SWITCH (SHOWN ON)

BATTERY

LAMP TERMINALS

BRAKE WARNING LAMP

PARKING-BRAKE SWITCH (SHOWN OFF)

BRAKE-WARNING-LAMP SWITCH (PRESSURE-DIFFERENTIAL SWITCH)

Fig. 6-44. A parking-brake warning-lamp circuit diagram.

REVIEW QUESTIONS

Select the *one* correct, best, or most probable answer to each question.

1. Technician A says that parking brakes are mechanical brakes because mechanical brakes are more effective than hydraulic brakes. Technician B says that parking brakes are mechanical brakes because, for safety, they must operate separately from the hydraulic brakes. Who is right?
   a. A only
   b. B only
   c. Both A and B
   d. Neither A nor B

2. In a parking-brake system, equal braking to each rear wheel is provided by the:
   a. parking-brake levers.
   b. ratchet assembly.
   c. cable adjuster.
   d. equalizer.

3. Technician A says that when the parking brake is fully applied on a duo-servo drum brake, only the primary shoe is forced against the drum. Technician B says that drum-brake parking brakes are self-energizing. Who is right?
   a. A only
   b. B only
   c. Both A and B
   d. Neither A nor B

4. On a drum-brake parking brake, the parking-brake adjuster assembly adjusts:
   a. the length of one of the cables.
   b. the position of the parking-brake levers.
   c. the position of the ratchet in the control unit.
   d. the length of the pedal travel.

5. Technician A says that when the parking brakes are applied on a car with Delco Moraine rear calipers, only the inner brake pad is forced against the rotor. Technician B says that when the brakes are applied, a screw applies force to both the piston and the caliper. Who is right?
   a. A only
   b. B only
   c. Both A and B
   d. Neither A nor B

6. On a car with an auxiliary drum brake used as a parking brake, the parking brake is adjusted by:
   a. changing the length of the control cable.
   b. changing the length of the rear cables.
   c. rotating an adjuster nut on the parking-brake assembly.
   d. adjusting the equalizer.

7. A car has a Delco Moraine rear caliper that includes a parking brake. All of the following occur when the parking brakes are applied *except*:
   a. The caliper moves inward.
   b. The adjuster screw is rotated.
   c. The piston moves outward.
   d. The piston is rotated.

8. All of the following are true of Ford rear calipers *except*:
   a. The thrust screw is prevented from rotating by an antirotation pin.
   b. Three steel balls apply force to the thrust screw.
   c. An adjuster mechanism is part of the piston assembly.
   d. The actuating lever turns the thrust screw.

9. On a car with duo-servo rear drum brakes, if the parking brakes are only partially applied, the car will roll in reverse because:
   a. only the secondary shoe and lining are forced against the drum.
   b. the secondary shoe does not apply force to the primary shoe.
   c. drum brakes are only self-energizing when the car moves forward.
   d. the primary shoe and lining are not forced against the drum.

10. Technician A says that the check valve in the piston of a Delco Moraine rear caliper (with parking brake) releases any brake fluid that leaks past the piston seal. Technician B says that the check valve releases any air pressure or moisture trapped between the cone and the piston. Who is right?
    a. A only
    b. B only
    c. Both A and B
    d. Neither A nor B

CHAPTER 7

VACUUM-ASSIST POWER BRAKES

OBJECTIVES

After you have studied this chapter, you should be able to:

1. Define air pressure and vacuum, and describe the methods used to measure them.

2. Name the components in a vacuum-assist power-brake system.

3. Describe the construction of a typical vacuum booster.

4. Describe the operation of a vacuum booster.

Power brakes assist the driver in applying the brakes. In a vacuum-assist power-brake system, a *vacuum booster* is located between the brake-pedal arm and the master cylinder (Fig. 7-1). The vacuum booster increases the force applied by the driver's foot. This makes the force required to apply the brakes less than on a car without power brakes. In addition, the brake-pedal travel required to apply the brakes is less than on a car without power brakes.

The vacuum booster is usually attached directly to the firewall (Fig. 7-1). A *brake-pedal pushrod*, or *valve*

rod, connects between the brake-pedal arm and the booster. Sometimes the vacuum booster is attached to the firewall with mounting brackets (Fig. 7-2). Then, the brake-pedal pushrod connects through a lever arrangement to the vacuum booster. All vacuum-assist power brakes use a combination of air pressure and vacuum for their operation.

AIR PRESSURE

Air is made of molecules, and molecules have weight. The air that surrounds the earth (the air we breathe) is the earth's *atmosphere*. The air molecules in the atmosphere push down on all objects on the surface of the earth. The weight of the air molecules pushing down on a surface is called *air pressure*. Air pressure not only pushes downward but also acts equally in all directions. Because these air molecules make up the earth's atmosphere, this pressure is called *atmospheric air pressure*. At sea level the atmospheric air pressure is 14.7 pounds per square inch (psi) [101.4 kilopascals (kPa)]. At higher altitudes the pressure is less; for example, at an altitude of 5,000 feet (ft) [1,524 meters (m)] above sea level, the atmospheric air pressure is 12.25 psi [84.5 kPa].

Air pressure can be raised above atmospheric pressure by an *air compressor*. A compressor is a pump used

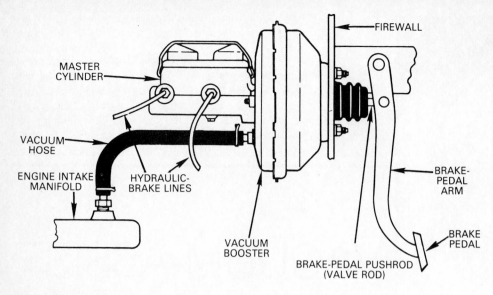

Fig. 7-1. A power-brake vacuum booster that mounts directly on the firewall. *(Bendix Aftermarket Brake Division)*

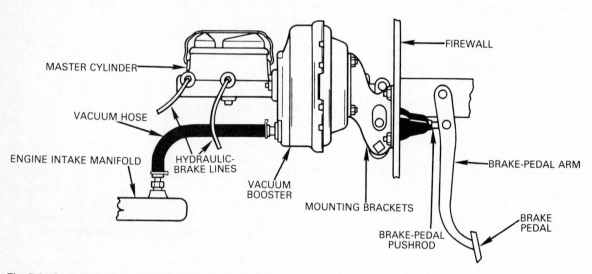

Fig. 7-2. A power-brake vacuum booster that attaches to the firewall with mounting brackets. *(Bendix Aftermarket Brake Division)*

to raise the pressure of a gas or vapor. When the pressure of air is raised above atmospheric pressure, the air is called *compressed air*. Compressed air is used to operate the air brakes on heavy trucks.

MEASURING THE PRESSURE

When a pressure gauge (Fig. 7-3) is not connected to a source of pressure, the gauge reads 0 psi [0 kPa]. If the gauge is connected to air or a liquid under a pressure of 20 psi [138 kPa], the gauge reading will be 20 psi [138 kPa], as shown in Fig. 7-4. This reading is the *gauge pressure*. It is sometimes written 20 psig [138 kPa gauge].

Another system of pressure measurement is called *absolute pressure*. It takes the atmospheric air pressure into account. When the gauge is unconnected and the

gauge pressure is zero, the absolute pressure is 14.7 psi [101.4 kPa]. This means that only atmospheric air pressure is acting on the gauge. This pressure is written 14.7 psia [101.4 kPa absolute]. When a pressure of 20 psi [138 kPa] is applied to the gauge, the absolute pressure is 34.7 psia [239.4 kPa absolute]. The absolute pressure is the atmospheric pressure added to the gauge pressure:

Absolute pressure = atmospheric pressure + gauge pressure
$$34.7 \text{ psia} = 14.7 \text{ psia} + 20 \text{ psig}$$
$$[239.4 \text{ kPa} = 101.4 \text{ kPa} + 138 \text{ kPa}]$$

At sea level the absolute pressure is always 14.7 psi [101.4 kPa] higher than the gauge pressure. Figure 7-5 shows a comparison between absolute pressure and gauge pressure.

A pressure reading given in psi is gauge pressure unless otherwise specified. Therefore, the notation *psi* is usually used instead of *psig*.

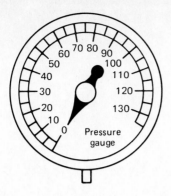

Fig. 7-3. An unconnected pressure gauge, indicating a pressure of 0 psi [0 kPa].

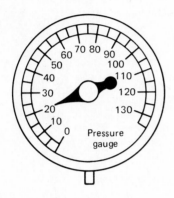

Fig. 7-4. A pressure gauge, indicating a pressure reading of 20 psi [138 kPa].

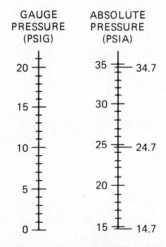

GAUGE PRESSURE (PSIG)	ABSOLUTE PRESSURE (PSIA)	
20	35	34.7
15	30	
10	25	24.7
5	20	
0	15	14.7

Fig. 7-5. A comparison between absolute pressure and gauge pressure.

VACUUM

A *vacuum* is the absence of air. A *perfect vacuum* is the complete absence of air, which means that there are no air molecules in a certain enclosed space. On Earth, only a nearly perfect vacuum can be achieved.

A *partial vacuum* means that there are some air molecules but that there are less than the number usually present. The intake manifold of a spark-ignition engine has a partial vacuum while the engine is running.

This vacuum is created in the cylinders as each piston moves downward on its intake stroke (Fig. 7-6). Then the volume above the piston in the cylinder increases rapidly. Air from the atmosphere flows past the throttle valve and into the intake manifold. From the intake manifold, the air flows past the open intake valve and into the cylinder. However, the air can never flow into the intake manifold quickly enough to fill it. As a result, there are fewer air molecules in the intake manifold than it would normally hold if the engine was not running. This shortage of air molecules causes a partial vacuum in the intake manifold. In a running engine this vacuum is called the *intake-manifold vacuum*. Many cars use intake-manifold vacuum to operate the vacuum booster.

VACUUM PUMPS

In addition to power brakes, intake-manifold vacuum may operate other accessories and devices on the car. These include heater and air-conditioner controls, the transmission modulator, the cruise control, and some emission control devices. Under some conditions, it may be difficult for the engine to maintain the proper vacuum to operate these devices. For this reason, some cars have a separate vacuum pump to ensure that there will be enough vacuum to operate the power brakes.

Figure 7-7 shows an electrically operated vacuum pump. This pump is designed to maintain sufficient vacuum for the power brakes. The pump connects between the vacuum booster (described later in this chapter) and the intake manifold (Fig. 7-8). Therefore, the pump increases the intake-manifold vacuum that is supplied to the vacuum booster. The pump does not operate continuously. It only runs when the vacuum drops below a specified level. There is a switch built into the pump assembly. If the vacuum drops below the specified level, the switch turns the pump on. When the vacuum rises to a sufficient level, the switch turns the pump off.

A belt-driven vacuum pump is shown in Fig. 7-9. This type of pump operates continuously and is driven by a V belt. The V belt is driven by the engine crankshaft. An alternator-driven vacuum pump is shown in Fig. 7-10. The pump bolts onto the alternator rear housing. The pump is driven by a part of the alternator rotor shaft that extends beyond the housing.

Diesel engines do not have a usable vacuum in the intake manifold. A vacuum pump provides the vacuum for the power brakes. A gear-driven vacuum pump for a diesel engine is shown in Fig. 7-11. This pump is driven by the engine camshaft.

MEASURING A VACUUM

The words *strong* and *weak* are often used to describe a vacuum. The fewer the air molecules in an enclosed space, the stronger the vacuum. The greater the number of air molecules, the weaker the vacuum. Three different systems are used to measure the strength of a vacuum. It can be measured in terms of *absolute pressure*, *inches of mercury*, and *negative air pressure*.

111

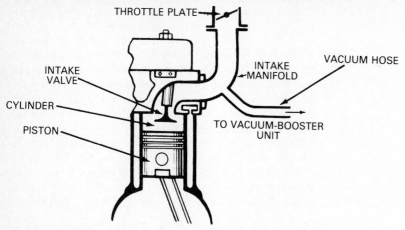

Fig. 7-6. An engine cylinder and intake manifold, showing the vacuum-hose connection for the vacuum booster. *(FMC Corporation)*

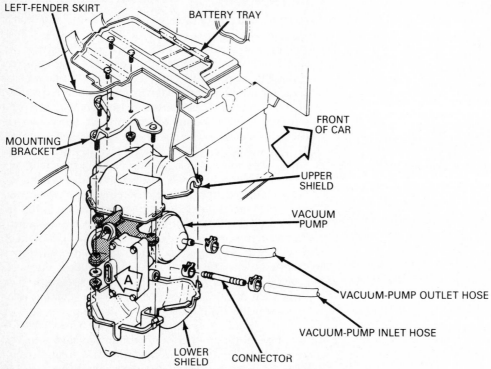

Fig. 7-7. An electric vacuum pump that mounts beneath the battery tray. *(Oldsmobile Division of General Motors Corporation)*

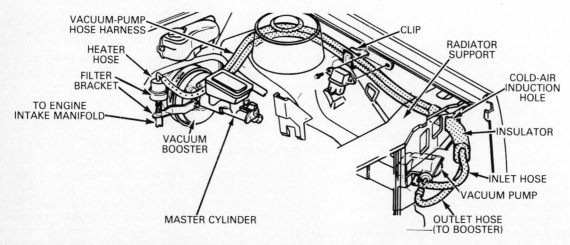

Fig. 7-8. The vacuum-hose routing for an electric vacuum pump. *(Oldsmobile Division of General Motors Corporation)*

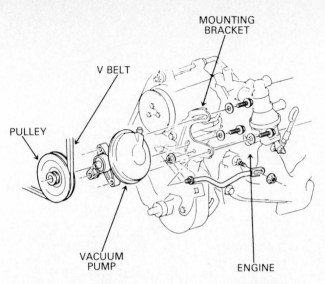

Fig. 7-9. A belt-driven vacuum pump. *(Oldsmobile Division of General Motors Corporation)*

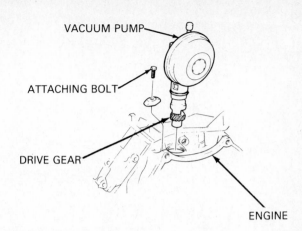

Fig. 7-11. A gear-driven vacuum pump. *(Oldsmobile Division of General Motors Corporation)*

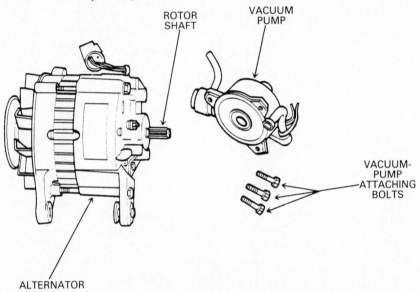

Fig. 7-10. A vacuum pump driven by an extension of the alternator motor shaft. *(Chevrolet Motor Division of General Motors Corporation)*

Absolute Pressure

If the absolute pressure is less than 14.7 psia [101.4 kPa] at sea level, a partial vacuum exists. If the absolute pressure is zero, there is a perfect vacuum. The lower the absolute pressure, the stronger the vacuum. The closer the absolute pressure is to 14.7 psia [101.4 kPa], the weaker the vacuum.

Inches of Mercury

The most common system of measuring vacuum is in inches of mercury. The chemical symbol for mercury is Hg; therefore, inches of mercury is abbreviated in. Hg. Mercury is a metal that is normally a liquid.

Figure 7-12 shows a glass tube that is filled with mercury and inverted in a bowl of mercury. The filling pro-

cedure is done carefully so that no air bubbles are allowed to enter the tube. The result is a column of mercury that is 29.9 inches (in.) [760 millimeters (mm)] higher than the level of mercury in the bowl. The space above the mercury in the tube has a nearly perfect vacuum (0 psia [0 kPa absolute]). The column is held up because the atmospheric pressure of 14.7 psia [101.4 kPa absolute] is pushing down on the mercury in the bowl, and 0 psia [0 kPa absolute] is at the top of the column.

If some air gets into the tube, then there would be only a partial vacuum above the mercury in the tube. The pressure difference from the top of the column to the bottom of the column would not be as great. The column of mercury would then drop to a lower level and would not be as high as when there was a nearly perfect vacuum in the tube.

The height of the column is a measure of the strength of the vacuum in the space above the column.

113

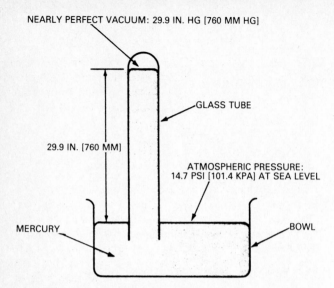

NEARLY PERFECT VACUUM: 29.9 IN. HG [760 MM HG]

GLASS TUBE

29.9 IN. [760 MM]

ATMOSPHERIC PRESSURE:
14.7 PSI [101.4 KPA] AT SEA LEVEL

MERCURY

BOWL

Fig. 7-12. A glass tube filled with mercury and inverted in a bowl filled with mercury. An atmospheric pressure of 14.7 psi [101.4 kPa] at sea level will support a column of mercury 29.9 in. [760 mm] high.

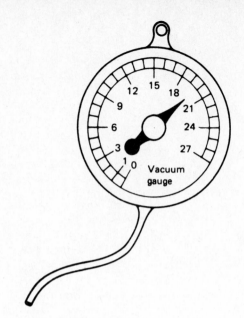

Vacuum gauge

Fig. 7-14. A typical vacuum gauge.

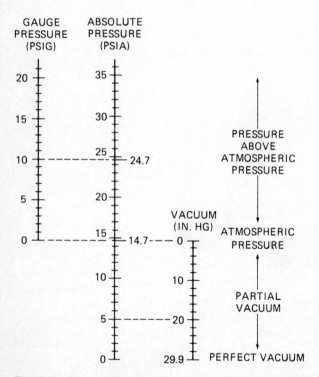

Fig. 7-13. The relationship between gauge pressure, absolute pressure, and vacuum.

Therefore, a nearly perfect vacuum is expressed as a vacuum of 29.9 in. Hg [760 mm Hg]. Normal air pressure (no vacuum) is expressed as a vacuum of 0 in. Hg [0 mm Hg]. A vacuum that is midway between a perfect vacuum and no vacuum at all is approximately 15 in. Hg [381 mm Hg]. Figure 7-13 shows the relationship between gauge pressure, absolute pressure, and vacuum.

With the engine running, the vacuum in the intake manifold is approximately 20 in. Hg [508 mm Hg]. Fig-

ure 7-14 shows the type of vacuum gauge used to measure engine intake-manifold vacuum. From Fig. 7-13, 20 in. Hg is equivalent to a pressure of 5 psia [34.5 kPa].

Negative Air Pressure

Vacuum is sometimes expressed as a negative air pressure, or an air pressure below zero. When this is done, the vacuum is measured in psi, or in the metric equivalent of kPa. A perfect vacuum would be a vacuum of −14.7 psi [−101.4 kPa]. Figure 7-15 compares vacuum measurements using inches of mercury and psi.

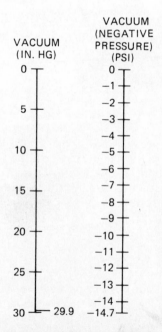

Fig. 7-15. The relationship between vacuum measured in inches of mercury and vacuum expressed as a negative pressure measured in psi.

BASIC OPERATION OF A VACUUM BOOSTER

Figure 7-16 shows a piston located in the center of a cylinder. The piston separates the cylinder into two separate chambers. The cylinder has openings into each chamber. If a partial vacuum is applied to the left chamber, and atmospheric air pressure is applied to the right chamber, the piston will move to the left. This is because the difference in pressure from one side of the piston to the other produces a force on the piston. The force acts from the high pressure to the low pressure.

Assume in Fig. 7-17 that the piston has a surface area of 75 square inches (in.^{2}) [484 square centimeters (cm^2)] and that the vacuum applied to the left chamber is 20 in. Hg (508 mm Hg). Atmospheric pressure is 14.7 psia [101.4 kPa absolute]. From Fig. 7-13, a vacuum of 20 in. Hg [508 mm Hg] is equivalent to 5 psia [34.5 kPa]. Therefore, there is a difference in pressure of 9.7 psi [66.9 kPa] from one side of the piston to the other:

$$14.7 \text{ psia} - 5 \text{ psia} = 9.7 \text{ psi}$$
$$[101.4 \text{ kPa} - 34.5 \text{ kPa} = 66.9 \text{ kPa}]$$

This is equivalent to a pressure of 9.7 psi [66.9 kPa] pushing the piston to the left. A pressure of 9.7 psi [66.9 kPa] acting on a piston with a surface area of 75 in.^{2} [484 cm^2] produces a force of 727.5 pounds (lb) [3,237 newtons (N)]:

$$\text{Pressure X area} = \text{force}$$
$$9.7 \text{ psi X } 75 \text{ in.}^2 = 727.5 \text{ lb}$$
$$[66.9 \text{ kPa X } 484 \text{ cm}^2 = 3,237 \text{ N}]$$

In a power-brake system, the chamber on one side of the piston has two valves (Fig. 7-18): a *vacuum valve* and an *air valve*, or *atmospheric valve*. The chamber on the other side of the piston has a port connected to the engine intake manifold or to a vacuum pump. When the brakes are not applied, there is vacuum on both sides of the piston. This is called a *vacuum-suspended booster*.

When the brakes are applied, the vacuum valve is closed and the air valve is opened (Fig. 7-19). Air under

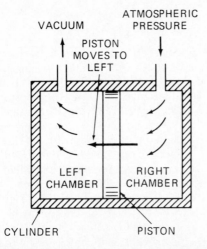

Fig. 7-16. A piston located in a cylinder. If atmospheric pressure is admitted to the right chamber of the cylinder and vacuum is admitted to the left chamber, the piston will move to the left.

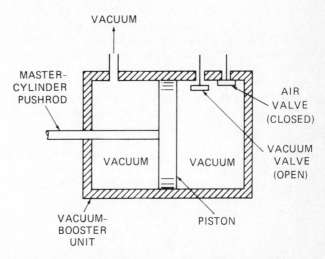

Fig. 7-18. A simplified vacuum booster. With the vacuum valve open and vacuum on both sides of the piston, no force is applied to the piston.

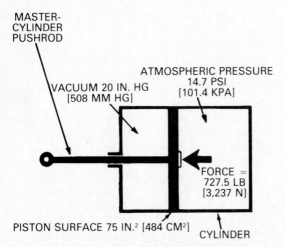

Fig. 7-17. The force on a piston caused by a difference in pressure from one side of the piston to the other. Atmospheric pressure is on one side of the piston, and a vacuum of 20 in. Hg [508 mm Hg] is on the other side. *(FMC Corporation)*

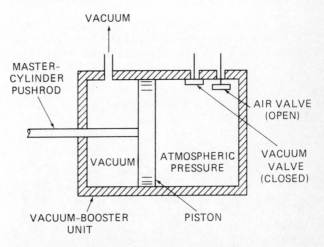

Fig. 7-19. A simplified vacuum booster. With the vacuum valve closed and the air valve open, there is vacuum on one side of the piston and atmospheric pressure on the other side. Therefore, there is a force applied to the piston.

atmospheric pressure flows into the right chamber. The difference in pressure from one side of the piston to the other applies a force to the piston. The piston, in turn, applies this force through a pushrod to the master cylinder. This causes hydraulic pressure to increase in the hydraulic brake system, applying the brakes.

It only requires a small brake-pedal force to move the valve rod. Therefore, with a vacuum-assist power-brake system, a small force applied to the brake pedal produces a large force at the master cylinder.

Some older cars had *atmospheric-suspended boosters*. With an atmospheric-suspended booster, when the brakes are not applied, there is atmospheric air pressure on both sides of the piston. Then, when the brake pedal is applied, vacuum is admitted to one side of the piston. Atmospheric-suspended boosters are slower-acting than vacuum-suspended boosters and are no longer installed in new cars.

VACUUM CHECK VALVE

Reliable power-brake operation depends on a sufficient vacuum in the vacuum booster. A hard vehicle acceleration will cause the intake-manifold vacuum to drop. This would prevent the power brakes from operating until manifold vacuum built up again. Therefore, a *check valve* is needed to hold vacuum in the booster (Fig. 7-20). The check valve allows air to flow through in one direction only. It allows air to flow from the vacuum booster to the intake manifold, but not from the manifold to the booster. Therefore, when the intake-manifold vacuum drops (the air pressure increases), air cannot flow to the booster. The check valve permits several power-assisted brake applications if the vacuum source fails to provide vacuum. Most check valves are included in the vacuum-hose connector in the booster (Fig. 7-21).

CONSTRUCTION OF A VACUUM BOOSTER

Figure 7-22 shows an exploded view of a vacuum booster. The internal components are enclosed by a front housing and a rear housing. The housings make up the outer

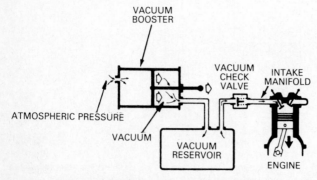

Fig. 7-20. The vacuum check valve used to hold vacuum in the booster. (*Wagner Division, Cooper Industries Inc.*)

116

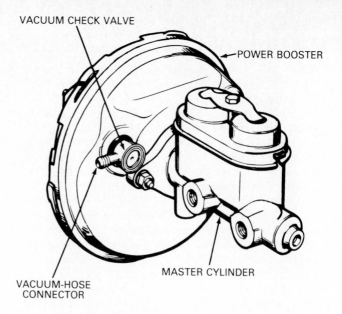

Fig. 7-21. A typical location of a vacuum check valve. (*Bendix Aftermarket Brake Division*)

shell of the booster. The housings lock together with tabs around their outer edges. When the housings are joined, a large seal called a diaphragm is clamped between the housings. The diaphragm separates the booster into two separate chambers (Fig. 7-23). The diaphragm is held in position by a diaphragm support plate. The power-piston assembly is attached to the support plate (Figs. 7-22 and 7-23). The power-piston assembly, diaphragm, and diaphragm support plate act together as a single unit.

A brake-pedal pushrod connects from the brake-pedal arm to the power-piston assembly (Figs. 7-22 and 7-23). A dust boot fits over the end of the booster, and the pushrod passes through an opening in the boot. The dust boot helps prevent dirt from entering the booster. When the brakes are applied, air is drawn into the booster past the pushrod. A filter prevents dirt particles from entering with the air. A silencer (Fig. 7-22) is used to minimize the rushing sound of the air as it enters the booster.

The power-piston assembly includes an air valve and a floating control valve (Figs. 7-24 and 7-25). The air valve is attached to the end of the brake-pedal pushrod. In some positions of the pushrod, the air valve seats against the floating control valve. When this occurs, the air valve blocks outside air flow into the rear chamber of the booster assembly.

In some positions of the pushrod, part of the floating control valve seats against a step in the inner diameter of the power piston. This step is the *control-valve seat* (Fig. 7-25). When the control valve contacts the control-valve seat, vacuum in the front chamber of the booster is prevented from reaching the rear chamber of the booster. This portion of the floating control valve is the vacuum valve.

Figure 7-23 shows a master cylinder bolted to the vacuum-booster assembly. When the master cylinder and vacuum booster are bolted together as one assembly, this is called an *integral-type* power-brake system. A *booster pushrod*, or *piston rod*, fits between the power piston

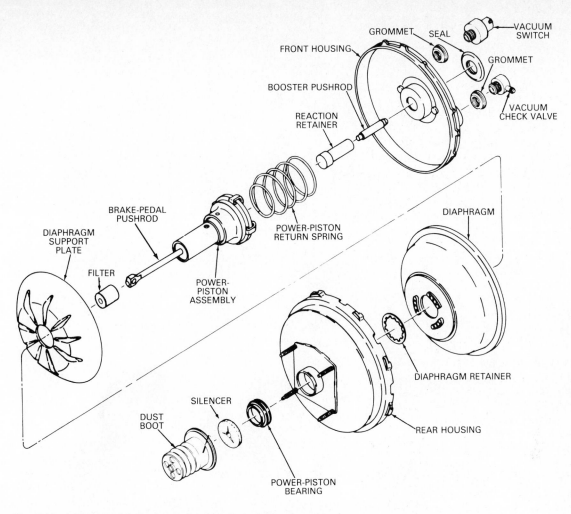

GROMMET SEAL VACUUM SWITCH

FRONT HOUSING GROMMET

BOOSTER PUSHROD VACUUM CHECK VALVE

REACTION RETAINER

BRAKE-PEDAL PUSHROD DIAPHRAGM

DIAPHRAGM SUPPORT PLATE POWER-PISTON RETURN SPRING

FILTER POWER-PISTON ASSEMBLY DIAPHRAGM RETAINER

REAR HOUSING

DUST BOOT SILENCER

POWER-PISTON BEARING

Fig. 7-22. A disassembled vacuum booster. *(Chevrolet Motor Division of General Motors Corporation)*

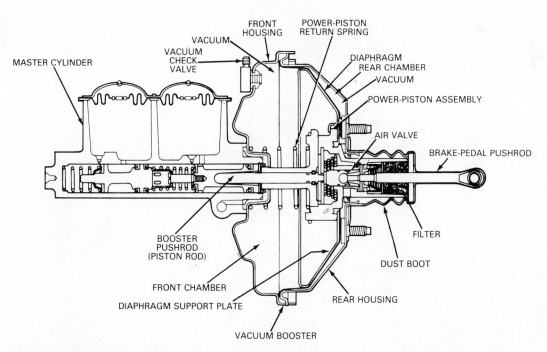

FRONT HOUSING POWER-PISTON RETURN SPRING

VACUUM DIAPHRAGM

MASTER CYLINDER VACUUM CHECK VALVE REAR CHAMBER

VACUUM

POWER-PISTON ASSEMBLY

AIR VALVE

BRAKE-PEDAL PUSHROD

FILTER

BOOSTER PUSHROD (PISTON ROD) DUST BOOT

FRONT CHAMBER

DIAPHRAGM SUPPORT PLATE REAR HOUSING

VACUUM BOOSTER

Fig. 7-23. An integral-type master cylinder and vacuum booster. *(Chevrolet Motor Division of General Motors Corporation)*

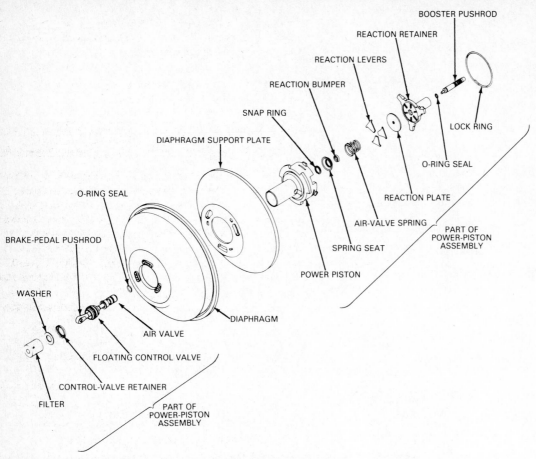

Fig. 7-24. A disassembled power-piston assembly that uses a reaction plate and three reaction levers. (*Pontiac Division of General Motors Corporation*)

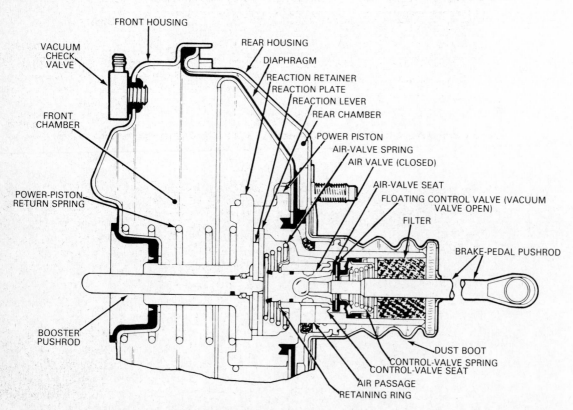

Fig. 7-25. A vacuum booster in the released position. (*Delco Moraine Division of General Motors Corporation*)

and the master cylinder. A power-piston return spring is located on the master-cylinder side of the power piston. The spring pushes the power piston to the right in Fig. 7-23.

Some boosters have a vacuum switch (Fig. 7-22). The switch is used on some cars to light a brake warning lamp on the instrument panel if there is a loss of vacuum in the booster.

OPERATION OF A VACUUM BOOSTER

Vacuum-booster operation is described under four conditions: brakes released, brakes being applied, brakes applied and holding, and brakes releasing.

Brakes Released

In Fig. 7-25 the brake pedal and the brake-pedal pushrod are in their released positions. In the booster the air valve is held against its seat on the floating control valve by the air-valve spring, and the floating control valve is away from its seat in the power-piston assembly. Therefore, the air valve is closed and the vacuum valve is open. When the vacuum valve is open, a passage is opened between the front and rear chambers of the booster. This allows air to be removed from the rear chamber of the booster.

The air flows from the rear chamber of the booster through air passages in the power piston, through the opening between the floating control valve and its seat in the power piston (the vacuum valve), and through an opening in the power piston into the front chamber of the booster. From the front chamber of the booster,

the air flows through the check valve and into the intake manifold or vacuum pump. Therefore, vacuum is present on both sides of the diaphragm. The power-piston return spring holds the power piston and diaphragm to the right in the unapplied position (Fig. 7-25). A simplified diagram of the operation of the vacuum booster in the released position is shown in Fig. 7-26.

Brakes Being Applied

When the brakes are applied, the brake-pedal pushrod is pushed to the left, as shown in Fig. 7-27. The floating control valve moves with the pushrod and is pushed against its seat in the power piston. When this occurs, the vacuum-valve opening between the front and rear chambers of the booster is closed.

Further movement of the pushrod pushes the air valve away from its seat on the floating control valve. Air under atmospheric pressure now flows through the filter and silencer and through the air-valve opening into the rear chamber of the booster. With vacuum in the front chamber and atmospheric pressure in the rear chamber, a force is applied to the diaphragm and power piston. The force of the power-piston return spring is overcome, and the diaphragm and power piston are pushed to the left in Fig. 7-27. The power piston applies force through the air-valve spring, the reaction levers, and the reaction plate, to the booster pushrod. This causes hydraulic pressure to increase in the master cylinder, applying the brakes.

The amount of force applied to the booster pushrod depends on the difference in pressure from the rear chamber of the booster to the front chamber. A simplified diagram of the operation of the booster while the brakes are being applied is shown in Fig. 7-28.

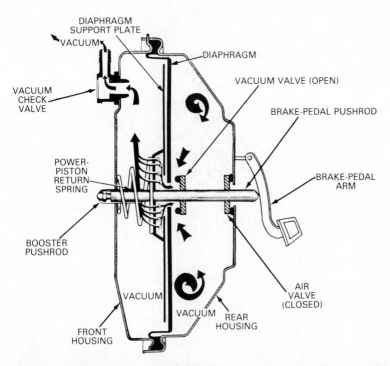

Fig. 7-26. Simplified operation of the vacuum booster in the released position. *(Pontiac Motor Division of General Motors Corporation)*

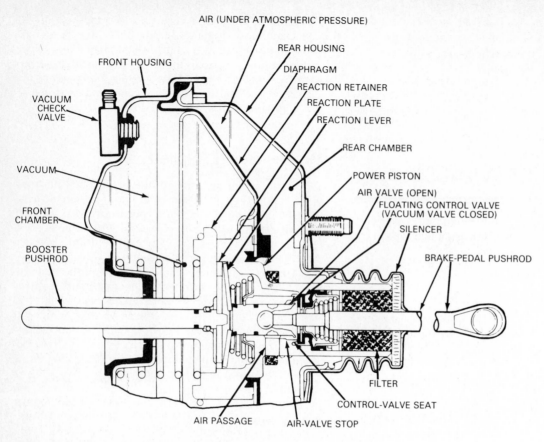

Fig. 7-27. **A vacuum booster in the applied position.** *(Delco Moraine Division of General Motors Corporation)*

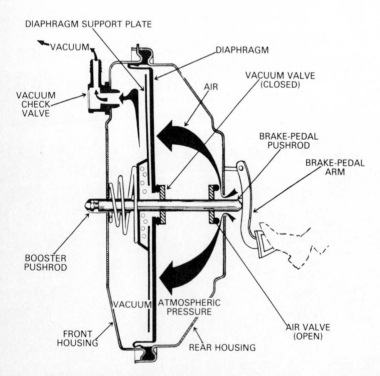

Fig. 7-28. **Simplified operation of the vacuum booster when the brakes are being applied.**
(Pontiac Motor Division of General Motors Corporation)

Brakes Applied and Holding

When the brakes are in the applied position, the power piston moves slightly farther to the left, as shown in Fig. 7-29. The vacuum valve remains closed, and the movement of the power piston pushes the floating control valve against the air valve. This closes the air valve. Now the air is trapped in the rear chamber. Under this condition, the power piston remains stationary and the brakes remain applied.

If more force is applied to the brake pedal, the brake-pedal pushrod will move farther to the left, again opening the air valve. Then more air will enter the rear chamber, and a greater force will be applied to the diaphragm and power piston. This will provide a greater braking force at the wheels. A simplified diagram of this operation of the booster is shown in Fig. 7-30.

Brakes Releasing

When the brake pedal is released, the air-valve spring pushes the air valve back against the floating control valve, which closes the air valve. Further movement of the air valve then pushes the floating control valve away from its seat in the power piston. When this happens, the vacuum valve opens (Fig. 7-25). Air flows from the rear chamber of the booster through air passages in the power piston, through the vacuum-valve opening, and through an opening in the power piston into the front chamber of the booster. From the front chamber of the booster, the air flows through the check valve and into the intake manifold or vacuum pump.

After the air is evacuated from the rear chamber, there is again vacuum on both sides of the diaphragm, and no force is acting on the diaphragm and power piston. The power-piston return spring pushes the power piston and diaphragm back to their released positions. This allows the booster pushrod to move back, which releases hydraulic pressure in the master cylinder and releases the brakes.

NON-POWER-ASSISTED BRAKE OPERATION

If the vacuum booster fails to provide a power assist, the brakes can still be applied. When the brake pedal is depressed, the brake-pedal pushrod moves to the left in Fig. 7-27. If there is a failure in the vacuum booster, the brake-pedal pushrod will continue to move until the air valve contacts a stop on the inside diameter of the power piston. Further movement of the brake pedal will then cause the power piston to apply force through the reaction levers and reaction plate to the booster pushrod. This will apply the brakes. When this occurs, the driver will have to apply a much greater force to apply the brakes than if the vacuum booster were operating normally.

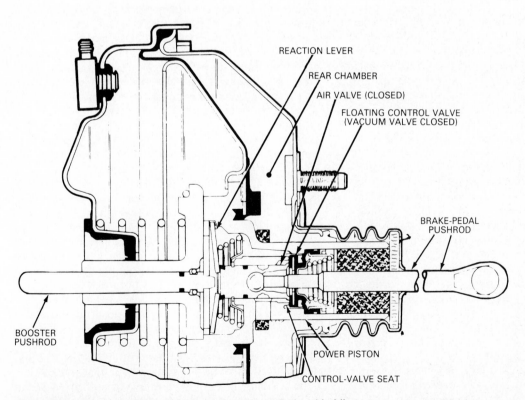

Fig. 7-29. A vacuum booster when the brakes are applied and holding. *(Delco Moraine Division of General Motors Corporation)*

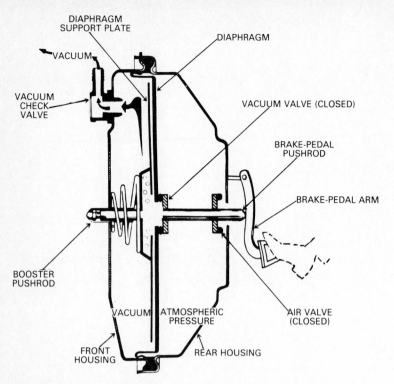

DIAPHRAGM
SUPPORT PLATE

DIAPHRAGM

VACUUM

VACUUM
CHECK
VALVE

VACUUM VALVE (CLOSED)

BRAKE-PEDAL
PUSHROD

BRAKE-PEDAL ARM

BOOSTER
PUSHROD

VACUUM   ATMOSPHERIC
PRESSURE

AIR VALVE
(CLOSED)

FRONT
HOUSING

REAR HOUSING

**Fig. 7-30. Simplified operation of the vacuum booster when the brakes are applied and
holding.** *(Pontiac Motor Division of General Motors Corporation)*

BRAKE FEEL

On a car without power brakes, when the driver depresses the brake pedal, the booster pushrod is pushed against the primary piston in the master cylinder. Hydraulic pressure then builds up in the master cylinder, and the pushrod cannot move farther with the same pedal force. The harder the driver presses on the brake pedal, the greater the hydraulic pressure, and the harder the pedal feels to the driver. The pedal pushes back against the driver's foot with the same force that the driver applies. The force against the driver's foot is called the *reaction force*. The driver judges how hard to depress the brake pedal based on the rate at which the car slows and on the feel of the reaction force in the brake pedal.

On a car with power brakes, the brake pedal operates the brake-pedal pushrod. There is no direct contact between the brake-pedal pushrod and the master cylinder. Therefore, there is no way for the driver to judge how hard to depress the brake pedal. For this reason, reaction components are built into the power-piston assembly. The vacuum booster shown in Fig. 7-24 has a reaction plate and three reaction levers. When the driver depresses the brake pedal, some of the force acting on the booster pushrod is transferred back through the reaction plate and reaction levers, and through the air valve and brake-pedal pushrod to the brake pedal (Fig. 7-27). This reaction force provides some brake "feel" to help the driver judge how hard to depress the brake pedal.

Figure 7-31 shows a vacuum booster that has a reaction disc and reaction piston. These function in a similar manner to the components shown in Fig. 7-24 to provide brake feel to the driver.

DUAL-DIAPHRAGM VACUUM BOOSTER

Figure 7-32 shows a *dual-diaphragm*, or *tandem, vacuum booster* that has two diaphragms and two diaphragm support plates, mounted one behind the other. The *primary diaphragm* is the diaphragm closest to the rear of the car. The *secondary diaphragm* is closest to the front of the car. Some dual-diaphragm vacuum boosters have two power pistons that are attached together. Other dual-diaphragm boosters use a single power piston.

A housing divider separates the vacuum booster into two sections (Fig. 7-33). Each section contains a diaphragm. Therefore, there are four separate chambers in a dual-diaphragm booster: a chamber in front of each diaphragm, and a chamber behind each diaphragm. The operation of a dual-diaphragm vacuum booster is similar to the operation of a single-diaphragm booster.

When the brakes are not applied (Fig. 7-33), there is vacuum in all four chambers. When the brakes are applied (Fig. 7-34), atmospheric air is admitted to the rear chamber of each diaphragm. With atmospheric pressure behind each diaphragm, and with vacuum in front of each diaphragm, a force is applied to both diaphragms. This force is applied to the power pistons, and the power pistons apply the force to the booster pushrod.

With two diaphragms, twice as much force is applied to the booster pushrod as there is with a single diaphragm of the same diameter. Therefore, a dual diaphragm vacuum booster can have a smaller diameter than a single-diaphragm booster and still provide the same braking force. Dual-diaphragm vacuum boosters take up less space in the engine compartment.

122

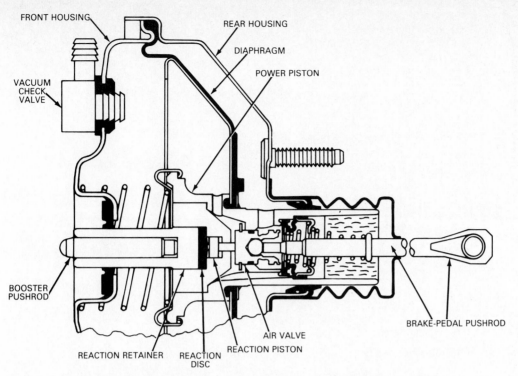

Fig. 7-31. A vacuum booster that uses a reaction disc and a reaction piston. *(Delco Moraine Division of General Motors Corporation)*

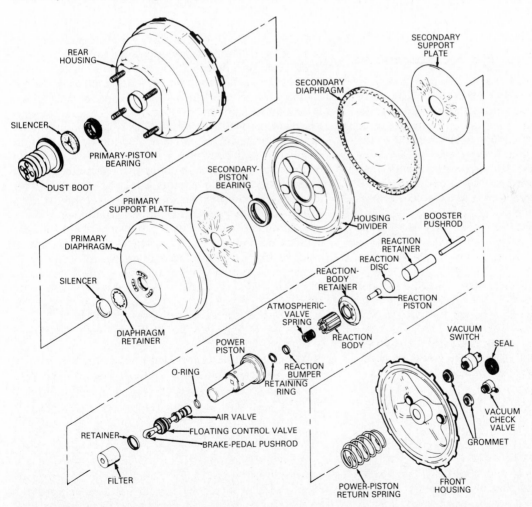

Fig. 7-32. A disassembled tandem vacuum booster. *(Chevrolet Motor Division of General Motors Corporation)*

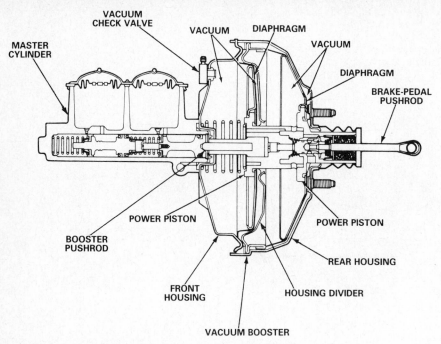

Fig. 7-33. A tandem vacuum booster in the released position. *(Chevrolet Motor Division of General Motors Corporation)*

REMOTE-MOUNTED VACUUM BOOSTER

A power-brake system with a *remote-mounted vacuum booster* is shown in Fig. 7-35. The booster is mounted some distance away from the master cylinder. A brake line connects the master cylinder to the booster, and brake lines connect a hydraulic cylinder in the booster to the wheel cylinders. The booster multiplies the hydraulic pressure produced by the master cylinder and applies this increased pressure to the wheel cylinders. For this reason, these systems are also called *multiplier-type power-brake systems.*

The remote-mounted vacuum booster uses a combination of vacuum and atmospheric pressure on opposite sides of a diaphragm (or piston) for its operation.

The operation is similar to that of an integral-type vacuum booster. The hydraulic pressure produced by the master cylinder controls valves in the booster. The valves control the vacuum and air pressure applied to the diaphragm (or piston). The difference in pressure from one side of the diaphragm (or piston) to the other produces a large force. This force is applied to a piston in the hydraulic cylinder in the booster. The force of the piston produces a high pressure in the cylinder. This pressure is transferred from the cylinder through brake lines to the wheel cylinders. Therefore, a relatively small hydraulic pressure from the master cylinder is multiplied into a high hydraulic pressure to operate the brakes.

Remote-mounted vacuum boosters are no longer used on passenger cars and light trucks. However, they are sometimes used on heavier trucks.

VOCABULARY REVIEW

Absolute pressure   The pressure compared to a perfect vacuum. It is the atmospheric pressure added to the gauge pressure.

Air compressor   A device used to raise the pressure of air above atmospheric pressure.

Air pressure   The force of air molecules on a surface, divided by the area of the surface.

Air valve   The valve in a vacuum booster that is opened to admit air under atmospheric pressure into one chamber of the booster.

Atmosphere   The air that surrounds the earth.

Atmospheric air pressure   The pressure of the air molecules in the earth's atmosphere acting on a surface.

Atmospheric-suspended power-brake booster   A vacuum brake booster that has atmospheric air pressure on both sides of the diaphragm when the brakes are not applied. Vacuum is admitted to one side of the diaphragm to apply the brakes.

Atmospheric valve   Another name for an air valve.

Booster pushrod   The rod that connects from the vacuum booster to the master cylinder.

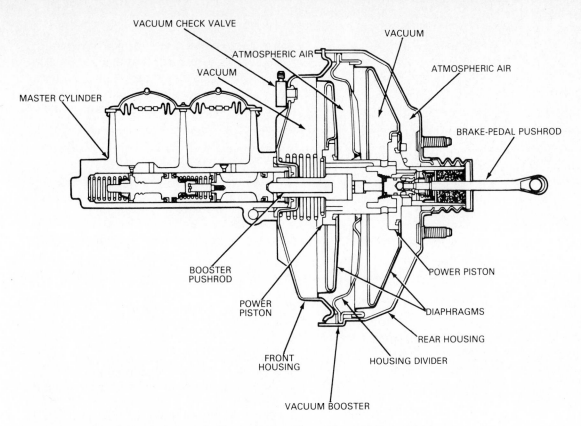

Fig. 7-34. A tandem vacuum booster in the applied position. *(Chevrolet Motor Division of General Motors Corporation)*

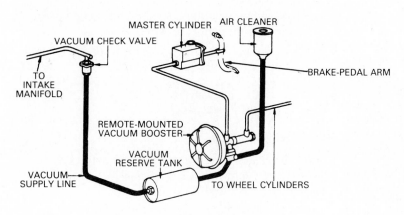

Fig. 7-35. A remote-mounted vacuum booster. *(Wagner Division, Cooper Industries Inc.)*

Brake-pedal pushrod The rod that connects from the brake-pedal arm to the vacuum booster.

Check valve A valve that permits air flow in one direction, but not in the other.

Compressed air Air that has been raised in pressure to above atmospheric pressure.

Gauge pressure The pressure indicated by a pressure gauge.

Intake-manifold vacuum The vacuum in the intake manifold of a running engine caused by the intake strokes of the pistons.

Integral-type power-brake system A power-brake system in which the master cylinder attaches directly to the vacuum-booster assembly.

Multiplier-type power-brake system A power-brake system which has a remote-mounted vacuum booster and which multiplies the hydraulic pressure from the master cylinder.

Partial vacuum A partial absence of air.

Perfect vacuum The complete absence of air.

Piston rod Another name for a booster pushrod.

Reaction force The force that the brake pedal applies to the driver's foot, equal and opposite to the force applied by the driver's foot to the brake pedal.

Tandem vacuum booster A vacuum booster that has two diaphragms, one behind the other.

Vacuum The absence of air.

Vacuum booster A device that uses the difference between vacuum and air pressure to increase the force of the driver's foot when applying the brakes.

Vacuum-suspended power-brake booster A vacuum brake booster that has vacuum on both sides of the diaphragm when the brakes are not applied. Air is admitted to one side of the diaphragm to apply the brakes.

Vacuum valve That valve in a vacuum booster which is opened to admit vacuum into one chamber of the booster.

Valve rod Another name for a brake-pedal pushrod.

REVIEW QUESTIONS

Select the *one* correct, best, or most probable answer to each question.

1. Technician A says that a vacuum-suspended brake booster has atmospheric pressure on both sides of the diaphragm when the brakes are not applied and that vacuum is admitted to one side of the diaphragm to apply the brakes. Technician B says that there is vaccum on both sides of the diaphragm and that atmospheric pressure is admitted to apply the brakes. Who is right?
   a. A only
   b. B only
   c. Both A and B
   d. Neither A nor B

2. In a vacuum-assist power-brake booster, what are the positions of the vacuum valve and air valve when the brakes are applied and holding?
   a. Both valves are open.
   b. The vacuum valve is open and the air valve is closed.
   c. The air valve is open and the vacuum valve is closed.
   d. Both valves are closed.

3. In a vacuum-assist power-brake booster, what are the positions of the vacuum valve and air valve when the brakes are being applied?

   a. Both valves are open.
   b. The vacuum valve is open and the air valve is closed.
   c. The air valve is open and the vacuum valve is closed.
   d. Both valves are closed.

4. A vacuum of 22 in. Hg [559 mm Hg] is approximately equivalent to what absolute pressure?
   a. 4 psia [27.6 kPa]
   b. 6 psia [41.4 kPa]
   c. 36 psia [248.4 kPa]
   d. 14.7 psia [101.4 kPa]

5. At sea level, if the gauge pressure is 8 psi [55.2 kPa], what is the absolute pressure?
   a. 6.7 psi [46.2 kPa]
   b. 0 psi [0 kPa]
   c. 22.7 psi [156.6 kPa]
   d. 14.7 psi [101.4 kPa]

6. The check valve in a vacuum booster:
   a. holds air pressure in the front chamber of the booster.
   b. allows air to flow from the booster to the intake manifold or vacuum pump.
   c. holds vacuum in the rear chamber of the booster.
   d. allows air to flow from the intake manifold or vacuum pump to the booster.

7. In a vacuum-assist power-brake booster, which valve closes first when the brakes are being applied?
   a. The check valve
   b. The control valve
   c. The air valve
   d. The vacuum valve

8. A vacuum of 10 in. Hg [254 mm Hg] is approximately equivalent to a pressure of
   a. -10 psi [-69 kPa].
   b. -5 psi [-34.5 kPa].
   c. -7.5 psi [-51.8 kPa].
   d. -14.7 psi [-101.4 kPa].

9. In a vacuum-assist power-brake system, brake feel is provided by:
   a. the power-piston return spring.
   b. springs in the power-piston assembly.
   c. the diaphragm.
   d. the reaction components.

10. **All of the following are true of a dual-diaphragm vacuum booster** *except:*
   a. There are four separate chambers
   b. There is vacuum on both sides of both diaphragms when the brakes are not applied
   c. There is atmospheric air pressure on both sides of both diaphragms when the brakes are applied and holding
   d. Atmospheric air is admitted to the rear chamber of each diaphragm when the brakes are applied

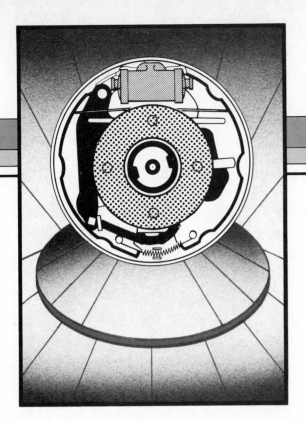

CHAPTER 8

HYDRAULIC-ASSIST POWER BRAKES

OBJECTIVES

After you have studied this chapter, you should be able to:

1. Name the components in a hydraulic-assist power-brake system.

2. Describe the components in a hydraulic-assist power-brake system.

3. Describe the operation of a hydraulic-assist power-brake system.

The hydraulic-assist power brakes covered in this chapter use pressurized power-steering fluid to increase the hydraulic pressure in the master cylinder. A hydraulic-assist power-brake system is shown in Fig. 8-1. The system includes the power-steering pump, hydraulic-brake booster, master cylinder, and power-steering hoses.

The hydraulic-brake booster described in this chapter is called the Hydro-Boost power-brake booster (Fig. 8-2). The booster is attached to the vehicle's firewall, and the master cylinder attaches to the booster (Fig. 8-3). The construction and operation of the master cylinder are described in Chap. 3.

When the driver depresses the brake pedal, the hydraulic booster increases the force of the driver's foot and applies this increased force to the master cylinder. Therefore, less brake-pedal force is required to stop the car than if the brake pedal operated the master cylinder directly.

POWER-STEERING PUMP AND HOSES

The power-steering pump is belt-driven from the engine crankshaft. The function of the power-steering pump is to provide high-pressure power-steering fluid for use in the power-steering system. In a hydraulic-assist power-brake system, the high-pressure power-steering fluid is pumped first to the hydraulic booster and then to the steering gear.

Hoses connect the power-steering pump with the hydraulic booster and power-steering gear (Fig. 8-4). The power-steering pump has one outlet (or high-pressure) hose and two return (or low-pressure) hoses. The outlet hose carries high-pressure power-steering fluid from the power-steering pump to the hydraulic booster. Another high-pressure hose carries the high-pressure fluid from the booster to the power-steering gear. One return hose carries power-steering fluid from the power-steering gear back to the power-steering pump. The other return

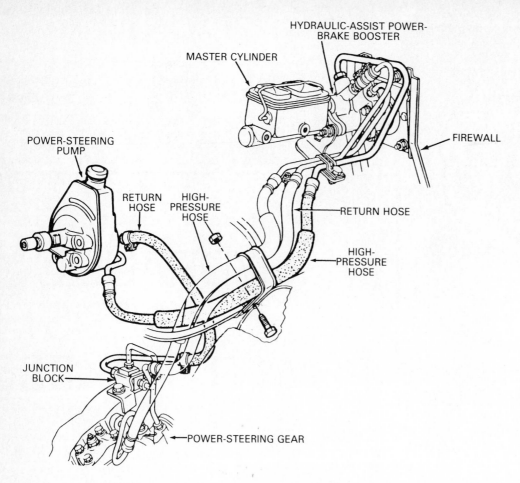

Fig. 8-1. The components of a hydraulic-assist power-brake system. *(FMC Corporation)*

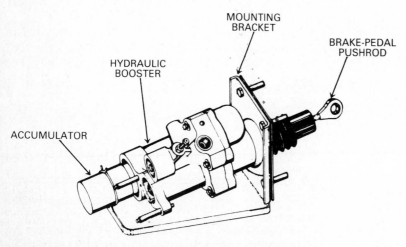

Fig. 8-2. A hydraulic-assist power-brake booster (Hydro-Boost). *(Bendix Aftermarket Brake Division)*

hose carries fluid from the booster back to the power-steering pump.

In some brake systems, the return hoses from the booster and the steering gear meet at a junction block (Figs. 8-5 and 8-1). Then a single return hose connects from the junction block to the pump.

The high-pressure hoses are rubber hoses reinforced with a nylon mesh. These hoses have steel lines and fittings attached to each end. The high-pressure hoses must

be able to hold a pressure of approximately 1,500 pounds per square inch (psi) [10,350 kilopascals (kPa)]. The return hoses are rubber hoses. These hoses, which do not have to hold high pressure, are clamped to fittings or steel lines with hose clamps.

The temperature of the power-steering fluid increases because it is pumped to a high pressure. On some cars the fluid is cooled by passing a steel line attached to the return hose in front of the radiator (Fig. 8-6). The power-

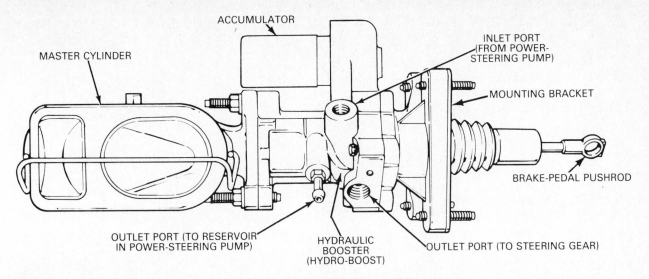

ACCUMULATOR

MASTER CYLINDER

INLET PORT
(FROM POWER-
STEERING PUMP)

MOUNTING BRACKET

BRAKE-PEDAL PUSHROD

OUTLET PORT (TO RESERVOIR
IN POWER-STEERING PUMP)

HYDRAULIC
BOOSTER
(HYDRO-BOOST)

OUTLET PORT (TO STEERING GEAR)

Fig. 8-3. A master cylinder shown attached to a Hydro-Boost power-brake booster. *(Ford Motor Company)*

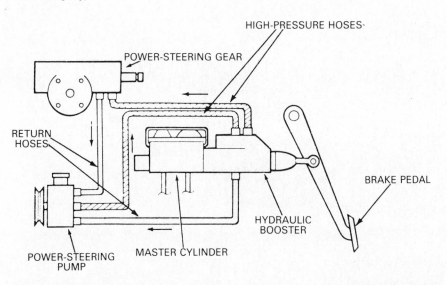

HIGH-PRESSURE HOSES

POWER-STEERING GEAR

RETURN
HOSES

BRAKE PEDAL

HYDRAULIC
BOOSTER

POWER-STEERING
PUMP

MASTER CYLINDER

Fig. 8-4. A power-steering-hose routing for a hydraulic-assist power-brake system. The pump shown has two return hoses. *(FMC Corporation)*

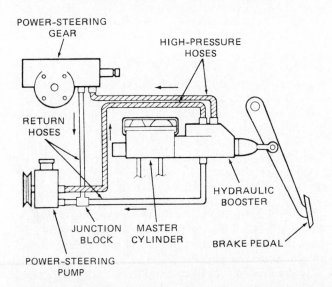

POWER-STEERING
GEAR

HIGH-PRESSURE
HOSES

RETURN
HOSES

HYDRAULIC
BOOSTER

JUNCTION
BLOCK

MASTER
CYLINDER

BRAKE PEDAL

POWER-STEERING
PUMP

Fig. 8-5. A power-steering-hose routing for a hydraulic-assist power-brake system. The pump shown has one return hose. *(FMC Corporation)*

steering fluid passes through this line on the way back to the power-steering-pump reservoir. The line is clamped to the radiator support, and the cooling air passes over the line before flowing through the radiator. Therefore, the fluid is cooled before it reaches the pump reservoir.

Power-steering fluid and brake fluid are not allowed to mix together. If power-steering fluid contacts the seals in the master cylinder, the seals will be damaged. If brake fluid contacts the seals in the hydraulic booster, those seals will be damaged. Therefore, the two hydraulic systems are completely separate.

HYDRAULIC BOOSTER

The main components of the hydraulic-brake booster are the housing, housing cover, power piston, spool valve, and accumulator (Fig. 8-7). The housing has two large holes, or *bores*, drilled in from one end (Fig. 8-8). The

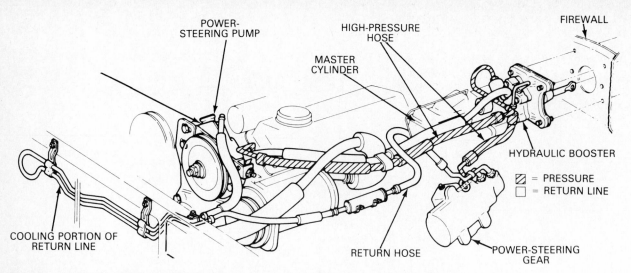

Fig. 8-6. A hydraulic-assist power-brake system that uses a section of the return line to cool the power-steering fluid. *(Ford Motor Company)*

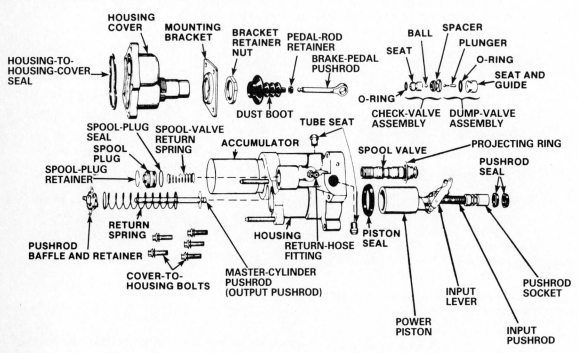

Fig. 8-7. A disassembled hydraulic-assist power-brake booster (Hydro-Boost I). *(Bendix Aftermarket Brake Division)*

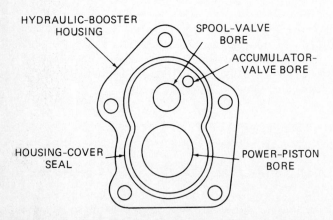

Fig. 8-8. The hydraulic-booster housing, showing the power-piston bore and the spool-valve bore.

bores are parallel to each other and are separated by a short distance. One bore has a larger diameter than the other bore. The larger bore holds the *power piston* and is called the *power-piston bore*. The power piston is acted on by pressurized power-steering fluid and applies force to the primary piston in the master cylinder. The smaller bore holds the *spool valve* and is called the *spool-valve bore*. The spool valve moves in its bore to control the flow of power-steering fluid.

Figure 8-9 shows a cutaway view of the hydraulic booster. When the housing cover is bolted to the housing, a *pressure chamber* is formed between the housing and the inside of the housing cover.

The brake-pedal pushrod (Fig. 8-2) connects from the brake-pedal arm to the pushrod socket in the open end of the power-piston bore (Fig. 8-9). The socket is in contact with one end of the input pushrod. The other

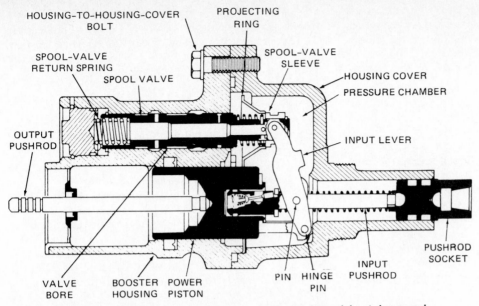

Fig. 8-9. A hydraulic-assist power-brake booster with the brake pedal not depressed. *(FMC Corporation)*

end of the input pushrod contacts the power-piston assembly. An output pushrod connects from the power-piston assembly to the primary piston in the master cylinder.

An input lever is located in the pressure chamber. The lever is hinged to the lower edge of the power piston with a pin and, in addition, is pinned to the input pushrod. The opposite end of the lever from the hinge contacts the spool valve. When the driver depresses the brake pedal, the input pushrod pushes the power piston. At the same time, the input lever moves the spool valve. The spool valve admits high-pressure power-steering fluid into the pressure chamber. The power-steering fluid applies force to the power piston and boosts the force that the driver applies to the power piston.

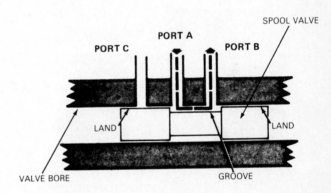

Fig. 8-10. A spool valve. *(Wagner Division, Cooper Industries Inc.)*

OPERATION OF THE SPOOL VALVE

Figure 8-10 shows the spool valve. There are three drilled passages, or *ports*, in the valve bore. In the position of the valve shown in Fig. 8-10, hydraulic fluid can flow from port A to port B, but port C is blocked.

In Fig. 8-10 one part of the spool valve has a smaller diameter than the rest of the valve. The smaller-diameter part is the *spool-valve groove*. The surfaces of the larger-diameter parts are *spool-valve lands*.

The spool valve shown in Fig. 8-10 has a hollow center, and drilled holes connect one of the lands with the center. The center of the spool valve opens into the booster pressure chamber.

The valve bore is in the upper portion of the booster, as shown in Fig. 8-9. The valve bore has sections with different diameters (Fig. 8-11). Three ports connect the outside of the booster to the valve bore. The outside openings of these ports are threaded. The threaded openings allow the power-steering-hose fittings to be attached to the booster.

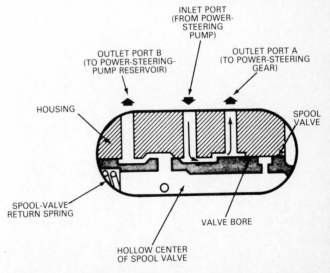

Fig. 8-11. A Hydro-Boost spool valve in its position when the brake pedal is not depressed. *(Wagner Division, Cooper Industries Inc.)*

131

The booster has one inlet port and two outlet ports. The brake hose from the power-steering pump connects to the inlet port. A hose connects one outlet port (outlet port A) to the steering gear. Another hose connects the other outlet port (outlet port B) back to the power-steering-pump reservoir.

Brakes Not Applied

When the brake pedal is not depressed, the spool valve is in the position shown in Fig. 8-11. Power-steering fluid flows from the power-steering pump to the inlet port of the booster. From the inlet port, the fluid flows into the groove of the spool valve. Then the fluid flows to outlet port A, and from port A it flows through a hose to the steering gear. When the spool valve is in this position, no pressure builds up in the booster. The power-steering fluid only passes through the booster on the way to the steering gear.

When the spool valve is in the position shown in Fig. 8-11, the center of the valve is open to outlet port B. Therefore, any power-steering fluid that is under pressure in the pressure chamber, or in the center of the spool valve, is returned to the pump reservoir.

Brakes Being Applied

When the brake pedal is depressed, the brake-pedal pushrod moves forward (to the left), as shown in Fig. 8-12. This movement causes the input pushrod and power piston to move forward. The motion of the input pushrod also causes the input lever to push the spool valve forward (Fig. 8-13).

When the spool valve is pushed forward, it blocks port B, preventing fluid flow back to the pump reservoir. In addition, fluid can now flow from the inlet port to the center of the spool valve. Fluid flows from the pump, through the inlet port, through the holes in the spool valve land, and into the center of the valve. Then

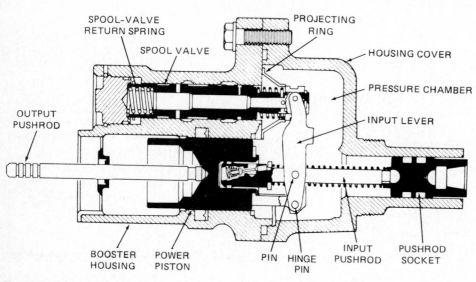

Fig. 8-12. A hydraulic-assist power-brake booster with the brake pedal depressed. *(FMC Corporation)*

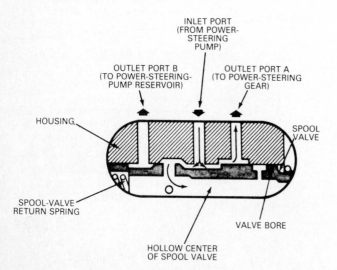

Fig. 8-13. A Hydro-Boost spool valve in its position when the brake pedal is depressed. *(Wagner Division, Cooper Industries Inc.)*

the fluid flows from the center of the valve into the pressure chamber.

The fluid in the pressure chamber applies force to the power piston and pushes it to the left, as shown in Fig. 8-12. The power piston applies this force through the output pushrod to the primary piston in the master cylinder. Then hydraulic pressure is built up in the brake fluid in the master cylinder to apply the brakes. The operation of the master cylinder is described in Chap. 3.

When the valve is in the position shown in Fig. 8-13, fluid continues to flow to the steering gear. However, the fluid flow is partially restricted by the spool valve. With continuous fluid flow to the steering gear, the steering is not affected when the brakes are applied.

The fluid flow is restricted by the spool valve. This causes the output pressure from the power-steering pump to increase. This increased pressure increases the force applied to the power piston. Therefore, a greater force than is applied to the brake pedal is applied to the power piston to operate the brakes.

Brakes Applied and Holding

When the brake pedal is depressed and held, the pressure of the power-steering fluid in the pressure chamber pushes the power piston forward. The input lever is hinged to the lower edge of the power piston (Fig. 8-14). When the power piston moves forward, the hinged portion of the lever is also pulled forward. This causes the lever to pivot in a clockwise direction around the pin that attaches it to the input pushrod. When this happens, the part of the lever that contacts the spool valve moves rearward. This movement pulls the spool valve rearward to the position shown in Fig. 8-15.

With the spool valve in this position, power-steering fluid is trapped in the center of the spool valve and in the pressure chamber. Because power-steering fluid cannot enter or leave the pressure chamber, the pressure in the chamber remains constant. Therefore, the power piston remains in a fixed position and applies a constant force to the primary piston in the master cylinder. This holds the brakes in the applied position.

When the spool valve is in the position shown in Fig. 8-15, power-steering fluid continues to flow to the steering gear. This ensures that the power steering will not be affected by the operation of the brakes.

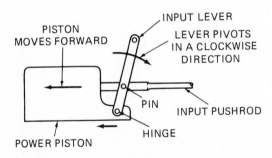

Fig. 8-14. The motion of the input lever when the power piston moves forward.

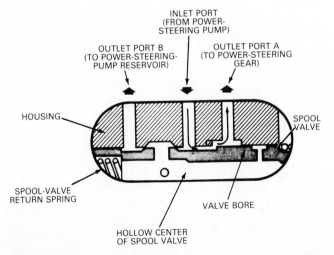

Fig. 8-15. A Hydro-Boost spool valve in its position when the brake pedal is applied and holding. (*Wagner Division, Cooper Industries Inc.*)

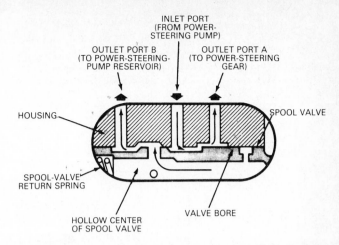

Fig. 8-16. A Hydro-Boost spool valve in its position when the brake pedal is released. (*Wagner Division, Cooper Industries Inc.*)

Brakes Releasing

When the brake pedal is released, the brake-pedal rod, pushrod socket, and input pushrod move rearward. This motion causes the input lever to pull the spool valve back to the position shown in Fig. 8-16. In this position, the center of the spool valve is open to outlet port B. Now power-steering fluid can flow from the pressure chamber and the center of the spool valve, through the holes in the spool valve land, through outlet port B, and to the power-steering-pump reservoir.

With no pressure in the pressure chamber, the power-piston return spring moves the piston rearward. This relieves the pressure in the master cylinder, and the brakes are released.

ACCUMULATOR

The *accumulator* is a fluid-storage container. It stores power-steering fluid under pressure, and it releases the fluid to the pressure chamber if there is a failure in the power-steering system. The accumulator is mounted on the outside of the booster housing (Figs. 8-2 and 8-7) and will provide from one to three power-assisted stops if the power-steering pump fails to supply fluid to the booster.

Fluid flow to and from the accumulator is controlled by the accumulator-valve assembly (Figs. 8-17 and 8-18). The valve assembly includes a check valve and a dump valve. The *check valve* allows power-steering fluid to flow into the accumulator, and it holds pressurized fluid in the accumulator. The *dump valve* releases pressurized power-steering fluid from the accumulator.

In Fig. 8-17 the accumulator-valve assembly is shown separated from the booster. This is done to simplify the drawing. The valve assembly is actually located in the booster housing, next to the spool-valve bore (Fig. 8-8). When the pressure in the accumulator is less than the pressure produced by the power-steering pump, the check valve in the accumulator-valve assembly is forced open. Power-steering fluid then flows into the accumulator.

133

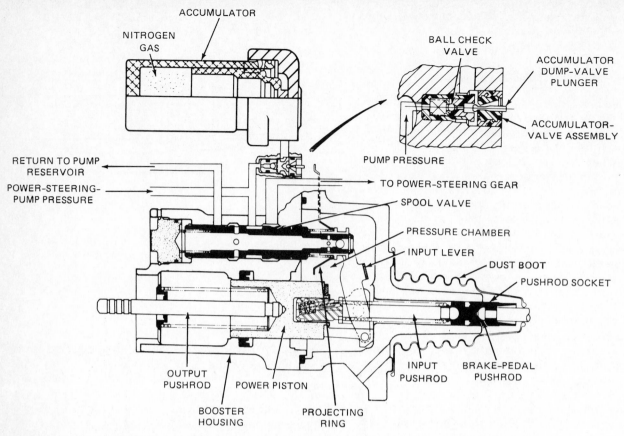

Fig. 8-17. A hydraulic-assist power-brake booster, showing the accumulator and the accumulator-valve assembly. *(Ford Motor Company)*

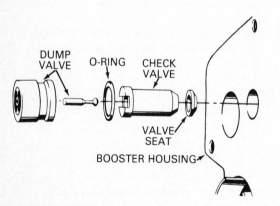

Fig. 8-18. A disassembled accumulator-valve assembly. *(Oldsmobile Division of General Motors Corporation)*

One type of accumulator (Figs. 8-17 and 8-19) has a chamber filled with nitrogen gas; as the power-steering fluid flows into the accumulator, the accumulator piston is pushed into the accumulator and the gas is compressed. Another type of accumulator (Fig. 8-20) has a large spring. As the power-steering fluid flows into the accumulator, the accumulator piston is pushed into the accumulator and the spring is compressed. In either type of accumulator, the power-steering fluid is stored under pressure and held in the accumulator by the check valve. The check valve holds pressure in the accumulator even if the power-steering-pump pressure drops below the accumulator pressure.

When the brake pedal is depressed, if there is no power-steering-pump pressure, the input lever moves a

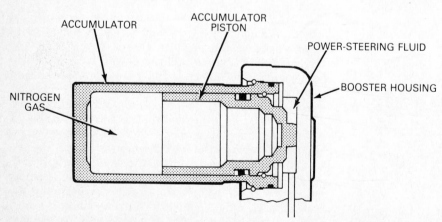

Fig. 8-19. An accumulator with a gas-filled chamber. *(Ford Motor Company)*

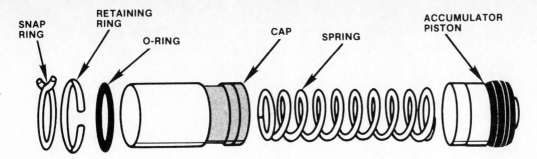

Fig. 8-20. A spring-loaded accumulator. *(Bendix Aftermarket Brake Division)*

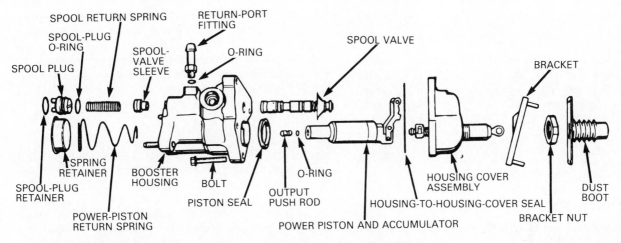

Fig. 8-21. A disassembled hydraulic-assist power-brake booster (Hyro-Boost II). *(Bendix Aftermarket Brake Division)*

projecting ring on the spool valve. The ring slides along the valve and pushes a plunger in the accumulator valve. This opens the accumulator dump valve, and the accumulator supplies pressurized power-steering fluid through the spool valve to the pressure chamber of the booster. Therefore, the power assist will continue to operate until the pressure in the accumulator is released.

If a failure occurs in the power-steering system and the car has been stopped from one to three times, there may be no pressure left in the accumulator, but the car can still be stopped without power assist. When the brake pedal is depressed, the force on the brake pedal is transferred through the brake-pedal pushrod, the pushrod socket, and the input pushrod directly to the power piston. The power piston then transfers this force to the primary piston in the master cylinder. However, the force applied to the brake pedal must be greater than if the power assist were operating normally.

The hydraulic booster that has been described has the accumulator mounted on the outside of the booster housing. This booster is called Hydro-Boost I. Another version, Hydro-Boost II, has the accumulator built into the power piston (Fig. 21). Accumulator operation is similar in both types.

VOCABULARY REVIEW

Accumulator A container for power-steering fluid in a hydraulic-brake booster. The accumulator stores pressurized power-steering fluid to operate the brakes if there is a failure in the power-steering system.

Check valve The valve which allows power-steering fluid to flow into the accumulator and which holds pressurized fluid in the accumulator.

Dump valve The valve that releases pressurized power-steering fluid from the accumulator.

Port A hole that leads from the outside of the hydraulic-booster housing to the spool-valve bore.

Power piston A piston which is acted on by pressurized power-steering fluid and which applies force to the primary piston in the master cylinder.

Power-piston bore The hole in the booster housing in which the power piston is located.

Pressure chamber The hollow chamber to the rear of the power piston that is formed when

135

the housing cover is bolted to the booster housing.

Spool valve　A spool-shaped part that moves to control the flow of hydraulic fluid.

Spool-valve bore　The hole in the booster housing in which the spool valve is located.

Spool-valve groove　That part of a spool valve which has a smaller diameter than the rest of the valve.

Spool-valve land　A large-diameter portion of a spool valve.

REVIEW QUESTIONS

Select the *one* correct, best, or most probable answer to each question.

1. Technician A says that the accumulator supplies pressurized power-steering fluid to the hydraulic booster whenever the output pressure from the power-steering pump is low. Technician B says that the accumulator-valve plunger must be depressed to release power-steering fluid from the accumulator. Who is right?
   a. A only
   b. B only
   c. Both A and B
   d. Neither A nor B

2. What part of the Hydro-Boost assembly moves the spool valve?
   a. The input lever
   b. The input pushrod
   c. The brake-pedal pushrod
   d. The accumulator-valve plunger

3. What part of the Hydro-Boost assembly permits at least one power-assisted stop if the power-steering pump fails to provide pressure?
   a. The power piston
   b. The spool valve
   c. The accumulator-valve plunger
   d. The accumulator

4. In Fig. 8-14, which of the following is true when the brakes are applied and holding?
   a. The input lever rotates in a counterclockwise direction.
   b. The power piston moves rearward.
   c. The spool valve moves forward.
   d. The accumulator-valve plunger is depressed.

5. All of the following are true when the brakes are being applied *except*:
   a. The spool valve opens the inlet port
   b. The spool valve moves forward
   c. The power piston moves forward
   d. The spool valve opens the outlet port

6. All of the following are true when the brakes are releasing *except*:
   a. The spool valve opens the outlet port
   b. The input pushrod moves rearward
   c. The spool valve moves forward
   d. The accumulator check valve remains closed

7. Technician A says that when the power-steering-pump pressure drops below the accumulator pressure, the accumulator check valve opens. Technician B says that a projecting ring on the spool valve must depress the accumulator-valve plunger to release power-steering fluid from the accumulator. Who is right?
   a. A only
   b. B only
   c. Both A and B
   d. Neither A nor B

8. In the Hydro-Boost system, the power-steering operation is not affected when the brakes are applied. Technician A says that this is because the spool valve always permits some fluid flow to the steering gear. Technician B says that this is because a power-steering hose connects from the pump to the steering gear. Who is right?
   a. A only
   b. B only
   c. Both A and B
   d. Neither A nor B

9. Technician A says that power-steering fluid and brake fluid do not mix in the Hydro-Boost system because brake fluid does not have a high enough boiling point. Technician B says that their viscosities are too different for them to mix properly. Who is right?
   a. A only
   b. B only
   c. Both A and B
   d. Neither A nor B

10. In the Hydro-Boost unit, the pressure of the power-steering fluid increases when the brakes are applied. Technician A says that the movement of the power piston causes the pressure to increase. Technician B says that the pressure increases because the spool valve restricts the power-steering-pump output. Who is right?
    a. A only
    b. B only
    c. Both A and B
    d. Neither A nor B

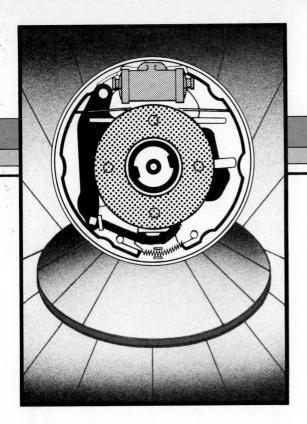

CHAPTER 9

ELECTRO-HYDRAULIC-ASSIST POWER BRAKES

OBJECTIVES

After you have studied this chapter, you should be able to:

1. Name the components in an electrohydraulic power-brake system.

2. Describe the construction of each major component in an electrohydraulic power-brake system.

3. Describe the operation of the electrohydraulic power-brake system.

Electrohydraulic-assist power brakes operate independently of either engine vacuum or power-steering fluid. This type of power brake has three separate hydraulic systems. Two hydraulic systems are controlled by the master cylinder, and these two operate the wheel cylinders to apply the brakes. This part of the operation is similar to that of the brake systems described previously. The fluid in these two systems is called the *apply fluid*.

The other hydraulic system has fluid that is pressurized by a pump driven by a small electric motor. The fluid in this system is the *booster fluid*. It assists the brake operation by increasing the pressure of the apply fluid

in the master cylinder. The electrohydraulic-assist power-brake system described in this chapter is used by General Motors and is called the Powermaster Brake System.

COMPONENTS OF AN ELECTROHYDRAULIC UNIT

An electrohydraulic-assist power-brake unit includes a main body, a fluid reservoir, an accumulator, a brake relay, a pressure-sensing switch, an electrohydraulic pump (called an E/H pump), and a check valve (Fig. 9-1). In addition, there are brake hoses, brake lines, electric wiring, and wiring connectors (Fig. 9-2).

Main Body

The main body of the power-brake unit includes the master cylinder and the power booster (Fig. 9-3). The master cylinder has primary and secondary pistons, piston seals, and piston return springs, as in other master cylinders. The power-booster section of the main body includes reaction components and a power-piston assembly. The power-piston assembly has a control valve and a discharge valve (Fig. 9-4).

137

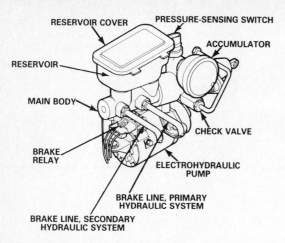

Fig. 9-1. An electrohydraulic power-brake unit. *(Chevrolet Motor Division of General Motors Corporation)*

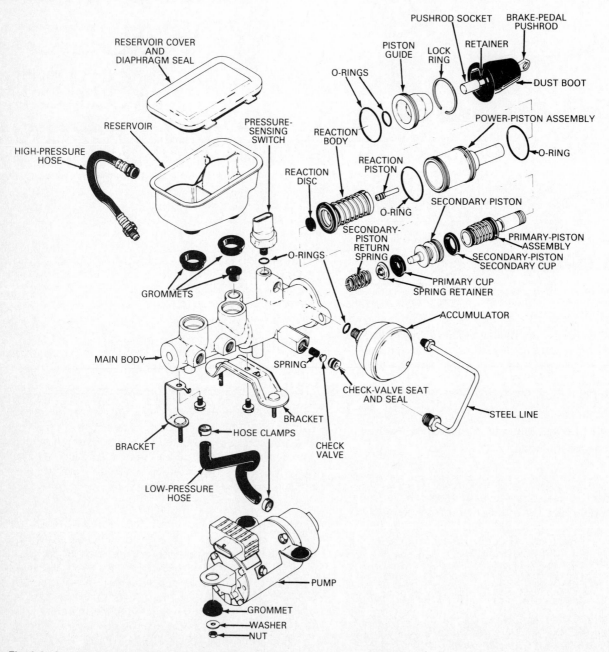

Fig. 9-2. An electrohydraulic power-brake unit. *(Pontiac Motor Division of General Motors Corporation)*

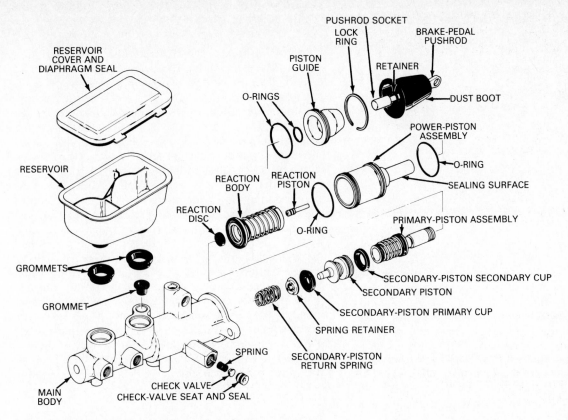

Fig. 9-3. The main body of the power-brake unit. *(Pontiac Motor Division of General Motors Corporation)*

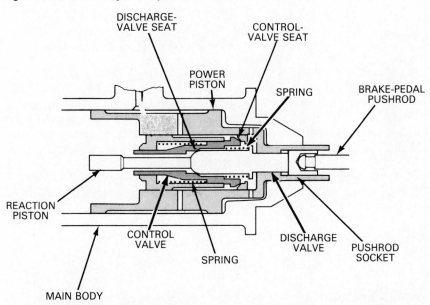

Fig. 9-4. The power-piston assembly, showing the control valve and the discharge valve. The brakes are in the released position and both valves are closed. *(Chevrolet Motor Division of General Motors Corporation)*

A pushrod connects from the brake-pedal arm to a pushrod socket. The socket contacts the discharge valve in the power-piston assembly. A dust boot fits over the end of the main body, and the pushrod fits through an opening in the boot. The dust boot helps prevent dirt from entering the main body. When the driver depresses the brake pedal, the pushrod operates the valves in the power-piston assembly to apply the brakes. The operation of these valves is discussed later in this chapter under "OPERATION OF AN ELECTROHYDRAULIC BRAKE SYSTEM."

Fluid Reservoir

The fluid reservoir (Fig. 9-5) has three compartments. One compartment is for booster fluid. The other two compartments are for apply fluid. One of these compart-

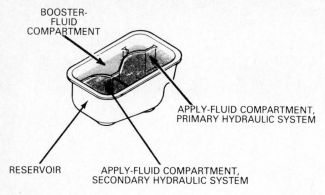

Fig. 9-5. The fluid reservoir, showing the apply compartments and the booster compartment. *(Chevrolet Motor Division of General Motors Corporation)*

ments has apply fluid for the primary hydraulic system, and the other compartment has apply fluid for the secondary hydraulic system.

The reservoir attaches to the main body with grommets. Three grommets are used because there are three fluid connections to the main body. One connection is for booster fluid, and two connections are for primary and secondary apply fluid. The same hydraulic-brake fluid is used for both the apply fluid and the booster fluid. But because of the operation of the system, the apply fluid and the booster fluid never mix.

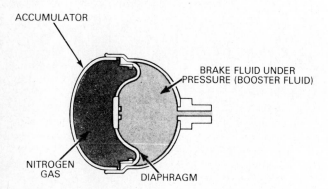

Fig. 9-6. The accumulator. *(Chevrolet Motor Division of General Motors Corporation)*

Accumulator

The *accumulator* (Fig. 9-6) threads into an *accumulator port* in the main body. The accumulator is a storage container for brake fluid. The fluid stored in the accumulator is the booster fluid. The accumulator has two chambers separated by a diaphgram. One chamber contains nitrogen gas. Brake fluid is pumped into the other chamber. The fluid pushes against the diaphragm and compresses the nitrogen gas. This causes the booster fluid to be stored under high pressure. The accumulator ensures that there is a large supply of brake fluid, at high pressure, to provide power assist quickly when the brakes are applied.

Brake fluid is pumped from the booster-fluid compartment in the reservoir to the accumulator. The amount of brake fluid in the accumulator and the reservoir varies with the operation of the brakes (Fig. 9-7). When the accumulator is discharged (has little fluid), the compartment in the reservoir is full (Fig. 9-7a). When the accumulator is charged (has a large supply of fluid), the compartment in the reservoir is nearly empty (Fig. 9-7b). The accumulator holds enough brake fluid for several power-assisted brake applications if there is a failure in the pump or in the vechicle's electrical system.

Brake Relay

A *relay* is a magnetic device that switches current in an electric circuit. The relay uses a magnet to operate one or more sets of switch contacts, or *relay contacts*.

All magnets are surrounded by a magnetic field (Fig. 9-8). A *magnetic field* is all the lines of force of a magnet taken together as a whole. A *line of force* is an imaginary line of magnetic force that passes from the north pole of a magnet, through the air surrounding the magnet, to the south pole of the magnet. The magnet shown in Fig. 9-8 is a permanent magnet. A *permanent magnet* is a magnet that is made of a material that retains its magnetism for a long period of time.

When electric current is passed through a coil of wire, the coil becomes a magnet (Fig. 9-9). If a metal such as iron is placed in the coil, the magnetism becomes

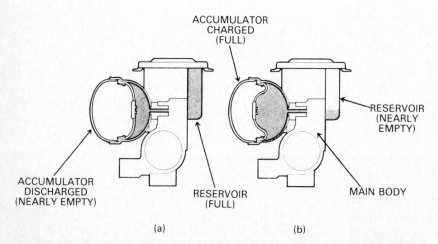

Fig. 9-7. Brake fluid in the accumulator and reservoir. *(a)* When the accumulator is discharged, the booster compartment in the reservoir is full; *(b)* when the accumulator is charged, the booster compartment in the reservoir is nearly empty. *(Chevrolet Motor Division of General Motors Corporation)*

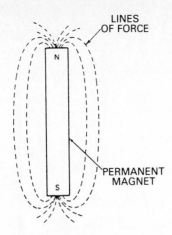

Fig. 9-8. The magnetic field of a permanent magnet.

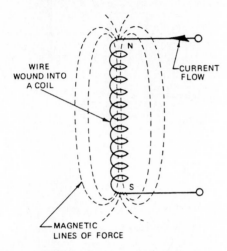

Fig. 9-9. The magnetic field of an electromagnet.

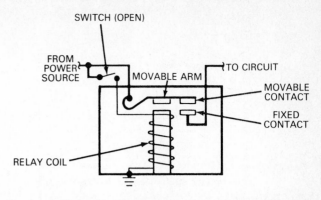

Fig. 9-10. A relay in its deenergized position. No current is flowing in the relay coil, and the contacts are open. *(Ford Motor Company)*

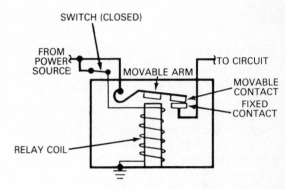

Fig. 9-11. A relay in its energized position. Current is flowing in the relay coil, and the contacts are closed. *(Ford Motor Company)*

stronger. The piece of iron is called the core. A magnet formed by passing current through a coil of wire is an *electromagnet.*

A relay is shown in Fig. 9-10. It has an electromagnet called the relay coil and a set of relay contacts. One contact is fixed, and the other contact is attached to a movable arm. The relay shown is a normally open relay. *Normally open* means that the contacts are apart when the relay is in its normal, or deenergized position. *Deenergized* means that there is no current flowing in the relay coil and therefore, the coil is not magnetized.

A switch in the relay-coil circuit controls the current flow in the coil. When the switch is closed, as in Fig. 9-11, the relay is energized. *Energized* means that there is current flowing in the relay coil and that the coil is magnetized. When the relay is energized, the movable arm is attracted to the core of the electromagnet. The movable contact then touches the fixed contact, closing the relay contacts.

Some relays are *normally closed* relays. Their contacts are touching when the relay is in its normal, or deenergized, position. Other relays have more than one set of contacts. The brake relay shown in Fig. 9-12 is a normally open relay with one set of contacts.

Pressure-Sensing Switch

The pressure-sensing switch (Fig. 9-13) threads into a hole in the main body, near the accumulator port. The switch senses accumulator pressure and energizes the brake relay when the pressure drops below a certain level. This turns on the pump. When the pump operates, it forces brake fluid from the booster compartment of the reservoir to the accumulator.

The switch energizes the relay and turns on the pump when the fluid pressure in the accumulator drops below 510 pounds per square inch (psi) [3,519 kilopascals (kPa)]. The switch deenergizes the relay and turns the pump off when the fluid pressure reaches 675 psi [4,658 kPa].

The pressure-sensing switch has an additional function. If the fluid pressure in the accumulator drops below 400 psi [2,760 kPa], the switch turns on the brake warning lamp on the instrument panel.

Pump

The pump (Fig. 9-14) attaches to brackets bolted to the main body. Rubber grommets between the pump and the brackets minimize the sound of the pump. Two rubber brake hoses and a steel brake line connect the pump to the main body. One hose connects from the booster compartment in the reservoir to the inlet fitting of the pump; this hose is the low-pressure hose. The other hose is

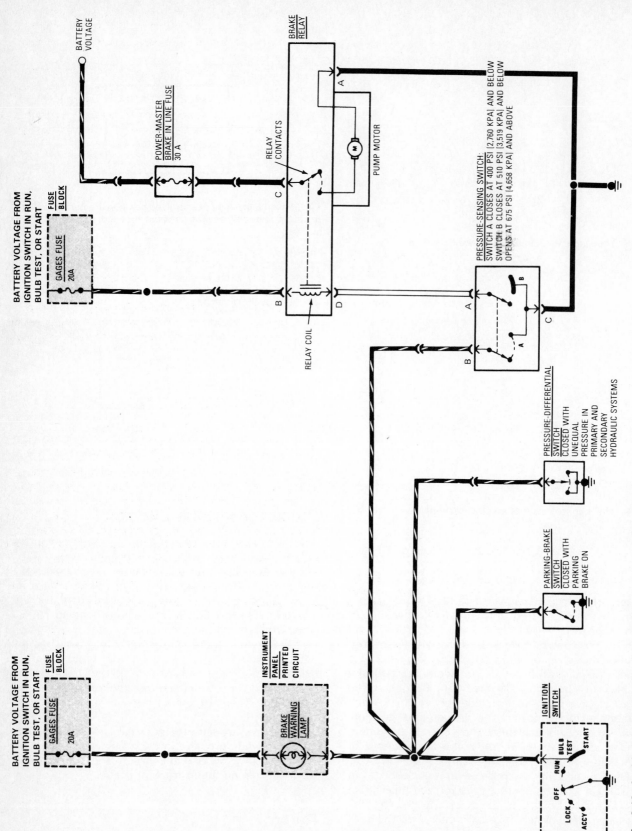

Fig. 9-12. A wiring diagram of an electrohydraulic power-brake system. *(Pontiac Motor Division of General Motors Corporation)*

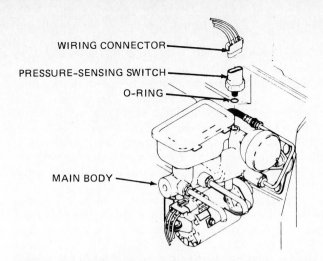

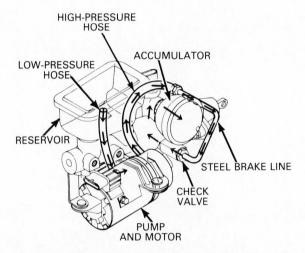

the high-pressure hose. It connects from the outlet of the pump to the steel brake line. The steel brake line connects to a fitting in the booster section of the main body.

When the pump operates, it draws booster fluid from the reservoir, through the low-pressure hose. Then the fluid is pumped through the high-pressure hose and steel line into the main body. As booster fluid is pumped into the main body, the fluid flows through a passage in the main body and fills the accumulator.

Check Valve

There is a check valve (Fig. 9-15) in the booster section of the main body. The valve is located in the fitting where the steel brake line attaches to the main body. The brake fluid from the pump must pass through the check valve before the fluid reaches the booster and accumulator. The check valve allows brake fluid to flow in one direction only. The check valve holds pressure in the booster and accumulator after the pump has turned off.

Power-Piston Assembly

The power-piston assembly is located in the booster section of the main body. The power-piston assembly has two valves: the control valve and the discharge valve (Fig. 9-4). The control-valve seat is located in the power piston. The discharge-valve seat is located in the center of the control valve. When a valve is seated (closed), brake fluid cannot flow through. When the valve opens, or moves away from its seat, brake fluid can flow through.

The control valve controls the admission of booster fluid from the accumulator to a chamber in the main body. This chamber is located at the rear of the power piston. The discharge valve releases booster fluid back to the fluid reservoir after the brakes are released.

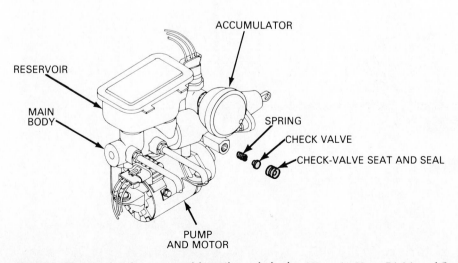

143

OPERATION OF AN ELECTROHYDRAULIC BRAKE SYSTEM

An electrohydraulic power-brake system operates under four conditions: brakes released, brakes being applied, brakes applied and holding, and brakes releasing.

Brakes Released

When the brakes are not applied, springs hold the power piston, control valve, and discharge valve in their nonapplied positions. The power piston is pushed to the right in Fig. 9-4. The control value is also pushed to the right, and held against its seat in the power piston. The discharge valve is open.

Brakes Being Applied

When the brake pedal is depressed, the pushrod moves to the left in Fig. 9-16. The pushrod socket is in contact with the discharge valve. Therefore, the motion of the pushrod pushes the discharge valve against its seat in the control valve and closes the discharge valve. This motion also causes the control valve to move to the left, away from its seat against the power piston. This opens the control valve. Now booster fluid flows from the accumulator, through the open control valve, and into the chamber at the rear of the power piston.

The booster fluid applies force to the power piston, pushing it to the left in Fig. 9-17. The power piston applies force through the discharge valve, reaction piston, and reaction disc to the primary piston in the master cylinder. This pressurizes the brake fluid in the master cylinder to apply the brakes (Fig. 9-18). The operation of the master cylinder is described in Chap. 3.

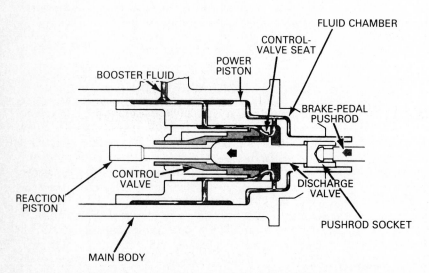

Fig. 9-16. The power-piston assembly when the brakes are being applied. The control valve opens to allow booster fluid to flow from the accumulator to the chamber at the rear of the power piston. The discharge valve is closed. *(Chevrolet Motor Division of General Motors Corporation)*

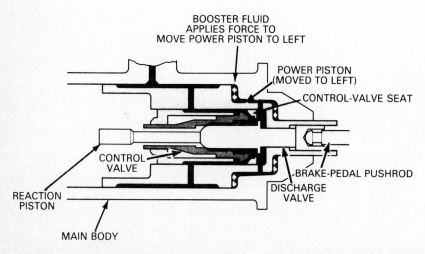

Fig. 9-17. The power piston moves to the left, to apply force to the pistons in the master cylinder. *(Chevrolet Motor Division of General Motors Corporation)*

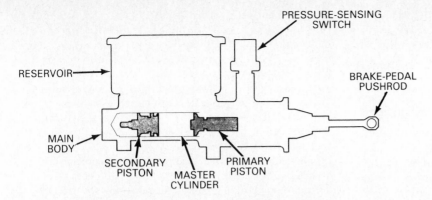

Fig. 9-18. The master-cylinder section of the power-brake unit, showing the primary and secondary pistons. *(Chevrolet Motor Division of General Motors Corporation)*

Brakes Applied and Holding

When the brakes are applied and holding, the booster fluid continues to move the power piston to the left (Fig. 9-19). The discharge valve and control valve remain in a fixed position. As the piston moves, the seat in the power piston is pushed against the control valve. This closes the control valve. Now booster fluid can no longer flow into the chamber behind the power piston. The booster fluid is trapped behind the power piston and continues to hold the brakes in the applied position.

Brakes Releasing

When the brake pedal is released, the pushrod moves to the right in Fig. 9-20. The discharge valve also moves to the right, which moves the valve away from its seat in the control valve. This opens the discharge valve. Now brake fluid flows from the chamber behind the power piston, through the open discharge valve, and back to the fluid reservoir.

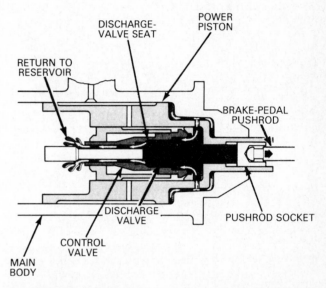

Fig. 9-20. The power-piston assembly when the brakes are releasing. The discharge valve is open, and booster fluid flows from the chamber at the rear of the power piston to the reservoir. *(Chevrolet Motor Division of General Motors Corporation)*

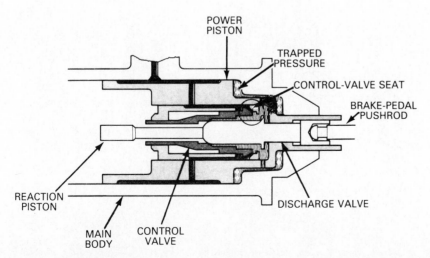

Fig. 9-19. The power-piston assembly when the brakes are applied and holding. Both the control valve and the discharge valve are closed. *(Chevrolet Motor Division of General Motors Corporation)*

When the fluid pressure is released from the chamber behind the power piston, the springs move the components to their nonapplied position, as shown in Fig. 9-4.

PUMP OPERATION

Each time the brake pedal is applied and released, a certain amount of booster fluid flows from the accumulator, through the booster section of the main body, to the reservoir. This causes a drop in pressure in the accumulator. When the pressure drops below approximately 510 psi [3,519 kPa] and the ignition switch is on, the pressure-sensing-switch contacts close and energize the brake relay. This turns on the pump (Fig. 9-21a). The pump operates until the pressure in the accumulator reaches approximately 675 psi [4,658 kPa]. Then the pressure-sensing switch contacts open and deenergize the brake relay. This turns off the pump (Fig. 9-21b).

ELECTRICAL OPERATION OF THE SYSTEM

Figure 9-12 shows an electrical wiring diagram of the electrohydraulic brake system. The main components are the brake relay, the pump motor, and the pressure-sensing switch. [Note that the abbreviation for ampere (a unit of electric current) is A; therefore, 20 A in Fig. 9-21 means 20 amperes.]

The brake relay is mounted on the pump motor. The relay has four terminals. Battery voltage is supplied from the ignition switch, through a fuse, to terminal B of the relay. Battery voltage is supplied directly from the battery, through another fuse, to terminal C of the relay.

The relay coil connects between terminals B and

D. Terminal D of the relay connects to terminal A of the pressure-sensing switch. One of the relay contacts connects to terminal C. The other relay contact is wired directly to the pump motor. The ground connection of the pump motor is wired directly to terminal A of the relay. Terminal A of the relay connects to vehicle ground.

When the pressure in the accumulator drops below approximately 510 psi [3,519 kPa], a set of switch contacts closes in the pressure-sensing switch. These contacts are labeled "contact set B" in Fig. 9-12. When the contacts close, terminal A and terminal C of the sensing switch are connected together. Terminal C of the switch connects to vehicle ground. Therefore, when the switch closes, terminal D of the brake relay is connected to ground. This energizes (magnetizes) the relay coil, and the relay contacts close. Then, battery voltage is connected from terminal C of the relay to the pump motor. This turns on the motor.

When the pressure in the accumulator reaches approximately 675 psi [4,658 kPa], the pressure-sensing-switch contacts open. This deenergizes the relay, which opens the relay contacts and turns off the motor.

Brake Warning Lamp

If the pressure in the accumulator drops below 400 psi [2,760 kPa], contact set A in the pressure-sensing switch closes (Fig. 9-12). This grounds the brake warning lamp on the instrument panel and lights the lamp (when the ignition switch is in the RUN position). The lamp is also lit under three other conditions:

- If the parking brake is applied, the parking-brake-switch contacts close. This grounds the warning lamp, and if the ignition switch is in the RUN position, the lamp will light.

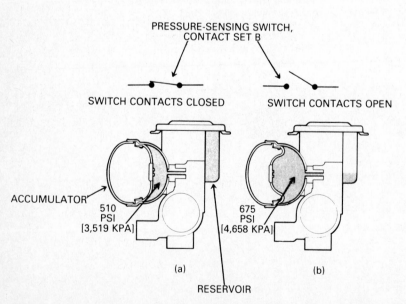

Fig. 9-21. The operation of the pressure-sensing switcch. (a) When the accumulator pressure drops below 510 psi [3,519 kPa], the switch closes and turns on the pump; (b) when the pressure reaches 675 psi [4,658 kPa], the switch opens and turns off the pump. (Chevrolet Motor Division of General Motors Corporation)

146

- If there is a loss of hydraulic pressure in one section of the hydraulic brake system, the pressure-differential-switch contacts close. This grounds the warning lamp, and if the ignition switch is in the RUN position, the lamp will light.
- When the ignition switch is turned to START, the switch passes through the BULB TEST position. When the switch is in the BULB TEST position, the warning lamp is grounded. This turns the lamp on and checks the bulb.

BRAKE FEEL

The reaction components provide some brake feel to the driver. When the brake pedal is depressed, the power piston moves to the left in Fig. 9-17 and pressurizes the brake fluid in the master cylinder. At the same time, the power piston pushes the reaction body against a step in the cylinder bore and compresses the reaction-body spring. This spring pushes back against the power piston, and this force is transmitted back to the driver's foot. The force against the driver's foot is the reaction force. The driver judges how hard to depress the brake pedal, based on how quickly the car stops and on the feel of the reaction force in the brake pedal.

BRAKE-SYSTEM FAILURE

If there is a failure in the power-assist system, the driver can still stop the car. When the driver depresses the brake pedal, force is applied to the pushrod and pushrod socket. This force is transferred from the pushrod socket through the discharge valve, reaction piston, and reaction disc to the primary piston in the master cylinder. The car will stop, but the pedal would have to be applied harder than if the power-assist system were functioning normally.

VOCABULARY REVIEW

Accumulator A container in which high-pressure brake fluid is stored.

Apply fluid The fluid in the master cylinder that operates the wheel cylinders to apply the brakes.

Booster fluid The fluid in an electrohydraulic-assist power-brake system that increases the hydraulic pressure of the apply fluid.

Deenergized The condition of a relay when its coil is not magnetized.

Electromagnet A magnet formed by passing electric current through a coil of wire.

Energized The condition of a relay when its coil is magnetized.

Line of force An imaginary line that passes from the north pole of a magnet, through the air surrounding the magnet, and to the south pole of the magnet.

Normally closed relay A relay in which the contacts are touching when the relay is in its normal, or deenergized, position.

Normally open relay A relay in which the contacts are apart when the relay is in its normal, or deenergized, position.

Permanent magnet A magnet made of a material that retains its magnetism for a long time.

Relay a magnet device that switches electric current in an electric circuit.

Relay contacts The electric contacts that are part of a relay.

REVIEW QUESTIONS

Select the *one* correct, best, or most probable answer to each question.

1. In an electrohydraulic-assist power brake, when the brakes are being applied:
   a. the control valve is open and the discharge valve is closed.
   b. both the control valve and the discharge valve are closed.
   c. both the control value and the discharge value are open.
   d. booster fluid is flowing through the discharge valve.

2. The pump turns on when the:
   a. reservoir is nearly empty.
   b. accumulator is empty.
   c. pressure in the accumulator reaches 675 psi [4,648 kPa].
   d. pressure-sensing-switch contacts close.

3. When the brakes are releasing:
   a. booster fluid flows from the accumulator to the reservoir.
   b. the control valve is open.
   c. the discharge valve is open.
   d. both the control valve and the discharge valve are closed.

4. Technician A says that the booster compartment of the reservoir is full when the accumulator is charged. Technician B says that it is full when the accumulator is discharged. Who is right?
   a. A only
   b. B only
   c. Both A and B
   d. Neither A nor B

5. When the brakes are applied and holding:
   a. both the control valve and the discharge valve are open.
   b. booster fluid is flowing from the accumulator to the chamber at the rear of the power piston.
   c. both the control valve and the discharge valve are closed.
   d. booster fluid is flowing from the accumulator to the reservoir.

6. All of the following are true concerning the pressure-sensing switch *except*:
   a. The switch turns the pump on when the pressure drops below 400 psi [2,760 kPa].
   b. The switch turns the pump off when the pressure reaches 675 psi [4,658 kPa].
   c. The switch turns the warning lamp on when the pressure drops below 400 psi [2,760 kPa].
   d. The pressure-sensing switch has two sets of switch contacts.

7. Technician A says that when the brake pedal is depressed, booster fluid applies force to the power-piston assembly. Technician B says that the pushrod and pushrod socket apply force directly to the discharge valve. Who is right?
   a. A only
   b. B only
   c. Both A and B
   d. Neither A nor B

8. Technician A says that in the electrohydraulic power-brake system, the brake warning lamp is lit when the accumulator pressure drops below 510 psi [3,519 kPa]. Technician B says that the lamp is lit when there is a leak in one section of the apply system. Who is right?
   a. A only
   b. B only
   c. Both A and B
   d. Neither A nor B

9. All of the following components are located in the main body *except*:
   a. The discharge valve
   b. The brake relay
   c. The primary-piston assembly
   d. The control valve

10. Technician A says that the check valve prevents booster-fluid flow from the accumulator to the pump. Technician B says that the check valve prevents booster-fluid flow from the chamber at the rear of the power piston to the accumulator. Who is right?
    a. A only
    b. B only
    c. Both A and B
    d. Neither A nor B

CHAPTER 10

ANTILOCK BRAKE SYSTEMS

OBJECTIVES

After you have studied this chapter, you should be able to:

1. Name the components in antilock brake systems.

2. Describe the components in antilock brake systems.

3. Describe the operation of integral-type and nonintegral-type antilock brake systems.

4. Describe the operation of rear antilock brake systems.

An antilock brake system (ABS) is a computer-controlled brake system that helps prevent wheel lockup during braking. When a wheel locks, it stops rotating and the tire skids or slides over the road surface. When a tire is skidding, the friction between the tire and the road surface is kinetic friction. When the wheel is not skidding, the friction is static friction. Kinetic friction is not as great as static friction; therefore, when skidding occurs, a car requires a greater distance to stop than if the tire were not skidding.

Skidding occurs more readily on a wet or slippery road surface than on a dry surface. This is because there is less static friction between the tires and the road surface when the road is wet or slippery than when the road is dry. Static friction tends to keep the tires rotating on the road surface; therefore, with less static friction, the wheels lock easily when the brakes are applied.

In addition to a greater stopping distance, the driver loses directional control of the vehicle when it skids. Therefore, to stop a car in the shortest possible distance and in as straight a line as possible, the wheels must be prevented from locking. To do this, the driver must pump the brake pedal when the car is about to skid. *Pumping* the brake pedal means alternately depressing and releasing the pedal. This helps prevent skidding, because if a wheel begins to lock, releasing the pedal allows the wheel to roll again.

In a computer-controlled brake system, the driver applies and holds the brake pedal. Then, if a wheel begins to lock, the computer pumps the brakes. It does this much more rapidly than the driver could, and it applies and releases the brakes at precisely the right time.

In some antilock systems, there is a sensor located at each wheel. The sensors sense the speed of rotation of the wheels, and this speed information is sent to the computer. If a wheel begins to lock during braking, the speed of rotation of that wheel begins to drop rapidly. The computer reacts to this rapid drop in wheel speed by removing the braking force from that wheel. When the wheel begins to roll again and its speed begins to increase, the computer restores the braking force to the wheel. If the wheel again begins to lock, the computer will again remove the braking force. In some antilock systems the computer can apply and release the brakes at each wheel as rapidly as 15 times per second.

Some antilock systems use only three wheel sensors. One sensor is used at each front wheel, and one sensor is located near the drive shaft to sense lockup at both rear wheels.

Some light trucks have an antilock system that prevents lockup at the rear wheels only. These are called rear antilock brake systems (RABS). A single speed sensor in the differential-gear assembly senses rear-wheel lockup.

WHEEL-SPEED SENSORS

Each wheel-speed sensor is positioned near a toothed ring. Figure 10-1 shows the sensor and ring locations for a front wheel on a rear-wheel-drive car. The ring is part of the hub-and-bearing assembly. Figure 10-2 shows the sensor and ring for a front wheel on a front-wheel-drive car. The ring is pressed onto the drive axle. Figure 10-3 shows the sensor and ring located for a rear wheel on a front-wheel-drive car. The ring is pressed onto the hub-and-bearing assembly.

The sensor is separated from the ring by a small gap. A typical sensor-to-ring gap is 0.026 inch (in.) [0.65 mil-

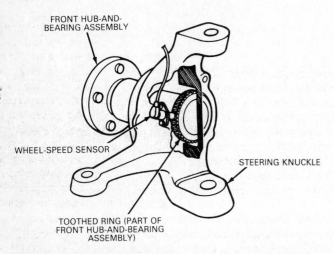

Fig. 10-1. The wheel-speed-sensor and toothed-ring locations for a front wheel on a rear-wheel-drive car. *(Chevrolet Motor Division of General Motors Corporation)*

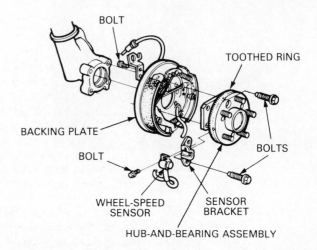

Fig. 10-3. The wheel-speed-sensor and toothed-ring locations for a rear wheel on a front-wheel-drive car. *(Chevrolet Motor Division of General Motors Corporation)*

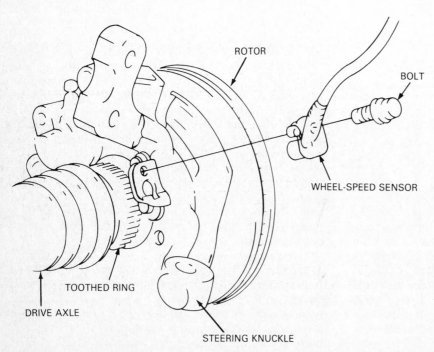

Fig. 10-2. The wheel-speed-sensor and toothed ring locations for a front wheel on a front-wheel-drive car. *(Chevrolet Motor Division of General Motors Corporation)*

150

limeter (mm)]. The sensor includes a permanent magnet and a coil of wire (Fig. 10-4).

As the wheel rotates, the ring moves past the sensor. In Fig. 10-4 the ring is shown with a tooth on the ring aligned with a tooth on the end of the sensor. Magnetic lines of force pass from one pole of the magnet, through the toothed ring, through the air, and back to the other pole of the magnet. Because the sensor coil surrounds the magnet, the lines of force also pass through the sensor coil.

The ring is made of a magnetic material. A *magnetic material* is a material, such as iron, that passes magnetic lines of force much more readily than air does. In the position of the ring shown in Fig. 10-4, the air gap between the ring and the sensor is small. With a small air gap, the lines of force easily pass to the ring. Because of this, there are many lines of force, and the magnetic field is strong.

Figure 10-5 shows the ring in a position when the teeth on the ring are not aligned with the tooth on the sensor. In this position, the air gap between the ring and the sensor is large. The lines of force do not readily pass through the larger gap, and thus the magnetic field is weak.

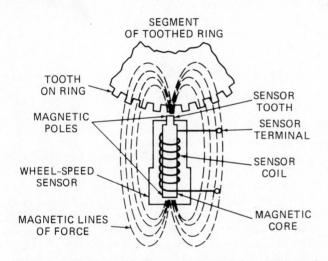

Fig. 10-4. A wheel-speed sensor and toothed ring, with a tooth on the ring aligned with the tooth on the sensor.

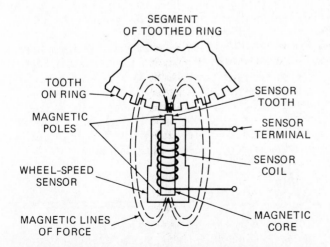

Fig. 10-5. A wheel-speed sensor and toothed ring, with the tooth on the ring not aligned with the tooth on the sensor.

When the wheel rotates, the ring spins past the sensor. As each tooth of the ring passes the tooth on the sensor, the magnetic field is alternately strengthened and weakened. Whenever a changing magnetic field passes a coil of wire, a voltage is generated in the coil. A small voltage is generated in the coil each time a tooth of the ring passes the coil. The voltage lasts only a very short time and is called a *voltage pulse*. One system used by Ford has 104 teeth on the ring; therefore, each revolution of the wheel produces 104 voltage pulses in the sensor coil. These voltage pulses are sent to the computer. The computer counts the pulses it receives per second from each wheel. The number of pulses per second is a measure of wheel speed. When the number of pulses per second drops rapidly, the computer determines that a wheel is about to lock. The number of pulses per second is called the *frequency* of the pulses.

MICROCOMPUTERS

A *computer* is an electronic device that stores and processes data (information). In addition to this, computers can control the operation of other devices. When computers were first developed, they were extremely large. One of the first computers used 18,000 vacuum tubes and filled an entire room. As vacuum tubes were replaced by transistors, computers became smaller. Improved manufacturing methods led to further reductions in size. Thousands of transistors and other components can now be placed on a small surface called a *chip* (Fig. 10-6). In fact, entire electronic circuits can be placed on a chip. Because all the components of the circuit are integrated together on a single chip, the resulting circuit is called an *integrated circuit (IC)*.

The small computers that use these tiny chips are called *microcomputers*. Figure 10-7 shows a block diagram of a typical microcomputer. The basic parts are the microprocessor, the memory, the input device, and the output device. Each part is described below.

Microprocessor

A *microprocessor* is also called a central processing unit (CPU). It contains an electronic clock that times all the operations of the computer. In addition, the microprocessor coordinates the movement of data from one part of the computer to another, and it ties all parts of the computer together. All the calculations and processing of data take place in the microprocessor.

Memory

A *memory* is the part of a computer that can store data. There are two different types of memories in a computer: a *read-only memory (ROM)* and a *random access memory (RAM)*.

A ROM has data stored in it when it is manufactured. The data will remain in the ROM for the life of the computer. The data in the ROM can be "read out" when it is needed. Reading out the data does not remove it from the ROM; the data can be read again

151

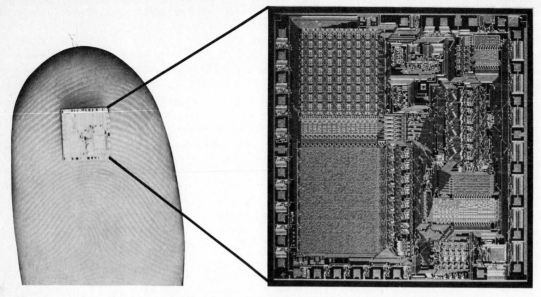

Fig. 10-6. A photograph of a chip, showing its relative size. *(Texas Instruments Incorporated)*

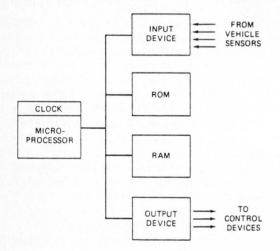

Fig. 10-7. A block diagram of a microcomputer.

and again. Data cannot be added to the ROM during the operation of the computer.

A RAM is also called a read-and-write memory because data can be added to the memory (written into it) and then read out when needed.

Input Device

An *input device* is the part of the microcomputer circuit that connects a sensor to the microcomputer. Sensors convert some measurement, such as wheel speed, into an electrical signal. Some sensors produce a varying voltage. A switch can also act as a type of sensor. Switch-type sensors provide a steady voltage under certain conditions, and no voltage under other conditions. The input device converts the output of the sensor into the type of data that a computer can use.

Output Device

An *output device* connects the microcomputer to a control device on the automobile. In an antilock brake system, an example of a control device is a valve that

controls the flow of brake fluid. The output device converts computer data into a signal that will operate the control device.

OPERATION OF A MICROCOMPUTER

During the operation of a microcomputer, the microprocessor controls everything. Its clock generates voltage pulses that time all the computer operations. A typical microprocessor clock rate is about 1 million clock pulses per second. This means that each separate computer operation is completed in only one-millionth of a second.

For a computer to perform any type of function, it must be programmed. A *program* is a set of instructions that tells the microprocessor what to do and when to do it. The program is stored in the ROM at the time of manufacture. The microprocessor tells the ROM to read out each program instruction in the proper sequence.

Information from the sensors is converted into computer data by the input device. This data is then supplied to the microprocessor. During the operation of the microcomputer, the microprocessor samples the input signals, performs calculations, compares numbers, and makes decisions on the basis of the program that is stored in the ROM. While the program is running, the RAM is used for temporary storage of data. When the final result of the program is reached, the data that represents the result is sent to the output device. It then converts the data into a signal that will operate a control device. Some common control devices used with antilock brake systems are motors, relays, and solenoids.

SOLENOIDS

A solenoid is an electromagnet with a movable core. In Fig. 10-8 a solenoid is shown in the deenergized position. *Deenergized* means that no current is flowing in the coil and that the electromagnet is therefore not mag-

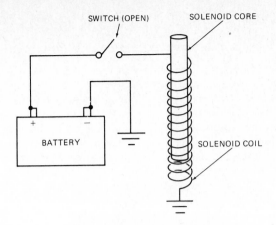

Fig. 10-8. A solenoid in the deenergized position.

netized. The core is shown partially inside the coil in Fig. 10-8.

When current flows through the coil, the resulting magnetism pulls the core into the coil (Fig. 10-9). When this occurs, the solenoid is said to be *energized*. The movable core is called a *plunger*. When a solenoid is energized, the movement of the plunger can be used to apply a force to operate a device. One type of solenoid-operated device used in an antilock brake system is the solenoid valve. A *solenoid valve* is an electrically operated valve that controls the flow of brake fluid.

OPERATION OF AN ANTILOCK BRAKE SYSTEM

The computer receives voltage pulses from each wheel-speed sensor and continually counts the number of pulses that it receives per second. When a wheel begins to lock, the frequency of the pulses drops rapidly. The computer is programmed to recognize this drop as the beginning of wheel lock. The computer then releases and applies the braking force at the wheels by operating solenoid valves.

Some antilock systems use two solenoid valves to control the braking force at a wheel. These solenoids are the inlet solenoid valve and the outlet solenoid valve. The *inlet solenoid valve* allows brake fluid to flow to a wheel cylinder or caliper to apply the brakes. The *out-*

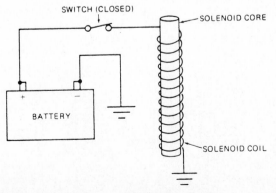

Fig. 10-9. A solenoid in the energized position.

let solenoid valve releases the brakes by allowing brake fluid to flow from the wheel cylinder or caliper. These solenoid valves are two-position valves; that is, they are either open or closed.

Other antilock systems use a three-position solenoid valve to control the braking force at a wheel. Whether two two-position valves are used or one three-position valve is used, the braking force is controlled the same way. When the brakes are applied and no wheel is about to lock, the brake-fluid flow to and from the wheel cylinders or calipers is the same as in a car without antilock brakes.

However, if the brakes are applied and a wheel is about to lock, the computer controls the braking force in two stages. In the first stage, the computer operates the solenoid valve or valves to trap the brake-fluid pressure in the wheel cylinder or caliper. Then the pressure in the wheel cylinder or caliper cannot increase even if the driver continues to apply force to the brake pedal.

This may be enought to stop the wheel from locking. However, if the wheel is still about to lock, then the computer operates the solenoid valve or valves to release brake-fluid pressure from the wheel cylinder or caliper. This is the second stage of control. Then, when the wheel is no longer about to lock, the computer again allows brake fluid to flow to the wheel cylinder or caliper to reapply the brakes. This entire operation can be repeated as often as 15 times per second to control wheel lockup.

On most four-wheel antilock brake systems, the front wheels are controlled independently, and the rear wheels are controlled together. The computer is programmed to react to the rear wheel that is slowing most rapidly. Therefore, if one rear wheel begins to lock, the computer controls brake-fluid flow to both rear wheels at the same time. The rear wheels are also controlled together on most rear-wheel antilock systems.

System Safeguards

Because of the need for safety in a brake system, several safeguards are programmed into the computer. These safeguards prevent the antilock system from operating if there is a malfunction in the system. For example, if a wheel-speed sensor malfunctions and sends the wrong information to the computer, a wheel could lock up at the wrong time. This could cause serious injury. For this reason, most antilock systems have a built-in internal test procedure. When the car is started, the computer begins the internal test procedure, testing the components in the antilock system. If a component is found to be defective, the computer is programmed to turn off the antilock system and light an antilock warning lamp. The brake system then acts like a power-brake system that does not have an antilock feature.

Some systems use two microporcessors. Both microprocessors receive the same information from the sensors, and both microprocessors are programmed to produce the same result. When the system is operating normally, both microprocessors do produce the same result and control the operation of the brake system.

However, if there is a malfunction in one of the microprocessors, then one microprocessor will produce a different result than the other. Another part of the microcomputer monitors the output of the microprocessors. The kind of data that a normally operating system should produce is programmed into the ROM. If the data from one microprocessor is different from that considered "normal," the monitor will reject the output of that microprocessor and accept the information from the other. Under some conditions it will reject the data from both microprocessors and turn off the antilock system.

The voltage supplied by the vehicle's electrical system to the microcomputer is critical. If the system voltage drops below a certain value, the antilock system will not operate properly. For this reason, most antilock brake systems continually monitor the electrical system's voltage. If the voltage drops too low, the antilock brake system is automatically turned off. Then the service brakes will operate without the antilock feature.

Lateral-Acceleration Switch

Some antilock systems use an additional sensor called a lateral-acceleration switch (Fig. 10-10). *Lateral acceleration* is a measure of the sideward movement of the vehicle. When a vehicle makes a sharp turn, the lateral acceleration is greater than if it makes a slight turn. In addition, the lateral acceleration is greater if it makes the turn at a high speed than if it makes the turn at a low speed. The lateral-acceleration switch signals the computer if the car is turning or is going around a curve. The switch consists of two normally closed switches. A *normally closed switch* is a switch that passes electric current in its normal, or unapplied, position.

The normally closed switches react to a combination of the speed and the sharpness of a turn. If the speed on a left turn exceeds a certain amount, or if the turn is sharp enough, one of the switches opens. If the speed on a right turn exceeds a certain amount, or if the turn is sharp enough, the other switch opens.

The computer is programmed to modify its control signals to the solenoid valve when the lateral-acceleration switch is operated. Therefore, the control signals when a car is braking around a curve differ from the signals when it is traveling in a straight line.

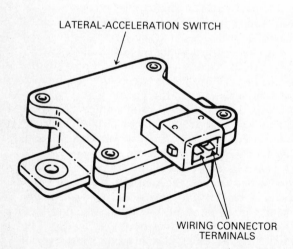

LATERAL-ACCELERATION SWITCH

WIRING CONNECTOR TERMINALS

Fig. 10-10. A lateral-acceleration switch. (*Chevrolet Motor Division of General Motors Corporation*)

154

TYPES OF ANTILOCK BRAKE SYSTEMS

There are three common types of antilock brake systems: (1) the four-wheel *integral type*, (2) the four-wheel *nonintegral type*, and (3) the rear-wheel type. In the integral type, the master cylinder, power booster, and antilock hydraulic unit are combined in a single unit. In the nonintegral type, the antilock hydraulic unit is separate from the master-cylinder-and-power-booster unit. Rear-wheel systems are usually nonintegral systems. These types of antilock brake systems are described below.

NOTE   When describing the operation of the switches and valves in these systems, the words *open* and *closed* are used. These words do not mean the same thing when applied to switches or when applied to valves. This can be confusing unless the following is understood: When describing a switch, *open* means that the contacts are apart and that the switch will not pass electric current (Fig. 10-11); *closed* means that the contacts are touching each other and that the switch will pass electric current. When describing a valve, *open* means that a passage through the valve is not obstructed and that the valve will pass a fluid (Fig. 10-12); *closed* means that the passage is obstructed and that the valve will not pass a fluid.

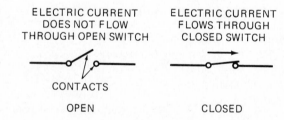

ELECTRIC CURRENT DOES NOT FLOW THROUGH OPEN SWITCH

ELECTRIC CURRENT FLOWS THROUGH CLOSED SWITCH

CONTACTS

OPEN

CLOSED

Fig. 10-11. A switch in the open and closed positions.

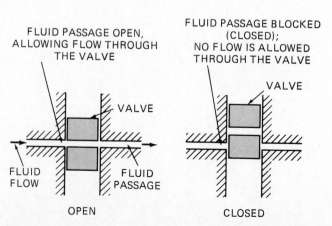

FLUID PASSAGE OPEN, ALLOWING FLOW THROUGH THE VALVE

FLUID PASSAGE BLOCKED (CLOSED); NO FLOW IS ALLOWED THROUGH THE VALVE

VALVE

VALVE

FLUID FLOW

FLUID PASSAGE

OPEN

CLOSED

Fig. 10-12. A valve in the open and closed positions.

FOUR-WHEEL INTEGRAL-TYPE ANTILOCK BRAKE SYSTEMS

The components in an integral-type antilock brake system are shown in Fig. 10-13. This system is manufactured by the Alfred Teves Corporation. The main components are the wheel-speed sensors, the electronic brake control module, the main relay, the hydraulic unit, the pump-motor relay, and the pressure and fluid-level switch.

An electrical diagram of this system is shown in Fig. 10-14. The diagram shows the components used in the system and the electrical connections between the components. Only one wheel-speed sensor and two solenoid valves are shown connected to the control module. This is done to simplify the diagram. The other sensors and solenoid valves connect to control-module terminals that are not shown.

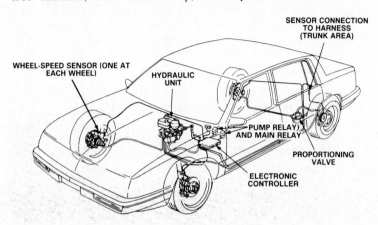

Fig. 10-13. The components of the Teves antilock brake system. *(Chevrolet Motor Division of General Motors Corporation)*

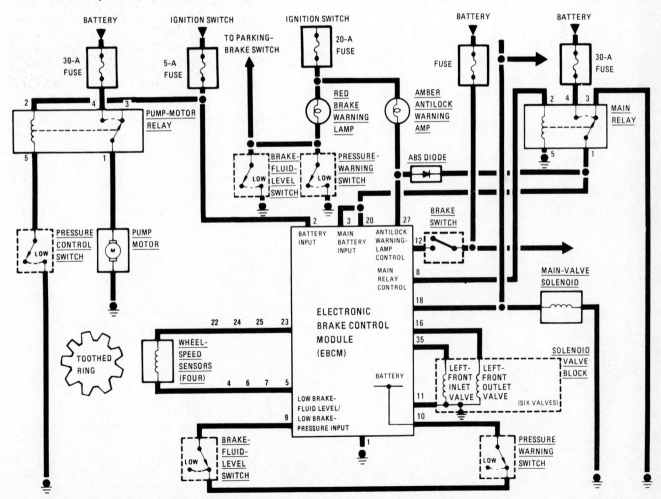

Fig. 10-14. An electrical diagram of the Teves antilock brake system. *(Chevrolet Motor Division of General Motors Corporation)*

155

Components

A description of the components used in the Teves system follows.

Wheel-Speed Sensors   The wheel-speed sensor operates the same as described earlier in this chapter under "WHEEL-SPEED SENSORS."

Electronic Brake Control Module (EBCM)

"Electronic brake control module" is the name given the microcomputer that controls the brake system (Fig. 10-15). The control module receives information from the wheel-speed sensors. Based on this information, the module controls the main relay, the main-valve solenoid, the solenoid valves, and the antilock warning lamp. The control-module terminal numbers are shown in Fig. 10-14.

Main Relay   Figure 10-16 shows a part of the diagram of Fig. 10-14. The main relay, the amber antilock warning lamp, a part of the control module, and an ABS diode are shown. A *diode* is a one-way current valve; that is, it allows electric current to flow through it in one direction only. The purpose of the ABS diode in this

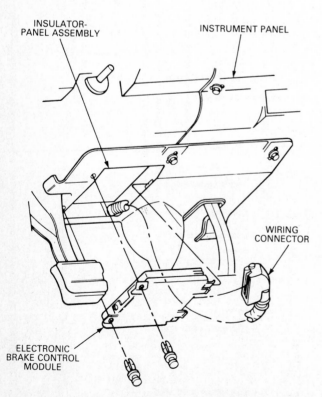

Fig. 10-15. The Teves electronic brake control module removed from beneath the instrument panel. (*Chevrolet Motor Division of General Motors Corporation*)

circuit is described later in this section under "System Operation." Parts of the control module are shown in two separate locations in Fig. 10-16; this is done to simplify the diagram.

The main relay includes the relay coil (terminals 2 and 5) and a set of relay contacts (terminals 1, 3, and 4). The contacts between terminals 1 and 3 are normally closed contacts. The contacts between terminals 1 and 4 are normally open.

The main relay is energized by the control module and supplies battery voltage to control-module terminals 3 and 20. The voltage at these terminals is used to operate the solenoid valves in the hydraulic unit. In addition, the main relay turns on the antilock warning lamp under certain conditions.

Hydraulic Unit   The hydraulic unit includes the master cylinder, the power booster, and the solenoid valve-block assembly (Figs. 10-17 and 10-18). The solenoid valve-block assembly contains three pairs of solenoid valves. These valves control brake-fluid pressure to the calipers or wheel cylinders.

A pair of solenoid valves consists of one inlet valve and one outlet valve. One pair of valves controls the left-front brake, the second pair controls the right-front brake, and the third pair controls the rear brakes. The inlet solenoid valve is a normally open valve; it allows brake fluid to flow to a wheel cylinder or caliper to apply the brakes when the valve is not energized. The outlet solenoid valve releases pressure from the wheel cylinder or caliper by allowing brake fluid to flow from the wheel cylinder or caliper. The outlet solenoid valve is a normally closed valve; that is, brake bluid cannot flow through this valve when it is not energized.

The master cylinder shown in Fig. 10-18 operates in a manner similar to that described in Chap. 3. However, the master cylinder is used in a different way than the master cylinders described in earlier chapters. The primary piston controls brake-fluid pressure to one front wheel, and the secondary piston controls pressure to the other front wheel. The rear brakes are operated by hydraulic pressure supplied from the booster section of the hydraulic unit. There is a proportioning valve (Fig. 10-13) that reduces brake-fluid pressure to the rear wheels on a hard brake application.

Some systems use a master cylinder that has a single piston. This piston controls brake-fluid pressure to both front wheels. As with the dual master cylinder, the rear brakes are operated by hydraulic pressure supplied from the booster section of the hydraulic unit. With a single-piston master cylinder, there is a proportioning-valve bypass. If there is a failure in the hydraulic system to the front wheels, the porportioning valve is bypassed, and full booster pressure is applied to the rear brakes.

There is a valve in the master-cylinder section of the hydraulic unit called the main valve (Fig. 10-18). The main valve is controlled by a solenoid operated by the control module. The main valve is used during antilock operation.

The booster is an electrohydraulic-assist power booster. It has an electric motor-and-pump assembly and an accumulator. The pump keeps the accumulator filled with brake fluid at a pressure of from 2,030 pouds per-

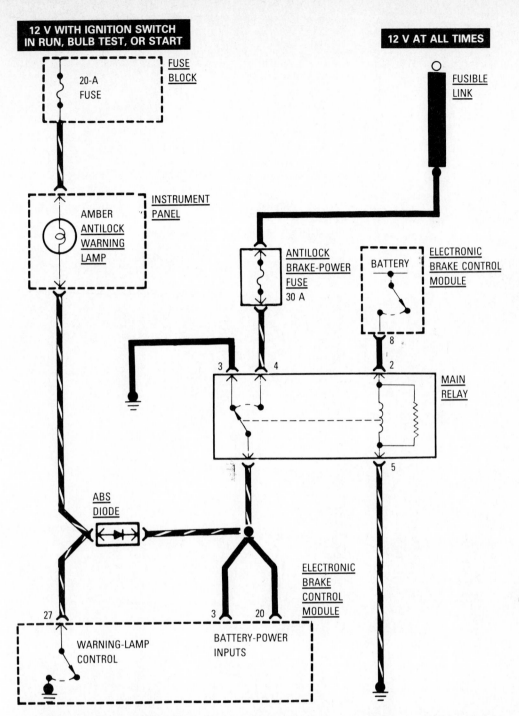

Fig. 10-16. A section of the Teves electrical diagram, showing the main relay, the amber antilock warning lamp, the electronic brake control module, and the ABS diode. *(Chevrolet Motor Division of General Motors Corporation)*

square inch (psi) [14,007 kilopascals (kPa)] to 2,610 psi [18,009 kPa]. The pump has a built-in pressure-relief valve (Fig. 10-18). This valve is needed for safety if a malfunction allows the pump pressure to increase above 2,610 psi [18,009 kPa]. If the pump pressure reaches 3,340 psi [23,046 kPa], the relief valve will open and relieve the pressure.

The operation of the booster is controlled by a spool valve. The spool valve is located in a bore that is parallel to the master-cylinder bore. A scissor-shaped lever mechanism contacts the spool valve. The brake-pedal

pushrod connects to the lever assembly. When the brake pedal is depressed, the lever assembly moves the spool valve to control the operation of the power booster.

The booster has a booster piston that has a pressure chamber behind it. When the brakes are applied, the spool valve allows brake fluid from the accumulator to fill the pressure chamber. The brake-fluid pressure in the chamber pushes the booster piston against the primary piston in the master cylinder. This pressurizes the brake fluid in the master cylinder to apply the brakes.

There are two fluid reservoirs used with this sys-

157

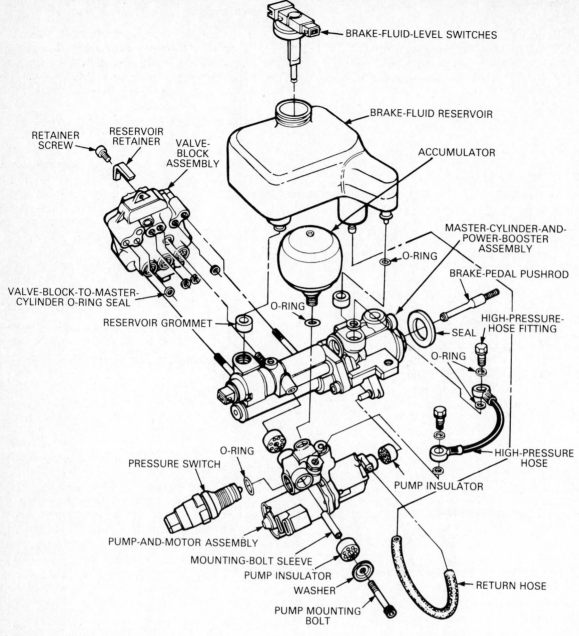

BRAKE-FLUID-LEVEL SWITCHES

BRAKE-FLUID RESERVOIR

RETAINER SCREW

RESERVOIR RETAINER

VALVE-BLOCK ASSEMBLY

ACCUMULATOR

MASTER-CYLINDER-AND-POWER-BOOSTER ASSEMBLY

BRAKE-PEDAL PUSHROD

VALVE-BLOCK-TO-MASTER-CYLINDER O-RING SEAL

O-RING

HIGH-PRESSURE-HOSE FITTING

SEAL

O-RING

RESERVOIR GROMMET

O-RING

HIGH-PRESSURE HOSE

PRESSURE SWITCH

O-RING

PUMP INSULATOR

PUMP-AND-MOTOR ASSEMBLY

MOUNTING-BOLT SLEEVE

PUMP INSULATOR

WASHER

RETURN HOSE

PUMP MOUNTING BOLT

Fig. 10-17. The Teves hydraulic unit. *(Chevrolet Motor Division of General Motors Corporation)*

tem. One reservoir is external (Figs. 10-17 and 10-18). This reservoir supplies brake fluid to the hydraulic unit. It is used when brake fluid is added to the system. The other reservoir is internal (Fig. 10-18) and is part of the master cylinder. The internal reservoir keeps the master cylinder filled with fluid and supplies brake fluid to the front calipers. The internal reservoir is supplied by the external reservoir.

Pump-Motor Relay The pump-motor relay controls the operation of the pump motor. When the pressure in the accumulator drops below 2,200 psi [15,180 kPa], the relay turns the pump on. When the pressure in the accumulator reaches 2,600 psi [17,940 kPa], the relay turns the pump off. The relay is operated by the pressure control switch.

Figure 10-19 shows the pump motor, pump-motor relay, and pressure switch. The pressure switch threads into the hydraulic unit and consists of three separate sets of switch contacts. These contacts are labeled 1, 2, and 3 in Fig. 10-19. The pressure switch is also shown in Fig. 10-14, but in that diagram it is shown as three separate switches; this is done to simplify the diagram.

In Fig. 10-19, contact set 2 is the pressure control switch. Battery voltage connects through a fuse located in the fuse block to one terminal of the pump-motor-relay coil. The other terminal of the relay coil connects to one terminal of the pressure control switch. The other terminal of the switch connects to ground. The pressure control switch senses the brake-fluid pressure in the accumulator. When the pressure in the accumulator drops below approximately 2,200 psi [15,180 kPa], the pres-

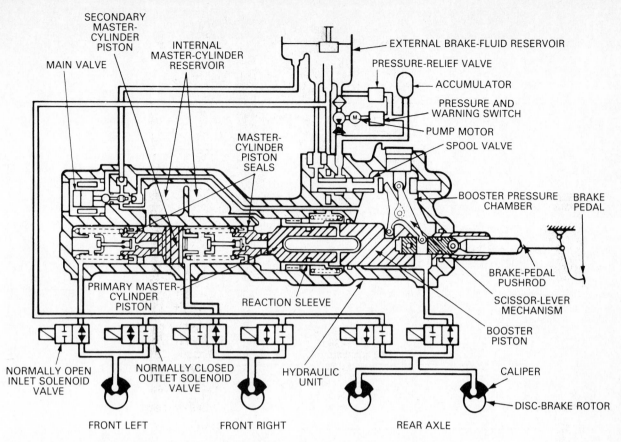

SECONDARY MASTER-CYLINDER PISTON
INTERNAL MASTER-CYLINDER RESERVOIR
MAIN VALVE
EXTERNAL BRAKE-FLUID RESERVOIR
PRESSURE-RELIEF VALVE
ACCUMULATOR
PRESSURE AND WARNING SWITCH
PUMP MOTOR
SPOOL VALVE
MASTER-CYLINDER PISTON SEALS
BOOSTER PRESSURE CHAMBER
BRAKE PEDAL
BRAKE-PEDAL PUSHROD
SCISSOR-LEVER MECHANISM
PRIMARY MASTER-CYLINDER PISTON
REACTION SLEEVE
BOOSTER PISTON
NORMALLY OPEN INLET SOLENOID VALVE
NORMALLY CLOSED OUTLET SOLENOID VALVE
HYDRAULIC UNIT
CALIPER
DISC-BRAKE ROTOR
FRONT LEFT
FRONT RIGHT
REAR AXLE

Fig. 10-18. The Teves hydraulic unit, showing its components and the connections to the solenoid valves. *(Chevrolet Motor Division of General Motors Corporation)*

sure control switch closes. This grounds the pump-motor relay and energizes it. This causes the relay contacts to close and supply battery voltage to the pump motor. When the pressure reaches approximately 2,600 psi [17,940 kPa], the pressure control switch opens. The relay is deenergized, which opens the relay contacts and turns the pump motor off. The operation of pressure-switch contact sets 1 and 3 is covered later in this section under "Warning Lamps."

System Operation

The system operation is broken down into four conditions: engine start-up, brakes not applied, brakes applied (antilock system not operating), and brakes applied (antilock system operating).

Engine Start-Up   When the ignition switch is turned to the RUN position, battery voltage is applied to terminal 2 of the control module, and to one terminal of the amber antilock warning lamp (Fig. 10-14). With battery voltage at terminal 2, the control module provides a ground at terminal 27, which turns on the amber antilock warning lamp. At the same time, the control module provides battery voltage at terminal 8.

Terminal 8 of the control module connects to one terminal of the main relay coil. The other terminal of the coil is grounded. Therefore, when battery voltage is supplied at terminal 8 of the control module, the main relay is energized (Fig. 10-20).

Then the relay contacts between terminals 1 and 3 of the relay open, and the contacts between terminals 1 and 4 close (Fig. 10-20). Battery voltage is connected through a fusible link and a fuse to terminal 4 of the main relay. Therefore, when the relay contacts between terminals 1 and 4 close, battery voltage is applied to terminals 3 and 20 of the control module. Voltage at these terminals allows the module to start the internal test procedure.

The control-module internal test procedure checks the main valve and the solenoid valves for proper operation. In addition, it checks the wheel speed sensors, and the internal circuitry of the module. If the control module determines that the system is operating properly, it removes the ground from terminal 27, which turns off the amber antilock warning lamp (Fig. 10-14).

If, during vehicle operation, the control module determines there is a problem with the antilock system, it can turn on the lamp in either of two ways. It can provide a ground at terminal 27, which grounds the lamp, or it can turn off the main relay by removing battery voltage from terminal 8. Deenergizing the main relay closes the contacts between terminals 1 and 3 (Fig. 10-21), and grounds the lamp. Then current flows from the ignition switch, through the lamp, the ABS diode, and relay contacts 1 and 3, to ground. This lights the lamp.

The ABS diode is used to protect the control module. When the main relay is energized, the relay supplies battery voltage to control-module terminals 3 and 20.

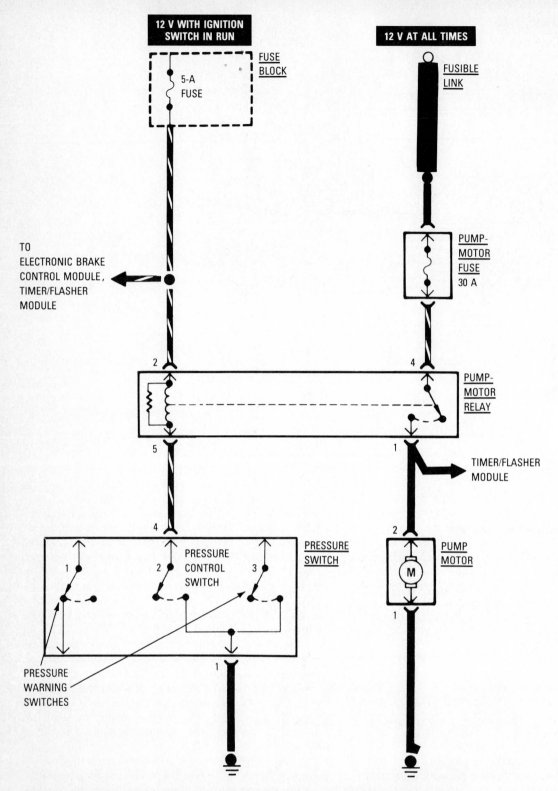

Fig. 10-19. A section of the Teves electrical diagram, showing the pump motor, the pump-motor relay, and the pressure switch. *(Chevrolet Motor Division of General Motors Corporation)*

The diode will not pass electric current from right to left in Fig. 10-16 (or Fig. 10-21). Therefore, battery voltage cannot reach terminal 27 of the control module. If battery voltage were connected to terminal 27 when the terminal was providing a ground, the control module would be damaged.

Brakes Not Applied   When the ignition switch is on, the electric motor and pump keep the brake fluid in the accumulator pressurized. When the brakes are not applied (Fig. 10-22), the spool valve prevents the pressurized fluid in the accumulator from reaching the pressure chamber in the hydraulic unit, or the rear brakes.

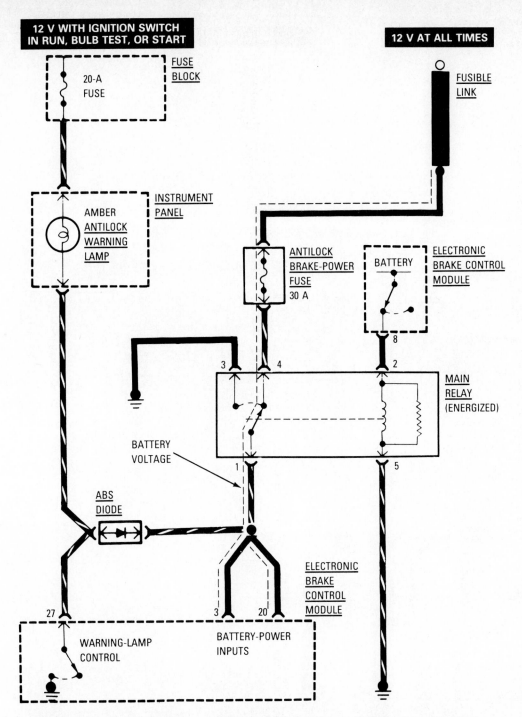

FUSE
BLOCK

20-A
FUSE

FUSIBLE
LINK

AMBER
ANTILOCK
WARNING
LAMP

INSTRUMENT
PANEL

ANTILOCK
BRAKE-POWER
FUSE
30 A

BATTERY

ELECTRONIC
BRAKE CONTROL
MODULE

8

3   4   2

MAIN
RELAY
(ENERGIZED)

BATTERY
VOLTAGE

1   5

ABS
DIODE

ELECTRONIC
BRAKE
CONTROL
MODULE

27

3   20

WARNING-LAMP
CONTROL

BATTERY-POWER
INPUTS

Fig. 10-20. Voltage being applied to control-module terminals 3 and 20 when the main relay is energized. *(Chevrolet Motor Division of General Motors Corporation)*

Brakes Applied (Antilock System Not Operating)

When the brake pedal is depressed, the brake-pedal pushrod moves the scissor-lever assembly, which in turn moves the spool valve (Fig. 10-23). The spool valve allows pressurized brake fluid to flow from the accumulator into the booster pressure chamber and to the rear-wheel cylinders or calipers. When more force is applied to the brake pedal, the spool valve moves farther to allow a greater fluid pressure in the booster chamber. This causes a greater pressure in the rear-wheel cylinders or calipers and causes a greater braking force to be applied at the wheels.

The pressurized brake fluid in the booster pressure chamber applies a force to the booster piston. It pushes against a reaction sleeve and the primary piston in the master cylinder. The reaction sleeve fits around the primary piston, as shown in Fig. 10-23. This action causes the brake fluid in the master cylinder to be pressurized to apply the front brakes.

When the antilock system is not operating, the inlet solenoid valves are open and the outlet solenoid valves are closed. With the valves in these positions, brake-fluid flows to and from the wheel cylinders or calipers in the same way as in a vehicle without an antilock system.

161

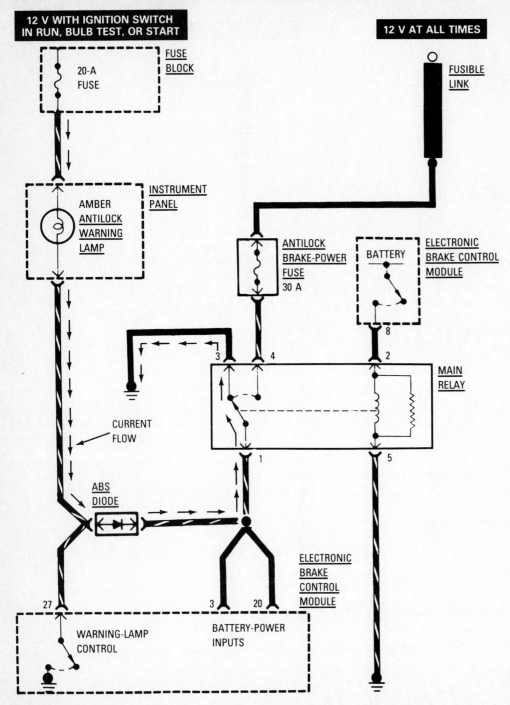

FUSE
BLOCK

20-A
FUSE

INSTRUMENT
PANEL

AMBER
ANTILOCK
WARNING
LAMP

CURRENT
FLOW

ABS
DIODE

27

WARNING-LAMP
CONTROL

12 V AT ALL TIMES

FUSIBLE
LINK

ANTILOCK
BRAKE-POWER
FUSE
30 A

BATTERY

ELECTRONIC
BRAKE CONTROL
MODULE

8

3   4   2

MAIN
RELAY

1   5

ELECTRONIC
BRAKE
CONTROL
MODULE

3   20

BATTERY-POWER
INPUTS

Fig. 10-21. The current flow through the amber antilock warning lamp when the main relay is deenergized. *(Chevrolet Motor Division of General Motors Corporation)*

Brakes Applied (Antilock System Operating)

When the brake pedal is depressed, and if a wheel is about to lock, the control module receives that information from the wheel-speed sensor. The control module then closes the inlet solenoid valve at the wheel that is about to lock. The outlet solenoid valve remains closed. With both valves closed, the pressure in that wheel cylinder or caliper cannot increase, and the brake fluid is held at that pressure. This may be all that is needed to prevent wheel lockup. However, if the control module continues to receive information from the

sensor that the wheel is about to lock, it opens the outlet solenoid valve. Then brake-fluid pressure is released from that wheel cylinder or caliper, and the brake fluid flows back to the external reservoir.

At the same time, the control module opens the main valve in the hydraulic unit (Fig. 10-24). This allows pressurized brake fluid to flow from the accumulator through the booster pressure chamber, through the internal reservoir of the master cylinder, and into chambers at the rear of the master-cylinder pistons. There are holes that pass through the pistons and connect these

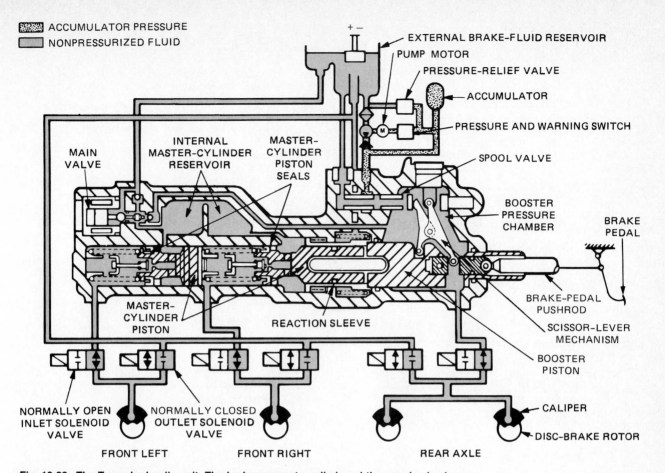

ACCUMULATOR PRESSURE
NONPRESSURIZED FLUID

EXTERNAL BRAKE-FLUID RESERVOIR
PUMP MOTOR
PRESSURE-RELIEF VALVE
ACCUMULATOR
PRESSURE AND WARNING SWITCH
SPOOL VALVE
BOOSTER PRESSURE CHAMBER
BRAKE PEDAL
BRAKE-PEDAL PUSHROD
SCISSOR-LEVER MECHANISM
BOOSTER PISTON
CALIPER
DISC-BRAKE ROTOR

MAIN VALVE
INTERNAL MASTER-CYLINDER RESERVOIR
MASTER-CYLINDER PISTON SEALS
MASTER-CYLINDER PISTON
REACTION SLEEVE

NORMALLY OPEN INLET SOLENOID VALVE
NORMALLY CLOSED OUTLET SOLENOID VALVE
FRONT LEFT
FRONT RIGHT
REAR AXLE

Fig. 10-22. The Teves-hydraulic unit. The brakes are not applied, and the spool valve is preventing the pressurized brake fluid in the accumulator from reaching the booster pressure chamber. *(Chevrolet Motor Division of General Motors Corporation)*

1. DYNAMIC — REGULATED ACCUMULATOR PRESSURE
2. STATIC — PRESSURE DEVELOPED BY MASTER-CYLINDER PISTONS

ACCUMULATOR PRESSURE
NONPRESSURIZED FLUID
PRESSURE PRODUCED BY ACCUMULATOR
PRESSURE PRODUCED BY MASTER CYLINDER

EXTERNAL BRAKE-FLUID RESERVOIR
PUMP MOTOR
PRESSURE-RELIEF VALVE
ACCUMULATOR
PRESSURE AND WARNING SWITCH
SPOOL VALVE
BOOSTER PRESSURE CHAMBER
BRAKE PEDAL
BRAKE-PEDAL PUSHROD
SCISSOR-LEVER MECHANISM
BOOSTER PISTON
CALIPER
DISC-BRAKE ROTOR

MAIN VALVE
INTERNAL MASTER-CYLINDER RESERVOIR
MASTER-CYLINDER PISTON SEALS
MASTER-CYLINDER PISTON
REACTION SLEEVE

NORMALLY OPEN INLET SOLENOID VALVE
NORMALLY CLOSED OUTLET SOLENOID VALVE
FRONT LEFT
FRONT RIGHT
REAR AXLE

Fig. 10-23. The Teves hydraulic unit. The brakes are applied, but the antilock system is not operating. The spool valve is allowing pressurized brake fluid from the accumulator to flow into the booster pressure chamber and to the rear-wheel calipers. *(Chevrolet Motor Division of General Motors Corporation)*

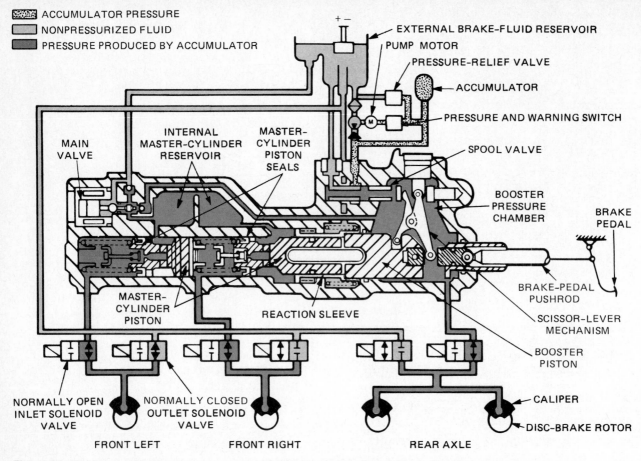

ACCUMULATOR PRESSURE
NONPRESSURIZED FLUID
PRESSURE PRODUCED BY ACCUMULATOR

EXTERNAL BRAKE-FLUID RESERVOIR
PUMP MOTOR
PRESSURE-RELIEF VALVE
ACCUMULATOR
PRESSURE AND WARNING SWITCH
SPOOL VALVE
BOOSTER PRESSURE CHAMBER
BRAKE PEDAL
BRAKE-PEDAL PUSHROD
SCISSOR-LEVER MECHANISM
BOOSTER PISTON

MAIN VALVE
INTERNAL MASTER-CYLINDER RESERVOIR
MASTER-CYLINDER PISTON SEALS
MASTER-CYLINDER PISTON
REACTION SLEEVE

NORMALLY OPEN INLET SOLENOID VALVE
NORMALLY CLOSED OUTLET SOLENOID VALVE
CALIPER
DISC-BRAKE ROTOR

FRONT LEFT   FRONT RIGHT   REAR AXLE

Fig. 10-24. The Teves hydraulic unit. The brakes are applied, and the antilock system is operating. The main valve in the hydraulic unit opens and allows pressurized brake fluid from the accumulator to flow into the internal master-cylinder reservoir to operate the front brakes. *(Chevrolet Motor Division of General Motors Corporation)*

chambers with the pressure chambers in front of the pistons. Therefore, brake fluid flows from the chambers at the rear of the pistons, through the holes in the pistons, and into the pressure chambers. Then pressurized brake fluid from the accumulator is available to operate the front brakes.

The brake fluid in the chamber at the rear of the primary piston does an additional job. It pushes the reaction sleeve rearward against the booster piston. This pushes the booster piston and brake-pedal pushrod rearward against the driver's foot. This alerts the driver that the antilock system has begun to operate. It also allows the piston return springs to push the piston rearward. Then, if the hydraulic system fails, there will be some piston movement available to apply the brakes.

When the control module receives information that the wheel is no longer locking, it restores braking force to that wheel. To do this, it closes the outlet valve and opens the inlet valve. This entire operation can take place as often as 15 times per second.

Warning Lamps

There are two warning lamps used with this system. One lamp is red; this is the brake warning lamp. The other lamp is amber; this is the antilock warning lamp.

Red Brake Warning Lamp   The red brake warning lamp is lit when any of the following conditions occur:

- The parking brake is applied, and the ignition switch is on.

- The ignition switch is in the START position.

- The fluid level in the hydraulic unit is low, and the ignition switch is on.

- The pressure in the accumulator drops below 1,500 psi [10,350 kPa], and the ignition switch is on.

A warning-lamp circuit diagram is shown in Fig. 10-25. Two switches are shown: the fluid-level switch and the pressure switch. The fluid-level switch consists of two separate switches, both located in the reservoir in the hydraulic unit. The switches are labeled 1 and 2.

The pressure-switch contacts are labeled 1, 2, and 3. Contact set 1 is a pressure warning switch, which opens when the accumulator pressure drops below 1,500 psi [10,350 kPa]. Contact set 2 is the pressure control switch described earlier in this chapter under "Pump-Motor Relay." Contact set 3 is a pressure warning switch, which closes when the accumulator pressure drops below 1,500 psi [10,350 kPa].

Battery voltage is supplied through a fuse in the fuse block to one terminal of the red brake warning lamp. If

164

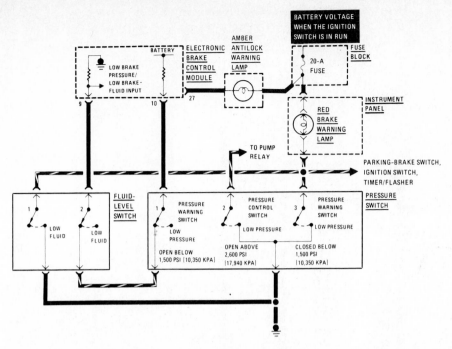

Fig. 10-25. A section of the Teves electrical diagram, showing the warning lamps and the pressure and fluid-level switches. *(Chevrolet Motor Division of General Motors Corporation)*

the other terminal of the lamp is grounded, the lamp will be lit. Therefore, all the switches that control the lamp are connected between this lamp terminal and ground. When any switch closes, the lamp is lit.

When the ignition switch is turned to the START position, or when the parking brake is applied, the lamp is grounded. This lights the lamp.

If the fluid in the reservoir of the hydraulic unit is low, fluid-level-switch contact set 1 closes. This gounds the lamp and lights it. If the accumulator pressure drops below 1,500 psi [10,350 kPa], pressure warning-switch contact set 3 closes. This grounds the lamp and lights it.

Amber Antilock Warning Lamp   The amber antilock lamp is lit when the antilock system is not operating. If the brake-fluid level in the reservoir of the hydraulic unit is low, or if the accumulator pressure is below 1,500 psi [10,350 kPa], the control module turns off the antilock system and lights the amber lamp.

In Fig. 10-25, terminal 10 of the control module is shown connected to one terminal of the pressure warning switch (pressure-switch contact set 1). The other terminal of the pressure warning switch connects to one terminal of fluid-level switch 2. The other terminal of fluid-level switch 2 connects to terminal 9 of the control module. These switches are connected in series. A *series* connection is one in which all the current that flows through one component must flow through the other components in the circuit.

The control module supplies voltage (which it receives from the vehicle battery) on terminal 10. Terminal 9 of the control module connects to ground (inside the control module). If both switches are closed, current flows from terminal 10, through both switches, to terminal 9. If either switch opens, the current flow stops.

The pressure warning switch opens when the accumulator pressure drops below 1,500 psi [10,350 kPa]. Fluid-level switch 2 opens when the brake fluid in the reservoir drops below a certain level. The control module senses a switch opening and provides a ground on terminal 27. This grounds one terminal of the antilock warning lamp and lights the lamp. When either switch opens, the computer turns off the antilock system.

The antilock warning lamp is also turned on when the main relay is deenergized. This part of the operation is described earlier in this chapter.

Flasher

Some systems have a flasher module (Fig. 10-26). The flasher module is powered by battery voltage, which is supplied to terminal C of the module. Terminal H of the module connects to the pump motor and receives battery voltage as long as voltage is supplied to the pump. If the pump motor runs (or voltage is supplied to it) for longer than 3 minutes, a timer in the module causes the module to provide an alternating ground on terminal F. One terminal of the red brake warning lamp is supplied with battery voltage, and the other terminal of the lamp is connected to terminal F of the module. Therefore, an alternating ground at terminal F causes the warning lamp to flash on and off. This alerts the driver that the pump has run for an excessive amount of time and that the brake system needs to be serviced.

Fault Detection

During vehicles operation, the control module continually checks the operation of the antilock system. If the control module detects a fault, it can turn the system off by removing battery voltage from control-module ter-

165

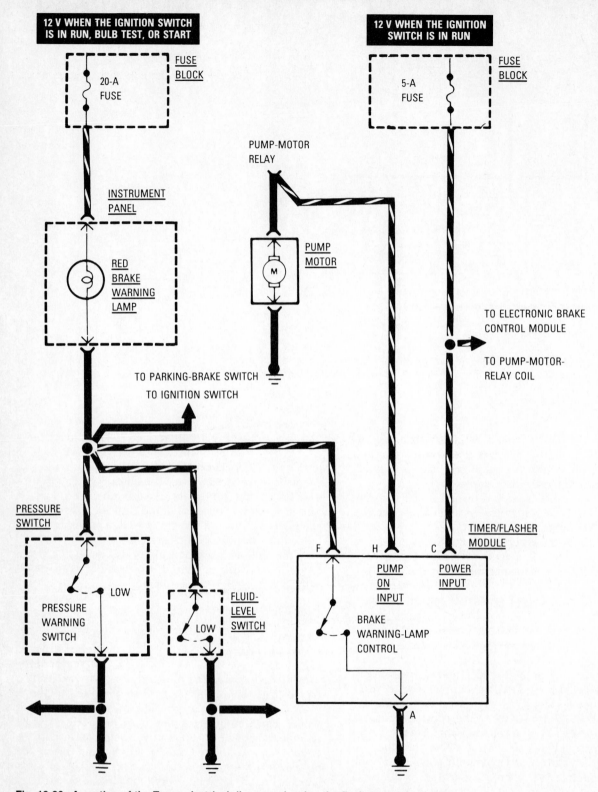

Fig. 10-26. A section of the Teves electrical diagram, showing the flasher-module circuit. *(Chevrolet Motor Division of General Motors Corporation)*

minal 8 (Fig. 10-16). This removes battery voltage from the main relay and deenergizes it. Then the antilock system will no longer operate, and the antilock warning lamp will be lit. The system will not operate and the lamp will remain on until the fault is repaired and the ignition switch is turned off and then on again.

If there is a temporary fault, such as interference from a radio transmitter, the control module will temporarily turn the system off. In addition, it will light the antilock warning lamp by providing a ground at terminal 27. When the interference is gone, the lamp will turn off and the system will resume its operation. The system is also turned off temporarily with low accumulator pressure or low brake fluid level.

Effect of Road Conditions

Sometimes wheel bounce on a bumpy road can be misinterpreted by the control module as the beginning of wheel lockup. The control module then attempts to start antilock operation even though the brakes are not applied. To prevent this from happening, some systems have a connection from the stoplamp switch to the control module. Then, when the brakes are not applied, the control module is programmed to minimize the effect of wheel bounce. In Fig. 10-14, for example, the stop lamp switch (brake switch) is shown connected to terminal 12 of the control module.

FOUR-WHEEL NONINTEGRAL-TYPE ANTILOCK BRAKE SYSTEMS

The components used in a nonintegral-type antilock brake system are shown in Fig. 10-27. This system is manufactured by the Robert Bosch Corporation. The power booster and master cylinder operate in a manner similar to that on a car without antilock brakes.

Four wheel-speed sensors provide information on wheel speed to the computer. The computer in the Bosch system is called the control module (Fig. 10-28).

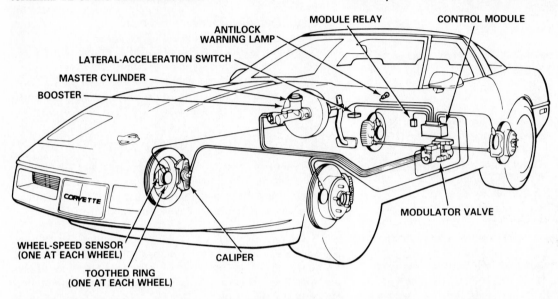

Fig. 10-27. The components of a Bosch antilock brake system. *(Chevrolet Motor Division of General Motors Corporation)*

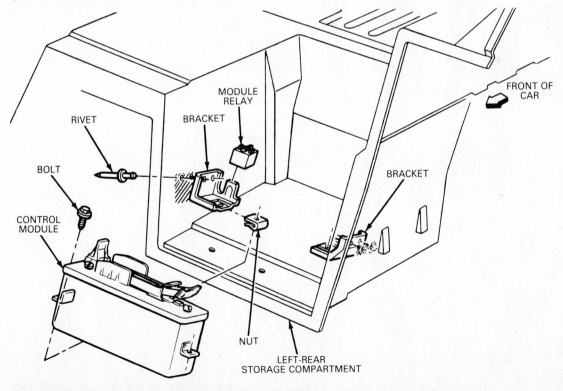

Fig. 10-28. The Bosch control module removed from the left-rear storage compartment. *(Chevrolet Motor Division of General Motors Corporation)*

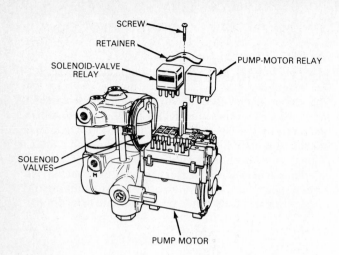

Fig. 10-29. The Bosch modulator-valve assembly. *(Chevrolet Motor Division of General Motors Corporation)*

The control module controls the braking force at the wheels by operating the modulator valve (Fig. 10-29). *Modulate* means to vary or change; therefore, the valve is given this name because it varies or changes the brake fluid pressure applied to the calipers.

The modulator valve includes a pump motor, a pump-motor relay, two accumulators, a solenoid-valve relay, and three solenoid valves. When the solenoid valves operate, they control the brake-fluid pressure to the calipers. There is one solenoid valve for each front wheel, and one solenoid valve for both rear wheels. The solenoid valves are three-postion valves. The positions are APPLY PRESSURE, HOLD PRESSURE, and RELEASE PRESSURE.

Figure 10-30 shows the locations of the control module and modulator valve for one car.

Other components that are part of the system are the lateral-acceleration switch (Fig. 10-31), the module relay (Figs. 10-28 and 10-30), the stoplamp switch, the ignition switch, an ABS diode, and the amber antilock warning lamp. The diode is connected between the warning lamp and the modulator valve. Its operation is described later in this section under "Output Signals from the Control Module."

The module relay also includes some diodes. These protect the control module from momentary high-voltage surges that may be generated in the vehicle's electrical system. In addition, the diodes protect the control module from reversed battery polarity, or from a charging voltage in excess of 24 volts.

An electrical diagram of the system is shown in Fig. 10-32. The diagram shows the components used in the system and the electrical connections between the components. The terminal numbers of the control module are included in the diagram.

Input Signals to the Control Module

The control module receives input signals from several components. These components are shown in Fig. 10-32, and the input signals are listed in Fig. 10-33. The control-module terminal numbers are also shown in Fig. 10-33.

Wheel-Speed Sensors   Four wheel-speed sensors, each located at a wheel, provide information on wheel speed to the control module. Only one wheel-speed sensor is shown in Fig. 10-32; this is done to simplify the diagram.

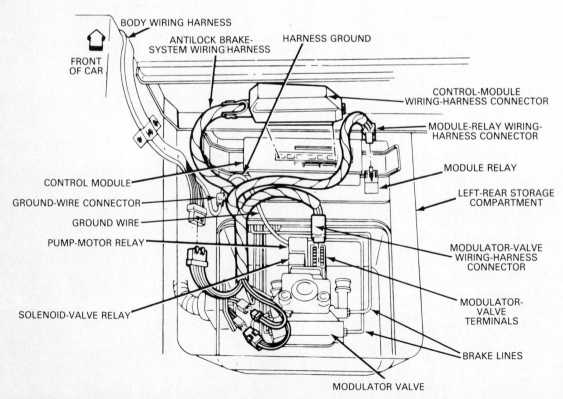

Fig. 10-30. The locations of the Bosch control module and modulator valve for one car. *(Chevrolet Motor Division of General Motors Corporation)*

168

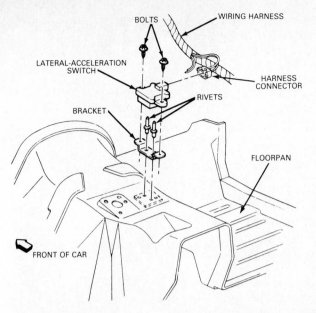

Fig. 10-31. The Bosch lateral-acceleration switch removed from the floorpan. *(Chevrolet Motor Division of General Motors Corporation)*

Ignition Switch The ignition switch provides a 12-V signal to the control module on terminal 15 when the ignition switch is turned to the START position. This voltage is also provided when the ignition switch is in the BULB TEST position. The BULB TEST position is a momentary ignition-switch position located between the RUN and START positions. As the ignition switch is turned from RUN to START, the BUS TEST position briefly lights the red brake warning-lamp bulb to check its operation.

Stoplamp Switch When the brakes are applied, the stoplamp switch turns on the stoplamps. In addition, it applies voltage to control-module terminal 25. Voltage at this terminal signals the control module that the brakes have been applied.

Module Relay When the ignition switch is in the RUN position, the module relay is energized. When this occurs, the module relay connects battery voltage to terminal 1 of the control module. Voltage on terminal 1 powers the control module.

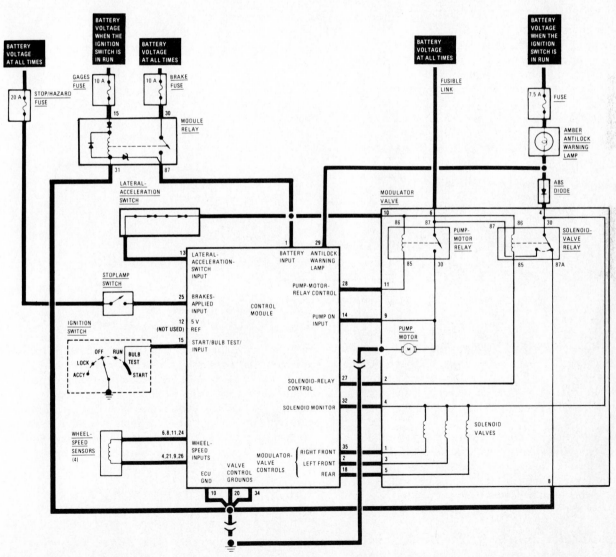

Fig. 10-32. An electrical diagram of the Bosch antilock brake system. *(Chevrolet Motor Division of General Motors Corporation)*

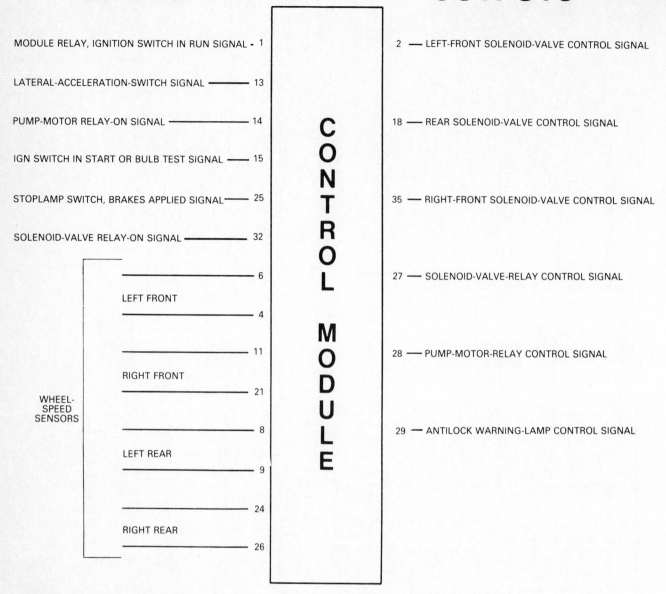

INPUTS

MODULE RELAY, IGNITION SWITCH IN RUN SIGNAL - 1

LATERAL-ACCELERATION-SWITCH SIGNAL —— 13

PUMP-MOTOR RELAY-ON SIGNAL ———— 14

IGN SWITCH IN START OR BULB TEST SIGNAL —— 15

STOPLAMP SWITCH, BRAKES APPLIED SIGNAL— 25

SOLENOID-VALVE RELAY-ON SIGNAL ———— 32

WHEEL-SPEED SENSORS

LEFT FRONT — 6 / 4

RIGHT FRONT — 11 / 21

LEFT REAR — 8 / 9

RIGHT REAR — 24 / 26

CONTROL MODULE

OUTPUTS

2 — LEFT-FRONT SOLENOID-VALVE CONTROL SIGNAL

18 — REAR SOLENOID-VALVE CONTROL SIGNAL

35 — RIGHT-FRONT SOLENOID-VALVE CONTROL SIGNAL

27 — SOLENOID-VALVE-RELAY CONTROL SIGNAL

28 — PUMP-MOTOR-RELAY CONTROL SIGNAL

29 — ANTILOCK WARNING-LAMP CONTROL SIGNAL

Fig. 10-33. Bosch control-module input signals and output control signals. *(Chevrolet Motor Division of General Motors Corporation)*

Pump-Motor Relay   When the pump-motor relay is energized, it turns on the pump. When this occurs, the relay also applies voltage to control-module terminal 14. The control module then receives a signal that voltage is being applied to operate the pump.

Solenoid-Valve Relay   When the solenoid-valve relay is energized, battery voltage is applied to one terminal of the solenoid valves. At the same time, voltage is also applied to terminal 32 of the control module. Voltage at this terminal signals the control module that voltage has been applied to the solenoid valves.

Lateral-Acceleration Switch   The lateral-acceleration switch consists of two normally closed switches connected in series. The lateral-acceleration switch connects between terminal 1 and terminal 13 of the con-

trol module. Normally, the switch connects battery voltage from terminal 1 to terminal 13. If the lateral acceleration of the vehicle is great enough, one of the normally closed switches will open. This breaks the connection between these two control-module terminals and removes voltage from terminal 13. An absence of voltage on terminal 13 signals the control module that the vehicle is going through a turn.

Output Signals from the Control Module

The control module controls a number of components. The components are shown in Fig. 10-32, and the control signals are listed in Fig. 10-33. The components and control signals are described on the pages that follow.

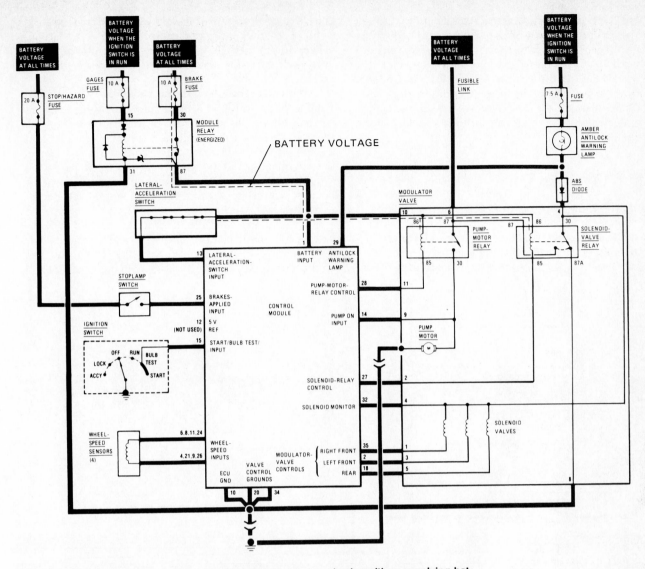

Fig. 10-34. The module relay in the Bosch system is the energized position, supplying battery voltage to the control module, the pump-motor relay, the solenoid-valve relay, and the lateral-acceleration switch. *(Chevrolet Motor Division of General Motors Corporation)*

Solenoid-Valve Relay   One terminal of the solenoid-valve-relay coil receives battery voltage from the module relay when that relay is energized (Fig. 10-34). The other terminal of the relay coil connects to terminal 27 of the control module. The control module energizes the solenoid-valve relay by providing a ground on terminal 27. When the solenoid-valve relay is energized, the relay contacts supply battery voltage to one terminal of each solenoid valve. However, this does not operate the solenoid valves. Another signal is required from the control module to operate the valves.

The amber warning lamp is connected to the solenoid-valve-relay contacts through the ABS diode. This diode prevents battery voltage from reaching terminal 29 of the control module when the solenoid-valve relay is energized. If voltage were applied to terminal 29, the control module would be damaged.

Solenoid Valves   The ground terminal of each solenoid valve connects to the control module. The left-front valve connects to terminal 2, the right-front valve connects to terminal 35, and the rear valve connects to terminal 18. The control module can provide any one of three signals to a solenoid. These signals are OPEN CIRCUIT, PARTIAL GROUND, or GROUND.

Pump-Motor Relay   One terminal of the pump-motor-relay coil receives battery voltage from the module relay when this relay is energized (Fig. 10-34). The other terminal of the relay coil connects to terminal 28 of the control module. The control module controls the operation of the pump-motor relay by providing a ground at terminal 28. A ground at terminal 28 energizes the relay. When the relay is energized, the pump motor turns on.

Amber Antilock Warning Lamp One terminal of the amber antilock warning lamp is supplied with battery voltage. The other terminal of the lamp connects to terminal 29 of the control module. If the control module detects a fault in the system, it provides a ground at terminal 29, which lights the lamp. In addition, the control module turns the antilock system off. When the lamp is lit, it alerts the driver that the antilock system is not operational.

System Operation

When the ignition switch is turned to the RUN position, battery voltage is applied to one terminal of the module-relay coil. The other terminal of the relay coil is grounded. Therefore, when the ignition switch is turned to the RUN position, the module relay is energized. This causes battery voltage to be applied to terminal 1 of the control module, to one terminal of the lateral-acceleration switch, to one terminal of the pump-motor-relay coil, and to one terminal of the solenoid-valve-relay coil.

With the ignition switch on RUN, and with battery voltage on terminal 1 of the control module, the control module is programmed to perform a brief test sequence. The control module does an internal check and a solenoid-valve-relay check. The solenoid-valve relay is not energized when the ignition switch is first turned to RUN. Therefore, the amber antilock warning lamp is lit because it is grounded through the solenoid-valve-relay contacts (Fig. 10-35).

If the control module determines that the antilock system is functional, it provides a ground at terminal 27. This energizes the solenoid-valve relay. The relay contacts then supply battery voltage to one terminal of each

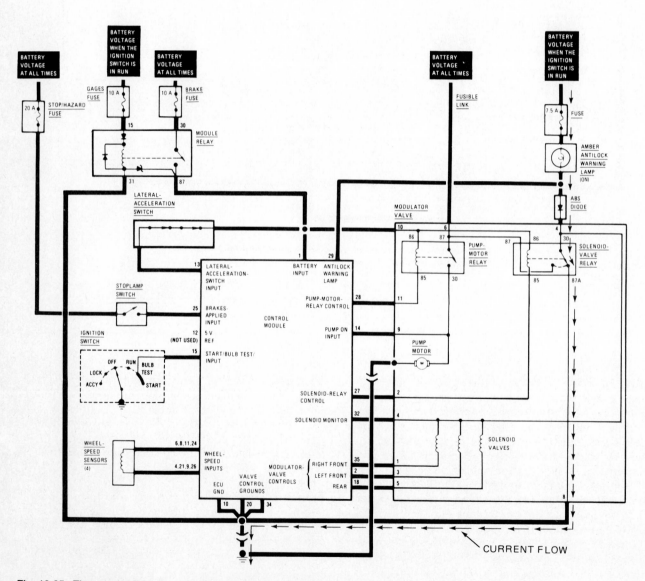

Fig. 10-35. The current flow through the amber antilock warning lamp in the Bosch system when the solenoid-valve relay is not energized. *(Chevrolet Motor Division of General Motors Corporation)*

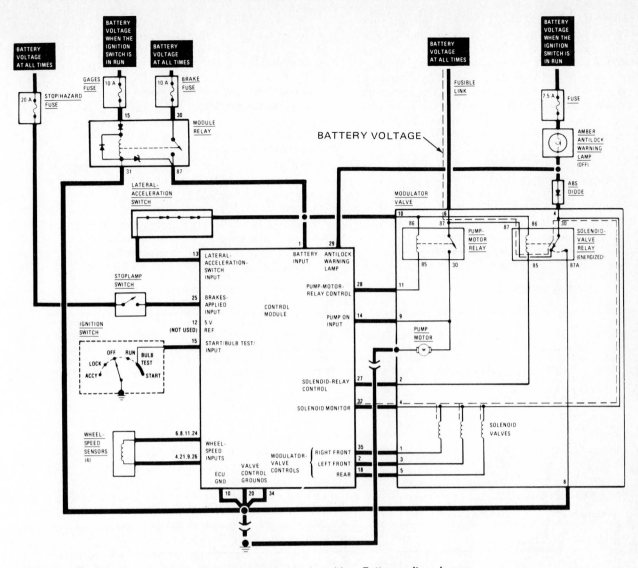

Fig. 10-36. The Bosch solenoid-valve relay in the energized position. Battery voltage is supplied to one terminal of the solenoid valves, and the amber antilock warning lamp is not grounded. *(Chevrolet Motor Division of General Motors Corporation)*

solenoid valve, and removes the ground from the warning lamp (Fig. 10-36). This turns the lamp off. The internal test procedure takes a few seconds to complete.

The amber warning lamp is also turned on when the ignition switch is turned to the BULB TEST or START positions. This is because the control module receives a signal from the ignition switch on terminal 15. The control module then grounds terminal 29 to light the lamp. The ignition switch also lights the red brake warning lamp when it is in the BULB TEST or START positions.

The control module is programmed to check the operation of the wheel-speed sensors, the solenoid valves, and the pump motor when the vehicle reaches a speed of between 3 and 11 miles per hour (mph) [5 and 17 kilometers per hour (kph)]. If the operation is not correct, the control module will turn on the amber lamp and disable the antilock system. The control module can

turn on the lamp by providing a ground on terminal 29 or by removing the ground from terminal 27 and de-energizing the solenoid-valve relay.

While the car is being driven, the wheel-speed sensors continually provide information on wheel speed to the computer. When the brakes are applied and none of the wheels is about to lock, the control module provides an open circuit at terminals 2, 18, and 35. Therefore, the three solenoid valves are not energized and remain in the APPLY PRESSURE position (Fig. 10-37). Then, when the brake pedal is depressed, brake-fluid pressure is applied to the calipers, and when the pedal is released, fluid pressure is released from the calipers. This operation is the same as on a vehicle without antilock brakes.

Suppose, for example, that the control module receives information from a sensor that the left-front wheel is about to lock. Then the control module provides a

173

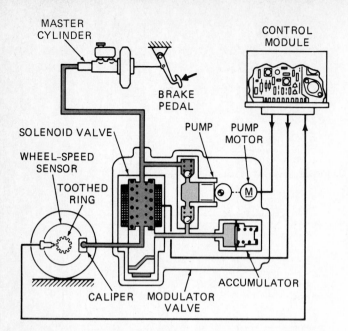

Fig. 10-37. The operation of the modulator valve in the Bosch system when the brakes are applied and none of the wheels are about to lock. The solenoid valve is shown in its apply pressure position. *(Chevrolet Motor Division of General Motors Corporation)*

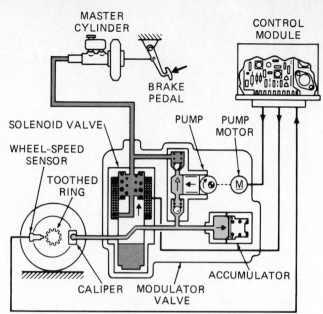

Fig. 10-39. The operation of the modulator valve in the Bosch system when the brakes are applied and a wheel is still about to lock. The solenoid valve is shown in its release pressure position. *(Chevrolet Motor Division of General Motors Corporation)*

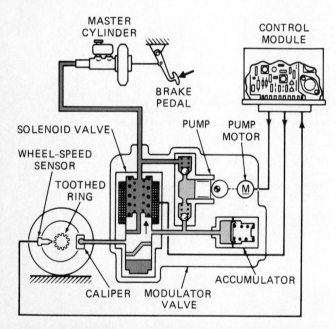

Fig. 10-38. The operation of the modulator valve in the Bosch system when the brakes are applied and a wheel is about to lock. The solenoid valve is shown in its hold pressure position. *(Chevrolet Motor Division of General Motors Corporation)*

moves to its RELEASE PRESSURE position (Fig. 10-39). Brake fluid is released from the caliper to release the braking force at the left-front wheel.

To ensure that the brake fluid is released quickly, there is a small chamber in the modulator valve into which the brake fluid can flow. This chamber is called an ACCUMULATOR (Fig. 10-39). There are two accumulators, one for the front brakes and one for the rear brakes. When the fluid flows into the accumulator, the braking force at the wheel is quickly released.

The pump is used to return the brake fluid from the accumulators back to the master cylinder (Fig. 10-39). The control module operates the pump by providing a ground at terminal 28. This energizes the pump-motor relay, which supplies battery voltage to the pump motor to turn it on. When the pump operates, the driver will feel a pulsation in the brake pedal as brake fluid is pumped back to the master cylinder.

When the wheel speed increases, indicating that there is no longer a tendency for the wheel to lock, the control module again provides an open circuit at terminal 2. This returns the solenoid valve to the APPLY PRESSURE position and again allows brake-fluid pressure to reach the caliper. This operation can repeat as often as 10 times per second to prevent wheel lockup.

REAR ANTILOCK BRAKE SYSTEMS (RABS)

Some light trucks have an antilock brake system that prevents lockup of the rear wheels only. The system shown in Fig. 10-40 includes an electrohydraulic control valve, a control module, and a wheel-speed sensor. A toothed ring is mounted on the differential ring gear (Fig. 10-41).

partial ground on terminal 2. This causes the left-front solenoid valve to move to a middle position (Fig. 10-38). In this position, the valve traps brake fluid in the caliper at a constant pressure. This is the HOLD PRESSURE position of the valve. When the valve is in this position, the pressure cannot increase in the caliper even if the driver continues to apply force to the brake pedal.

If the control module continues to receive information from the sensor that the wheel is about to lock, it provides a ground on terminal 2. Now the solenoid valve

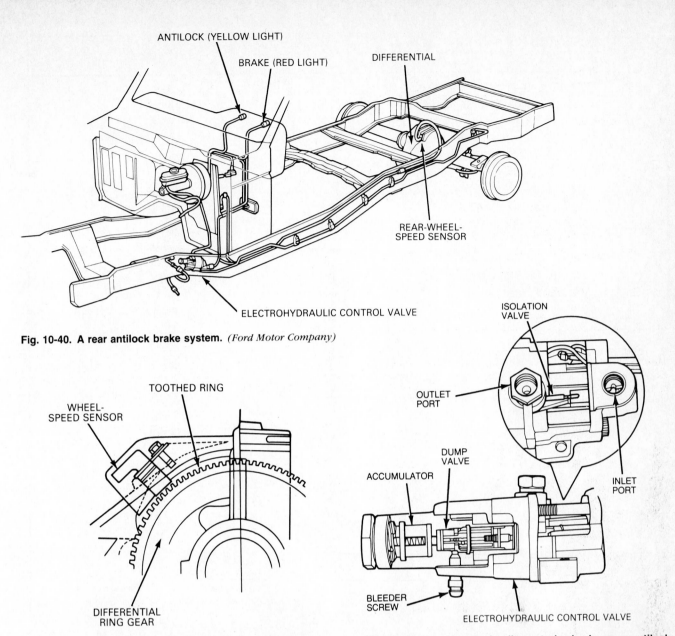

Fig. 10-40. A rear antilock brake system. *(Ford Motor Company)*

Fig. 10-41. A wheel-speed sensor located in the differential-gear assembly in a rear antilock brake system. *(Ford Motor Company)*

Fig. 10-42. The electrohydraulic control valve in a rear antilock brake system. *(Ford Motor Company)*

The wheel-speed sensor fits in the differential housing and is located near the toothed wheel. The sensor supplies wheel-speed information to the control module. If the rear wheels begin to lock up, the ring-gear speed drops and the control module receives this information from the sensor.

When this occurs, the control module operates a solenoid that closes an *isolation valve* in the control-valve assembly (Fig. 10-42). Hydraulic pressure is then trapped in the rear-wheel cylinders and cannot increase. If the wheels are still about to lock, the control module operates a solenoid that opens a dump valve, and this releases hydraulic pressure from the wheel cylinders. Brake fluid is released from the wheel cylinders, and flows into an accumulator in the control valve (Fig. 10-42).

When the control module senses that the wheels are no longer about to lock up, it allows hydraulic pressure to be applied to the wheel cylinders. At the same time, the spring in the accumulator pushes a piston, which pushes the brake fluid stored in the accumulator back into the master cylinder.

SELF-TEST

Some antilock brake systems have a self-test feature. When a malfunction occurs, the location of the problem is sensed by the computer, and a service code is stored in the computer memory. The code must then be retrieved from the memory. The service code is in the form of a one- or two-digit number. It provides information on the location of the problem and on where to begin testing.

On some vehicles, a diagnostic tester is used to obtain the code. The tester is plugged into the vehicle's

175

Service code	Test step
11 (Electronic Controller)	AA1
12 (Electronic Controller-Replacer)	AA2
21 (Main Valve)	BB1
22 (Left-Front Inlet Valve)	CC1
23 (Left-Front Outlet Valve)	CC2
24 (Right-Front Inlet Valve)	CC3
25 (Right-Front Outlet Valve)	CC4
26 (Rear Inlet Valve)	CC5
27 (Rear Outlet Valve and Ground)	CC6
31 (Left-Front Sensor)	DD1
32 (Right-Front Sensor)	DD5
33 (Right-Rear Sensor)	DD9
34 (Left-Rear Sensor)	DD13
35 (Left-Front Sensor)	DD1
36 (Right-Front Sensor)	DD5
37 (Right-Rear Sensor)	DD9
38 (Left-Rear Sensor)	DD13
41 (Left-Front Sensor)	DD1
42 (Right-Front Sensor)	DD5
43 (Right-Rear Sensor)	DD9
44 (Left-Rear Sensor)	DD13
51 (Left-Front Outlet Valve)	EE1
52 (Right-Front Outlet Valve)	EE3
53 (Rear Outlet Valve)	EE5
54 (Rear Outlet Valve)	EE7
55 (Left-Front Sensor)	DD1
56 (Right-Front Sensor)	DD5
57 (Right-Rear Sensor)	DD9
58 (Left-Rear Sensor)	DD13
61 (FLI and PWS Circuit)	FF1
71 (Left-Front Sensor)	EE1
72 (Right-Front Sensor)	EE3
73 (Right-Rear Sensor)	EE5
74 (Left-Rear Sensor)	EE7
75 (Left-Front Sensor)	DD1
76 (Right-Front Sensor)	DD5
77 (Right-Rear Sensor)	DD9
78 (Left-Rear Sensor)	DD13
99 (Electronic Controller)	AA1

Fig. 10-43. An example of the service codes for an antilock brake system with a self-test feature.
(Ford Motor Company)

wiring harness, and the code is read out on the tester's digital display. Figure 10-43 is a list of the service codes for one vehicle and of the tests to be performed for each code. For example, if code 21 appeared, you should perform test BB1 (Fig. 10-44) and check the main valve.

On other vehicles, a diagnostic connector on the control module (Fig. 10-45) must be grounded in order to obtain the service code. The amber antilock warning lamp then flashes out the code. For example, if after grounding the connector, the lamp flashes four times, this is a code 4. The vehicle's service manual lists the codes and the tests that should be performed for each code.

TEST STEP	RESULT ▶	ACTION TO TAKE
BB1 SERVICE CODE 21: CHECK MAIN VALVE		
• Disconnect main valve 2-Pin plug. • Measure resistance between the main valve electrical Pins 1 and 2. PIN NO. 1 PIN NO. 2	2 to 5.5 ohms (OK) ▶ Any other reading (O̶K̶) ▶	REPLACE or SERVICE cable harness (Circuit 430E or 493). REPLACE actuation assembly.

Fig. 10-44. The test procedure to be followed for a service code 21 in Fig. 10-43. *(Ford Motor Company)*

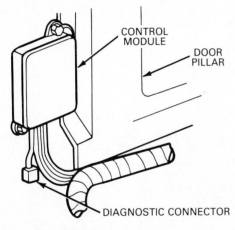

CONTROL MODULE

DOOR PILLAR

DIAGNOSTIC CONNECTOR

Fig. 10-45. An antilock-brake-system control module with a self-test diagnostic connector. *(Ford Motor Company)*

VOCABULARY REVIEW

ABS Antilock brake system.

Accumulator In the Teves system, a container in which high-pressure brake fluid is stored. In the Bosch system, a chamber where brake fluid can flow when the control module releases brake-fluid pressure from the calipers.

Chip A small surface on which transistors and integrated circuits are placed.

Closed In a switch, closed means that the contacts are together and that the switch will pass electric current. In a valve, it means that the valve will not allow a fluid to flow through it.

Computer An electronic device that stores and processes data.

Deenergized In a solenoid, this means that no current is flowing in the coil and that the coil is not magnetized.

Diode An electronic component that acts as a one-way current valve.

EBCM Electronic brake control module.

Energized In a solenoid, this means that current is flowing in the coil and that the coil is magnetized.

Frequency The number of voltage pulses per second produced by a wheel-speed sensor.

Inlet solenoid valve In an antilock brake system, the solenoid valve that controls brake-fluid flow to a wheel cylinder or caliper in order to apply the brakes.

Input device The part of a computer that connects a sensor to the computer.

Integral antilock brake system An antilock brake system in which the master cylinder, power booster, and antilock hydraulic unit are combined in a single unit.

Integrated circuit (IC) An electronic circuit made from a number of different types of components placed on a single chip.

Lateral acceleration A measure of the sideward movement of a vehicle.

Memory The part of a computer that stores data.

Microcomputer A miniature computer.

Microprocessor The part of a microcomputer that controls all the operations of the microcomputer. Also called a *central processing unit (CPU)*.

Modulate To vary or change.

Nonintegral antilock brake system An antilock brake system in which the antilock hydraulic unit is separate from the master cylinder and power booster.

Open In a switch, open means that the contacts are apart and that the switch will not pass electric current. In a valve, it means that the valve will allow a fluid to flow through it.

Outlet solenoid valve In an antilock brake system, the solenoid valve that controls brake-fluid flow from a wheel cylinder or caliper in order to release the brakes.

Output device The part of a computer that connects the computer to a control device.

Plunger The movable core of a solenoid.

Program A set of instructions that tells the microprocessor what to do and when to do it.

Pump the brakes To depress and release the brake pedal alternately in order to help prevent wheel lockup.

RABS Rear antilock brake system.

Random access memory (RAM) The part of a computer where data can be added (written in) and read out.

Read-only memory (ROM) The part of a computer that contains stored data.

Series An electric-circuit connection in which all the current that flows through one component also flows through the other components.

Solenoid An electromagnet with a movable core.

Solenoid valve An electrically operated valve that controls the flow of a liquid.

Voltage pulse A voltage that lasts only for a short time.

REVIEW QUESTIONS

Select the *one* correct, best, or most probable answer to each question.

1. All of the following are true of a Bosch modulator valve *except:*
   a. It has three solenoid valves.
   b. The solenoid valves are two-position valves.
   c. Each solenoid valve controls brake-fluid flow to and from the calipers.
   d. It has two accumulators.

2. Technician A says that the Teves accumulator acts as a temporary storage reservoir for brake fluid when the brakes are releasing. Technician B says that the Bosch accumulator stores brake fluid under high pressure to be used to apply the rear brakes. Who is right?
   a. A only
   b. B only
   c. Both A and B
   d. Neither A nor B

3. The module relay in the Bosch antilock brake system supplies battery voltage to all of the following components *except:*
   a. The solenoid-valve relay
   b. The pump-motor relay
   c. The control module
   d. The solenoid valves

4. Technician A says that on most antilock brake systems, when one rear wheel begins to lock, the computer controls the braking force at both rear wheels at the same time. Technician B says that the computer controls the rear wheels independently. Who is right?
   a. A only
   b. B only
   c. Both A and B
   d. Neither A nor B

5. If the amber antilock warning lamp is lit while the car is being driven, this means that:
   a. the antilock system is operating normally.
   b. the parking brake is partially applied.
   c. the computer has turned the antilock system off.
   d. a wheel is about to lock.

6. When the brakes are applied on a car with an antilock brake system, the driver feels a pulsation in the brake pedal. Technician A says that the pump is faulty. Technician B says that one wheel (or more) is being prevented from locking by the computer. Who is right?
   a. A only
   b. B only
   c. Both A and B
   d. Neither A nor B

7. Technician A says that the pump in the Bosch system pumps brake fluid from the accumulators to the master cylinder. Technician B says that the pump in the Teves system pumps brake fluid from the accumulator to the solenoid valves. Who is right?
   a. A only
   b. B only
   c. Both A and B
   d. Neither A nor B

8. What component in the Bosch antilock brake system allows the control module to control the brakes differently on a turn than on a straight road?
   a. A rear wheel-speed sensor
   b. The module relay
   c. The lateral-acceleration switch
   d. The ABS diode

9. All of the following are operated by the Bosch control module *except:*
   a. The pump-motor relay
   b. The module relay
   c. The solenoid-valve relay
   d. The amber antilock warning lamp

10. The Bosch control module receives input signals from all of the following components *except:*
    a. The ignition switch
    b. The module relay
    c. The solenoid-valve relay
    d. The solenoid valves

11. Technician A says that when a wheel is about to lock, the computer first causes the solenoid valve or valves to hold pressure in the wheel cylinder or caliper at the wheel that is about to lock. Technician B says that the first action is to release pressure from the wheel cylinder or caliper at the wheel that is about to lock. Who is right?
    a. A only
    b. B only
    c. Both A and B
    d. Neither A nor B

12. The signal that the computer in an antilock brake system receives from a wheel-speed sensor is:
    a. a steady voltage that becomes smaller as the wheel speed decreases.
    b. a magnetic line of force.
    c. a series of voltage pulses.
    d. a ground.

13. Technician A says that in a Teves antilock brake system, the brakes at the rear wheels are operated by accumulator pressure. Technician B says that the brakes at the rear wheels are controlled by the secondary piston in the master cylinder. Who is right?
    a. A only
    b. B only
    c. Both A and B
    d. Neither A nor B

14. A typical accumulator operating pressure in a Teves antilock brake system is:
    a. 150 psi [1,035 kPa].
    b. 2,400 psi [16,560 kPa].
    c. 3,500 psi [24,150].
    d. 1,500 psi [10,350].

15. When the main valve opens in the Teves hydraulic unit:
    a. brake fluid flows from the internal master-cylinder reservoir and through the main valve to operate the front brakes.
    b. brake fluid flows from the booster pressure chamber and through the main valve to operate the rear brakes.
    c. brake fluid flows from the outlet solenoid valves and through the main valve into the reservoir.
    d. brake fluid flows from the booster pressure chamber and through the main valve into the internal master-cylinder reservoir.

INDEX

GREAT EXPEDITIONS

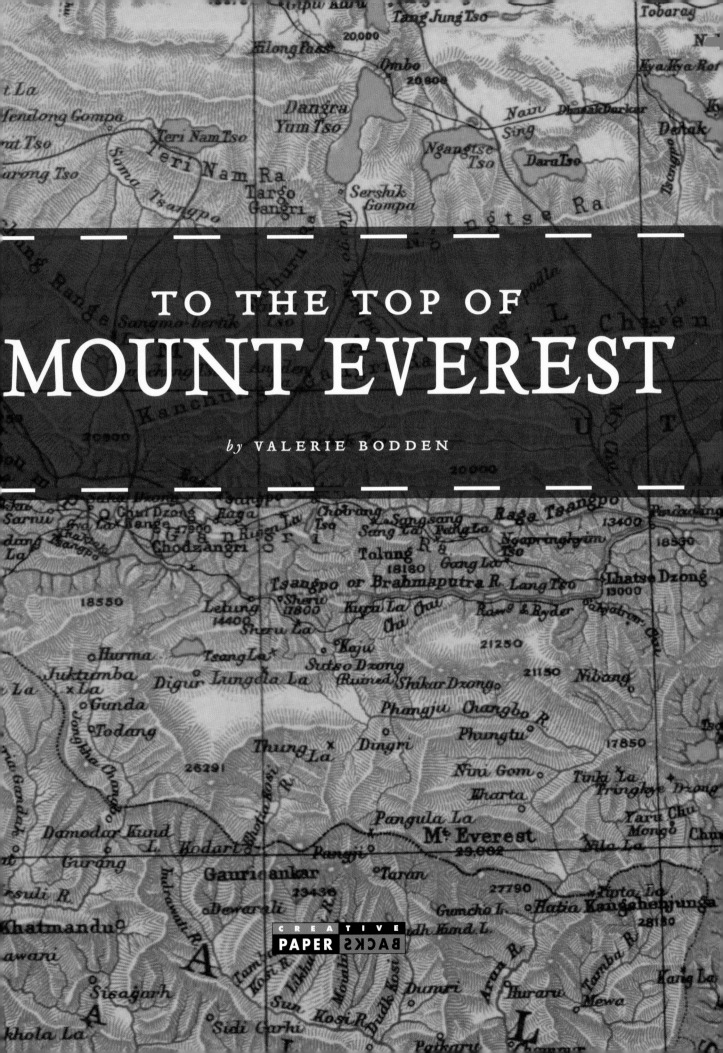

TO THE TOP OF
MOUNT EVEREST

by VALERIE BODDEN

CREATIVE PAPER BACKS

PUBLISHED BY Creative Paperbacks
P.O. Box 227, Mankato, Minnesota 56002
Creative Paperbacks is an imprint of The Creative Company
www.thecreativecompany.us

DESIGN AND PRODUCTION BY Ellen Huber
ART DIRECTION BY Rita Marshall
PRINTED BY Corporate Graphics
in the United States of America

PHOTOGRAPHS BY
Alamy (Royal Geographical Society), Corbis (Association Chantal Mauduit Namaste,
Hulton Deutsch Collection, Galen Rowell, STR/Keystone),
Getty Images (AFP, Express Newspapers, Keystone, Roger Mear, Matt Olson,
Popperfoto, Fred Ramage/Keystone, Three Lions),
The Granger Collection, NYC (Ullstein Bild), iStockphoto (Mike Bentley, Brandon
Laufenberg), Library of Congress, Royal Geographical Society

THE LIBRARY OF CONGRESS HAS CATALOGED THE HARDCOVER EDITION AS FOLLOWS:
Bodden, Valerie.
To the top of Mount Everest / by Valerie Bodden.
p. cm. — (Great expeditions)
Includes bibliographical references and index.
*Summary: A history of Edmund Hillary and Tenzing Norgay's 1953 summit of
Mt. Everest, detailing the challenges encountered, the individuals involved, the discoveries made,
and how the expedition left its mark upon the world.*

ISBN 978-1-60818-070-7 (hardcover)
ISBN 978-0-89812-668-6 (pbk)
1. Hillary, Edmund, 1919–2008—Juvenile literature. 2. Tenzing Norkey,
1914–1986—Juvenile literature. 3. Mountaineers—Everest, Mount
(China and Nepal)—Biography—Juvenile literature.
4. Mountaineering—Everest, Mount (China and Nepal)—History. I. Title.

GV199.92.H54B63 2011
796.5220922—dc22 2010033553
CPSIA: 043012 PO1572

2 4 6 8 9 7 5 3

TABLE OF CONTENTS

CHOMOLUNGMA

For hundreds of years, people have climbed mountains out of necessity, to get from one place to another. But during the 18th century, adventurers in Europe began to scale mountains for sport, and soon peaks around the world were being summited. It was not until the 1920s, however, that mountaineers began to set their sights on the highest mountain in the world: Mount Everest. Located on the border of Nepal and Tibet, this 5.5-mile-high (8.9 km) peak had defeated climbers for more than 30 years before New Zealander Edmund Hillary and Nepalese Sherpa Tenzing Norgay stood on its summit in 1953. The "roof of the world" had finally been reached.

For more than four centuries before Hillary and Tenzing successfully summited Everest, Tenzing's people, the Sherpas, had lived in its foothills. The Sherpas, whose name means "eastern people," had migrated from Tibet to a region of northeastern Nepal known as Solu-Khumbu in the 15th century. Here, at the foot of Everest, a

Trekking through the Himalayas was a common, everyday occurrence for the Nepalese people before the advent of professional climbing.

mountain they called Chomolungma (meaning "mother goddess of the world" or "goddess of the valley" in Tibetan), Sherpas grew potatoes and barley and raised yaks for the animals' milk and hides. Although their crops were planted at altitudes of up to 14,000 feet (4,267 m), and they took their yaks as high as 17,000 feet (5,182 m) to graze, Sherpas did not climb the great peaks of the Himalayas before Europeans arrived. Informed by the most ancient traditions of Tibetan Buddhism, they believed that the mountains were the homes of gods and goddesses. Chomolungma itself was known as the home of the goddess Miyolangsangma, whom the Sherpas believed offered good fortune and wealth.

The 1921 British expedition to Everest was famous climber George Mallory's first attempt at finding a route to the mountain's summit.

The lamas (Buddhist monks, or spiritual leaders) of Solu-Khumbu warned that climbing the mountains would bring bad luck from the gods.

The first people to consider scaling Mount Everest were the British, who SURVEYED India and the Himalayas during the mid-19th century and discovered that, at 29,002 feet (8,840 m), Everest was the highest mountain in the world. (Subsequent measurements have shown that the mountain is even higher—29,035 feet, or 8,850 m.) In 1921, the British mounted their first expedition to Everest, although they could not approach the mountain from Solu-Khumbu, since Nepal was closed to foreigners at the time. Instead, they attempted to find a route up the mountain from Tibet, to the north, which had granted

EXPEDITION JOURNAL

Edmund Hillary
April 26, 1953

After a couple of hours Tenzing and I departed [Camp IV] for Base Camp. We reached Camp III in one hour.... We descended to Camp II in 33 minutes on a perfect track. We met George Lowe with a team of porters at II and had a pleasant yarn.... Tenzing and I left Camp II with a great rush which was suddenly checked when under the weight of a hearty jump from me a large ice block sheared off and descended with me down a crevasse. Only lively work with my flailing CRAMPONS *and a fortunately quick rope from Tenzing stopped an unfortunate experience. We continued to Base in 55 minutes. Tenzing is an admirable companion—fit, energetic, capable and with excellent rope technique.*

them permission to climb. As they worked on scaling the north side, the climbers came to a high pass from which they were able to look down on the southern, or Nepalese, side of the mountain. What they saw—towering blocks of ice, yawning abysses, and steep slopes—led them to declare that Everest was impassable from that direction.

The 1921 British expedition marked the first time that Sherpas climbed Mount Everest for pay. Since the early 1900s, Sherpas had been working as porters, carrying loads in and out of the mountains for British expeditions in the region, and many had moved to Darjeeling, India, the departure point for Himalayan expeditions. This expedition to Everest—like all those to come—required porters to carry supplies and equipment to the remote mountain. Having lived in the Himalayas all their lives, Sherpas were well-adapted to carry out such demanding work.

The yak is a large, wild ox native to high-altitude Tibet that is often used for transporting heavy items up and down the mountainsides.

The goal of the 1921 British expedition was not to summit Everest but to explore potential routes to the peak. The next year, another British expedition set out for the mountain, this time with the goal of reaching the top. Although it did not succeed, two members of the party made it to 27,300 feet (8,321 m), higher than anyone had ever ascended on any mountain on Earth. The 1922 expedition also saw the first deaths on Everest, as seven Sherpas were killed in an avalanche. Tragedy marked the next British expedition, in 1924, as well, when climbers George Mallory and Andrew Irvine disappeared near the summit. (Mallory's body would not be found until 1999.) Before their disappearance, fellow climber Edward Norton had reached a record altitude of 28,100 feet (8,565 m), less than 1,000 feet (305 m) from the summit. During the 1930s, four more British groups made attempts on Everest, but none of them managed to surpass Norton's record.

With the onset of World War II in 1939, attempts to summit Everest were put on hold, and there were no expeditions for the next 10 years. By the time mountaineers were ready to return to Everest, Tibet had been taken over by China and its borders closed to WESTERNERS. At the same time, a revolution in Nepal had opened that country to foreigners again. As a result, anyone wanting to scale Everest now had to do so from the south. In 1950, a small party of British and American climbers traveled to Nepal to evaluate the possibility of finding a southern route up the mountainside. What they saw led them to agree

Mountaineers who attempted Everest in the early 1900s were often familiar with other tall peaks, such as France's Aiguille Verte.

1953 Everest Expedition Profile: Edmund Hillary

Edmund Hillary was born in Auckland, New Zealand, on July 20, 1919, and grew up in the small town of Tuakau. He got his first taste of the mountains at age 16 during a trip to New Zealand's Mount Ruapehu. After two years studying math and science at the University of Auckland, Hillary dropped out to join his father's beekeeping business. In 1950, he traveled to the European Alps, and in 1951, he made his first trip to the Himalayas. After summiting Mount Everest, Hillary made expeditions to other Himalayan mountains, as well as to Antarctica and the North Pole. In 1960, he founded the Himalayan Trust to help improve the lives of Sherpas in Nepal, and he continued to work with the trust until his death in January 2008.

with the findings of the 1921 expedition: it was likely impossible to ascend this side of Everest.

Undeterred, the British sent a RECONNAISSANCE mission to Everest in 1951. This time, an energetic New Zealander named Edmund Hillary joined the expedition. Peering at Everest from the slopes of a nearby mountain, Hillary and expedition leader Eric Shipton were able to pick out a potential route to the top. The expedition eventually managed to scale Everest's first obstacle, a region of precariously balanced ice blocks and deep chasms known as the Khumbu Icefall. The team was confident that the next year it would reach the summit.

Eric Shipton, a veteran of the 1930s Everest expeditions (pictured opposite), was chosen to lead the 1951 trek but was passed over in 1953.

The expedition was not to have a chance, however. Although only the British had been granted access to Everest up to that point, in 1952, Nepal gave Switzerland permission to mount the only two expeditions of the year. Tenzing Norgay (who had been a porter for three of the British attempts during the 1930s) accompanied both Swiss expeditions. On the first, he and Swiss climber Raymond Lambert reached about 28,000 feet (8,534 m) before turning back. On the second expedition, faced with fierce winds and deadly cold, they didn't make it even that far. That meant there was still a chance for the British to be the first to summit the mountain. As a new team headed to Everest in the spring of 1953, their odds looked better than ever, as joining the expedition were two Everest veterans—Hillary and Tenzing.

To Base Camp

LIKE ALL PREVIOUS BRITISH EXPEDITIONS TO EVEREST, THE 1953 EXPEDITION WAS SPONSORED BY THE HIMALAYAN COMMITTEE (FORMERLY KNOWN AS THE EVEREST COMMITTEE), A JOINT VENTURE OF GREAT BRITAIN'S ROYAL GEOGRAPHICAL SOCIETY AND ALPINE CLUB. IN SEPTEMBER 1952, THE COMMITTEE INVITED 42-YEAR-OLD JOHN HUNT, A COLONEL IN THE

British army, to lead the expedition. Although Hunt had never been on Everest, he had taken part in previous expeditions in other parts of the Himalayas. He accepted the invitation and quickly set about selecting expedition members. He wanted men between the ages of 25 and 40 who were strong and had experience climbing snow and ice.

Edmund Hillary, then 33 years old, fit the requirements exactly, as he was known to be a strong climber with a wealth of experience on the snow- and ice-covered mountains of New Zealand. He had also scaled a number of Himalayan peaks, in addition to taking part in the 1951 reconnaissance mission to Everest. Fellow

Cameraman Tom Stobart's inclusion in the 1953 expedition proved to be invaluable, as he was able to capture much of the action on film.

New Zealander George Lowe was also invited to join the expedition. Other team members included British climbers Charles Evans, Tom Bourdillon, Alfred Gregory, Michael Ward, Charles Wylie, George Band, Michael Westmacott, and Wilfrid Noyce, along with cameraman Tom Stobart, physiologist Griffith Pugh, and reporter James Morris.

Joining the group as sirdar, or leader of the Sherpa porters, would be Tenzing, on his seventh expedition to the mountain. (In addition to joining the British and Swiss expeditions, he had also led an illegal attempt by Canadian-born Earl Denman in 1947.) Unlike most Sherpas, Tenzing climbed not only for money

Michael Westmacott (left) first experimented with the use of oxygen systems while climbing in Great Britain and the Alps.

but also for the joy of climbing, and he was determined to finally get to the top of Everest. As sirdar, Tenzing hired hundreds of porters to carry supplies to the lower slopes, along with 20 climbing Sherpas to help transport equipment to camps higher up the mountain.

With the team selected, each member's thoughts turned to how he would survive in Everest's extreme conditions. Because the mountain is the highest in the world, one of the biggest factors affecting the expedition's performance would be the altitude. Differences in AIR PRESSURE make the air "thinner," or less dense, at high altitudes than it is at sea level. Although all air on Earth is made up of 21 percent oxygen, in thinner air, the oxygen MOLECULES are more spread out, so a person breathes in less oxygen with each breath. This creates a condition in the body known as hypoxia, or oxygen deprivation. If climbers increase their altitude slowly, their bodies can usually adjust, or acclimatize, to the altitude, but insufficient acclimatization can lead to headaches, nausea, fatigue, shortness of breath, or life-threatening CEREBRAL EDEMA. Even with a proper acclimatization period, the body never fully adjusts to altitudes above about 21,000 feet (6,400 m)—still a mile and a half (2.4 km) below Everest's summit—making even the act of putting one foot in front of the other a strenuous task. The thin air also affects the brain's ability to think clearly.

EXPEDITION JOURNAL

Tenzing Norgay
May 29, 1953 (from his 1955 autobiography Tiger of the Snows)

Many times I think of that morning at Camp Nine. We have spent the night there, Hillary and I, in our little tent at almost 28,000 feet, which is the highest that men have ever slept. It has been a cold night. Hillary's boots are frozen, and we are almost frozen too. But now in the gray light, when we creep from the tent, there is almost no wind. The sky is clear and still. And that is good. We look up. For weeks, for months, that is all we have done. Look up. And there it is—the top of Everest. Only it is different now: so near, so close, only a little more than a thousand feet above us. It is no longer just a dream, a high dream in the sky, but a real and solid thing, a thing of rock and snow, that men can climb. We make ready. We will climb it.

In order to help them deal with the extremely high altitudes they would be facing on Everest, the members of the expedition would use supplementary oxygen—carried in tanks on their backs—when scaling the highest mountain slopes. Although the oxygen wouldn't completely eliminate the effects of altitude, it would allow the climbers to work more efficiently, think more clearly, and even stay warmer. For the 1953 expedition, three types of oxygen systems were ordered: open-circuit (in which oxygen is blown across the face to supplement the surrounding air), closed-circuit (in which pure oxygen is breathed through a mask), and sleeping sets (worn at night to help climbers get more rest).

Expedition members had to wear many articles of protective clothing, in addition to regular climbing gear and oxygen support.

Along with a lack of oxygen, the expedition would face frigid weather conditions on Everest's high slopes, where temperatures regularly plunge well below 0 °F (-17.8 °C), and winds often blow at more than 100 miles (161 km) per hour year round. Clothing for such conditions included wool underclothing, shirts, and sweaters; down pants and jackets; and an outer, windproof covering, along with three pairs of gloves and lightweight, well-insulated boots. The expedition members' tents were made of wind-resistant material, and their double-layer sleeping bags were filled with down.

Climbing gear such as crampons, ropes, and ice hammers and axes would help the climbers get up the mountainside, and radios would allow them to monitor weather reports. Food for the expedition included biscuits, jam, cheese, soup, cocoa, and lemonade powder, as well as a few "luxury" items, such as tinned fruit and meat. Portable stoves were taken to heat the food and to melt snow for water.

By March 1953, the expedition's 18 tons (16.3 t) of gear and food had been sent to Kathmandu, Nepal's capital city, where the climbers gathered to begin their journey. After sorting through the equipment and piling it onto the backs of the 350 porters, the expedition set out on March 10 for the base of Mount Everest, nearly 200 miles (322 km) away. For 17 days, they traveled through the high ridges and deep valleys of northern Nepal, following rocky paths over mountain passes, crossing raging rivers on rickety hanging bridges, and trekking through forests of tall trees, fragrant flowers, and colorful birds.

On March 25, the expedition arrived in Namche Bazar, the largest Sherpa village, and then proceeded on to Tengboche Monastery. Located at an elevation of 12,700 feet (3,871 m), Tengboche offered an amazing view of Everest. Although the mountain's lower slopes were hidden by the neighboring peaks of Nuptse and Lhotse, its summit towered above all the other mountains. A plume of windblown snow could be seen unfurling from its highest reaches.

The expedition set up a temporary base at Tengboche, and the party spent the next three weeks climbing to around 20,000 feet (6,096 m) on several of the region's lower peaks in order to practice with the equipment and acclimatize before going higher. In early April, Hunt asked Hillary, Lowe, Band, and Westmacott to forge ahead and establish Camp I, or Base Camp, on the Khumbu GLACIER at the bottom of Everest. The group ascended to 17,900 feet (5,456 m) and set up camp on a relatively flat area of rock and ice. Then they prepared for the real work ahead.

1953 EVEREST EXPEDITION PROFILE:
TENZING NORGAY

Born in May 1914, Tenzing Norgay was the 11th of 13 children.
He grew up in the Sherpa village of Thami in the Khumbu
region of Nepal. There was no school in Khumbu, so Tenzing
spent his time helping his father tend their yaks. In 1932, at
the age of 18, he moved to Darjeeling, India, where he became
a porter for Himalayan expeditions. He took part in his first
Everest expedition in 1935 and embarked on five more trips
up the mountain before successfully reaching the summit in
1953. In 1954, Tenzing joined the newly established Himalayan
Mountaineering Institute, where he worked as director of field
training until 1976. Afterward, he became a guide for trekking
expeditions in Nepal and nearby countries. Tenzing died in 1986.

To the east of
Mount Everest
is the fifth-highest
peak in the world
(at 27,766 feet,
or 8,463 m),
Mount Makalu,
which was first
ascended in 1955.

UP THE MOUNTAIN

Because a mountain as large as Everest couldn't be climbed in a single day, the plan for reaching the summit was to set up a series of eight camps at progressively higher altitudes, with a final, ninth camp close enough to the summit that the remaining distance could be covered in a day. Hunt arranged the schedule so that the expedition members would take turns with the hardest work, such as establishing new routes. That way, while some worked on the mountain and slept at the higher camps, the others could carry supplies between camps and spend at least some evenings at the lower camps to keep their bodies in better shape.

It fell to Hillary, along with Westmacott, Band, and Sherpa Ang Namgyal, to forge a route up the Khumbu Icefall. Though Hillary had previously scaled the icefall in 1951, he found it much changed. Huge ice towers had tumbled and shifted, and new crevasses, or cracks, had opened in the ice. Although Hillary thought the icefall looked almost impassable, he

The success of the expedition can be credited in large part to the Sherpas who worked tirelessly to transport all the necessary supplies.

and his team managed to establish a route through it in five days, cutting steps into the ice and fastening ropes to aid climbing in the most difficult areas. Camp II was installed halfway up the icefall, and Camp III was established at its top.

Above the icefall, the climbers bolted together 3 aluminum ladders, each 6 feet (1.8 m) long, to serve as a makeshift bridge across a 16-foot-wide (5 m) crevasse. On the other side of the crevasse was a valley known as the Western Cwm (*KOOM*). Sweating in the intense sunlight reflected off the Cwm's glacier, the members of the expedition wound their way through hidden crevasses. Here, Hillary and Tenzing roped together for the first time (the rope ensured that if one man fell, the other would catch him) and discovered that they made a good team.

In the middle of the Western Cwm, the climbers set up Camp IV, or Advance Base Camp, from which further work on the mountain would be carried out. The next section of the route, leading up the steep, icy face of Lhotse, was forged by Lowe, Westmacott, and Band, along with Sherpas Ang Nyima and Annullu. The hard work of cutting steps into sheer ice at such altitudes was complicated by bad weather, and it was more than a week before the route was completed. Finally, the team reached the top of the Lhotse face and descended slightly onto the South Col, a large plateau—or high, flat plain—separating the peaks of Lhotse and Everest. At 26,000 feet (7,925 m), the South Col's icy, rock-strewn surface was almost constantly pummeled by hurricane-force winds. On this barren plain, Camp VIII was established (camps V, VI, and VII having been set up on the Lhotse face). More than 700 pounds (318 kg) of gear had to be hauled to this high camp by the climbers and 17 Sherpas.

By May 26, everything was ready for the first summit attempt. Earlier, Hunt had announced that Bourdillon and Evans would make up the first summit team, with the goal of reaching the South Summit (about 300 feet, or 91 m, below the true summit). They would be followed by Hillary and Tenzing, the strongest, most acclimatized members of the group, who would try to reach the top. On the 26th, Bourdillon and Evans set out from the South Col for the South Summit, using the still-experimental closed-circuit oxygen system. That same day, Hillary and Tenzing ascended to the South Col, where they greeted an exhausted—but successful—Bourdillon and Evans.

EXPEDITION JOURNAL

Edmund Hillary
May 29, 1953

I really felt now that we were going to get to the top and that nothing would stop us. I kept frequent watch on our oxygen consumption and was encouraged to find it at a steady rate. I continued on, cutting steadily and surmounting bump after bump and CORNICE *after cornice looking eagerly for the summit. It seemed impossible to pick it and time was running out. Finally I cut around the back of an extra large hump and then on a tight rope from Tenzing I climbed up a gentle snow ridge to its top. Immediately it was obvious that we had reached our objective. It was 11:30 A.M. and we were on top of Everest!*

Now it was Hillary and Tenzing's turn. On May 27, high winds and drifting snow pinned them to the camp on the South Col, but the next day they were ready to begin their summit assault. At 7:30 A.M., they met with Gregory, Lowe, and Ang Nyima, the support team that would help them carry gear to a final camp below the South Summit. All five climbers were using open-circuit oxygen and carrying loads of 40 to 50 pounds (18–23 kg), which would increase to 60 pounds (27 kg) after they picked up additional supplies that had been dropped for them by Bourdillon and Evans's team. The support team set off first, breaking a trail in order to allow the summit pair to conserve their energy for the final push. About an hour later, Hillary and Tenzing followed, climbing almost straight up to the southeast ridge of the mountain more than 1,000 feet (305 m) above the South Col. Here, they caught up with their support team, and the five men mounted the narrow snow- and rock-covered ridge together, with steep slopes plunging down on either side of them.

Before setting off from Advance Base Camp, Hillary and Tenzing double-checked each other's oxygen equipment.

At 27,900 feet (8,504 m), they decided to set up Camp IX on a small ledge. As the support team headed back down the mountain, Hillary and Tenzing carved out two small shelves—each only six and a half feet (2 m) long and three feet (1 m) wide—across which they set up their tent. Finally, after laboring for several hours, they crawled into the tent and ate chicken noodle soup, tinned apricots, sardines, biscuits, and dates. They also drank plenty of hot lemonade-flavored water and coffee to keep from becoming dehydrated. Then Tenzing lay on the bottom ledge of the tent, almost hanging out over the sheer rock face below, while Hillary scrunched himself onto the top ledge. For two

Although Hillary and Tenzing had not met prior to the 1953 expedition, they quickly formed a bond built on mutual respect.

separate two-hour periods, they used the sleeping sets of oxygen, which allowed them to sleep for at least a little while; the rest of the time they were cold and miserable in the -17 °F (-27 °C) tent.

Finally, dawn broke. At 4:00 A.M., the two men peered outside to see that weather conditions were perfect for climbing. After drinking some more lemonade water and eating a few biscuits, they put on every piece of clothing they had with them and thawed Hillary's boots (which had frozen during the night) over the cooking stove. By 6:30 A.M., they had strapped their crampons to their boots and their oxygen tanks to their backs and were ready to set out for the summit.

1953 Everest Expedition Profile: John Hunt

Born on June 22, 1910, in India (then part of the BRITISH EMPIRE), John Hunt began climbing mountains at the age of 15. During the 1930s, he served with the British army in India and took part in expeditions to the Himalayas. During World War II (1939–45), Hunt served in Egypt, Italy, and Greece and also taught classes in mountain and snow warfare. After being knighted for his leadership of the 1953 British expedition to Mount Everest, Hunt returned to the army, serving until 1956. From 1963 to 1966, he served as head of the University of Aberdeen in Scotland, before becoming chairman of the Parole Board for England and Wales. Hunt also continued climbing after the Everest expedition, taking part in several expeditions around the world, including others in the Himalayas. He died in 1998.

ON TOP OF THE WORLD

FROM CAMP IX, HILLARY AND TENZING BEGAN TO WORK THEIR WAY UP THE STEEP, NARROW RIDGE TOWARD THE SOUTH SUMMIT. TAKING TURNS LEADING, HILLARY AND TENZING STRUGGLED UPWARD THROUGH "BREAKABLE CRUST"—A THIN CRUST OF SNOW THAT SUPPORTED THEIR WEIGHT FOR ONLY A FEW SECONDS BEFORE SENDING THEM STAGGERING

into the powdery snow beneath. As they neared the South Summit, 800 feet (244 m) above Camp IX, the ridge widened but became steeper, requiring Hillary and Tenzing to climb almost vertically. The slope's loose snow often sent them sliding dangerously backwards. At 9:00 A.M., they reached the top of this slope and stepped with relief onto the South Summit.

After only 10 minutes, they set out again. To their left was a sheer rock precipice dropping 8,000 feet (2,438 m) into the Western Cwm, while on the right, snow cornices overhung a 10,000-foot (3,048 m) drop to the Kangshung Glacier. While one person climbed, the other

Carrying packs that weighed about 30 pounds (13.6 kg), Tenzing and Hillary were ready to begin the last stage of the climb on May 29.

wrapped the rope that joined them together around his ice ax, which he dug into the snow to serve as an anchor in case the climber slipped. About halfway between the South Summit and the true summit, Hillary and Tenzing came to a 40-foot-high (12 m) rock. Rather than climbing straight up the rock, which would have been nearly impossible at such an altitude, Hillary wedged himself into a crack between the rock and an overhanging ice cornice. Then he wiggled and JAMMED his way to the top, grabbing the rock with his hands and stabbing his crampons into the ice behind him. Tenzing followed Hillary up what is now known as the Hillary Step. Beyond the rock, the pair scaled a series of snowy humps, and finally, just as both were wondering if they would ever reach the top, they looked up to see open sky ahead of them.

At 11:30 A.M., Hillary and Tenzing stepped onto the snowy, dome-shaped summit of Mount Everest. Hillary turned to shake hands with Tenzing, who threw his arms around his partner in an exuberant hug. Then Hillary took off his oxygen mask, proving that human beings could survive at such altitudes without supplementary oxygen (no one had known if this was possible before). As sharp ice crystals borne on the wind stung his face, Hillary pulled out his camera and took a snapshot of Tenzing standing on the summit and holding up his ice ax, with the flags

Since Hillary was the only one of the pair familiar with working a camera, he photographed Tenzing standing atop the mountain.

EXPEDITION JOURNAL

George Lowe
letter home, May 31, 1953

Don't imagine our band of thirteen rolling and rollicking in an ecstasy brought on by victory. If you were at Base Camp now you would see nine sahibs [the Sherpa word for foreign members of an expedition] and about fifteen Sherpas lying listlessly around the tents with bloodshot and glazed eyes, thin, dirty and bewildered. Ed [Hillary] is now sleeping as he has done for hours and hours. Charles [Evans] is just smoking and tired; the talk is very desultory and dull; everyone is quite played out.... Two days ago we were on the South Col urging ourselves to the very limit—and now like pricked balloons all our reserves are gone.

NEWS CHRONICLE

No. 33,381   TUESDAY, JUNE 2, 1953   PRICE 1½d.

T
QUE
DR
TO
Back

THE CROWNING GLORY: EVEREST IS CLIMBED

Tremendous news for the Queen

HILLARY DOES IT

GLORIOUS Coronation Day news! Everest—Everest the unconquerable—has been conquered. And conquered by men of British blood and breed.

The news came late last night that Edmund Hillary and the Sherpa guide, Tensing, of Colonel Hunt's expedition had climbed to the summit of Earth's highest peak, 29,002 feet high.

Queen Elizabeth the Second, resting on the eve of her crowning, was immediately told that this brightest jewel of courage and endurance had been added to the Crown of British endeavour. It is understood that a message of royal congratulation was sent to the climbers.

Announcers broke into U.S. radio and television programmes last night to relay the news.

Hillary, a 34-year-old New Zealander, and Bhotia Tensing, 38-year-old leader of the Sherpa guides and bearers, are said to have made the final 1,000-foot ascent from Camp Eight on the upper slopes.

The feat was apparently accomplished on Monday.

A year ago Bhotia Tensing climbed to within 800 feet of the summit with Raymond Lambert of the unsuccessful Swiss expedition.

NEWS BY RUNNER

The latest news of the progress of the expedition hitherto—despatched by runner and received in London yesterday—was that the climbers were ready, as soon as the weather was suitable, to set out from Camp Seven, established high on the South Col at about 26,000 feet, to pitch Camp Eight high up near the summit.

David Weller, below, describes how the conquest is likely to have been accomplished.

The two figures are in wind-proof smocks of different colours, double-lined with nylon, and each wears two hoods beneath the visors the eyes peer out on the roof of the world from goggles greased against frosting.

Down in the night ties Tibet and to the left Nepal, while death in a variety of forms, none pleasant, lurks on every side.

At such a height no man can survive without extra oxygen, involving 28lb. of dead weight, where every ounce can count. In the endurance-time of this oxygen, carried on the back to the summit, is estimated at five hours.

Hands are cased in three sets of gloves : outer gauntlets of windproof cotton enclose mittens made of down. Next to

The new Elizabethan

EDMUND HILLARY, whose conquest of Everest sets the seal on the new Elizabethan age, is a 34-year-old bee farmer from New Zealand.

He learned his mountaineering in the Alps of the little Dominion and was a pioneer in introducing winter ski-ing there.

Hillary's rugged independence made him one of this expedition's most valuable members long before the final assault.

He and George Lowe, the other New Zealander of the party, were making a free-lance climb in the Himalayas when Eric Shipton—look, see expedition arrived in 1951 to choose a route up Everest.

Hillary and Lowe dropped their own project and trailed halfway across the vast range to join them. Shipton was so impressed by their performance that he gave them their places in the Coronation year attempt.

Shipton said last night : This is splendid. Once the South Col camp was established it seemed there was nothing to stop them, and I have been waiting for the good news.

SMILING, mountain - wise Bhotia Tensing, is the leader of the Sherpa guides and porters who accompanied the expedition.

He is 38 and a veteran of four previous attempts on Everest by the northern route. His Sherpa comrades call him the Tiger.

On May 28 last year Tensing climbed to 28,215 feet with Raymond Lambert of the unsuccessful Swiss expedition before the failure of their

Prophet Vicky

Here the forecast is rain—hail—sun—storm, BUT the crowds are singing in the rain SO—

WHO CARES NOW IF IT SNOWS?

CORONATION DAY FORECAST : Northerly winds, sunny spells, showers with hail and thunder, cold. Mid-day temperature 55 deg.

NEWS CHRONICLE REPORTERS

REPEATED heavy showers lashed the packed campers lining the Royal Way last night—and the temperature dropped 13 degrees in a few hours.

Yet the drenched campers refused to quit for fear of losing their places—and moment by moment the throng grew as 18,000 cars an hour converged on London. And the trains had yet to come. . . .

Thousands of cheering people surrounded the Queen Mother and Princess Margaret as they drove from Buckingham Palace after spending two hours with the Queen in her private apartments—a last visit before the Coronation.

Reinforced police could not clear a way : the car was halted for 15 minutes beside the Victoria Memorial.

The Queen Mother, in a white feathered gown and off-the-face white hat, and Princess Margaret, in a low-cut smoke-blue gown, waved. Motor-cycle police came to the rescue. But a little later more crowds ran from their pitches and blocked the route to Clarence House.

DAMP DANCES IN THE MALL

The Mall looked like a gigantic refugee camp. Over 30,000 people were bedding down along the pavements. Twenty-thousand more were trying to find places.

Thousands sat in puddles of water hanging out their clothes.

Camping up to 12-deep on either side after squatting there all day they were thoroughly soaked by the intermittent storms. But not one gave up his pitch.

Of all ages, from toddlers to over-70s, they sheltered as best they could, some under improvised tents of tarpaulin slung between the trees.

Groups were singing, others dancing in impromptu fancy dress. Quieter parties listened to portable radios or played cards. A chain of motl,e cafes issued tea, coffee and buns.

It was the same among the 6,000-7,000 camped out along Whitehall.

They seemed to have thought of everything. If the sun shines today—well, some had brought parasols. If it gets very cold ! There were thick blankets and heavy coats.

400 watch sea rescue

Watched by her 400 passengers, three brothers were taken aboard the Isle of Man steamer Snaefell from their crippled sailing boat, in a storm eight miles off the island yesterday.

The brothers, Christopher, Frank and Ian Whipp, of Rochdale, had ridden the storm, which dismasted their sloop, for 10 hours.

After the brothers had been taken aboard the steamer the heavy seas claimed Douglas lifeboat took the sloop in tow.

TENT TOWN

But it was raining a slow, miserable, penetrating drizzle. And from Trafalgar Square to Parliament Square the kerbs were lined with people huddled under tarpaulins, blankets, newspapers, umbrellas—some

---

map: EVEREST 29,002 ft., LHOTSE 27,890 ft., NORTH COL, ICE FALL

Stabbed girl dead in Thames

A MURDERED girl was found in the Thames yesterday and last night the police feared her girl companion had been killed too.

The girl in the river was 18-year-old Barbara Songhurst, a chemist's assistant, of Princes Road, Teddington. She was stabbed three times in the back after being assaulted on Lovers Towpath at Ham, Surrey.

On Sunday Barbara went cycling with her friend, 18-year-old Christina Reed, of Roy Crescent, Hampton Hill.

See Page Five

Flash crick

Lightning struck two workers dead at a match factory through the roof of a soap factory infam, near Mal-...

The men Jack Taylor, 44, Henry 37, and George Stokes, 32, of Cadishead.

CENTRAL WEATHER

short sunny in, temp. 50-55. R a.m.-0.04 a.m., sets 8.10 o. p.m.-3.64 p.m. in water at 1. a.m.-5.5 ...

Weather ma...

---

advertisement

"A SMITHS CLOCK my dear, is the *Unforgettable Gift for Coronation Year"*

Here is indeed a gift that will be a constan... for years and years to come with this 'out... period in our history. Whether it is fo... wedding or a birthday, or a reminder fro... 'back home' that British Craftsmanship i... the best... give Smiths Clocks in Coronat...

Sold in a great variety of beautiful design... by leading Jewellers everywhere...

of the United Nations, India, Nepal, and Britain streaming from its handle. Then Hillary snapped pictures of the view from the top. To the north was the dry plateau of Tibet, while to the east, the men could look down on the peaks of other Himalayan giants such as Makalu, Kanchenjunga, and Lhotse. Digging a hole in the snow of the summit, Tenzing left a small bag of sweets for the gods he believed lived on the mountain, while Hillary left a crucifix Hunt had given to him. By 11:45, the two were ready to tackle the long descent.

The achievement of reaching the top of the world was viewed as a triumph for the entire nation of Britain and its new queen, Elizabeth II.

Hillary and Tenzing began to make their way carefully down the narrow summit ridge. Following the tracks they had made on the way up, they found the journey down much easier, and by 2:00 P.M. they had arrived back at Camp IX. They rested there briefly before heading back to the South Col, where they spent the night with their support team. The next day, they continued down the mountain to rejoin the rest of the party, who had already descended to Advance Base Camp. When the other members of the expedition realized that Hillary and Tenzing had been successful, they ran out to greet the pair with hugs and congratulatory slaps on the back. Within a few hours, James Morris, the expedition's special correspondent from *The Times* of London, was on his way to communicate the news to the world. Hillary, who had been sure the achievement would interest only mountaineers, was stunned to turn on the radio at Base Camp a couple of days later and hear announcers on the British Broadcasting Corporation (BBC) network declare that Everest had at last been summited.

After nearly two months on the mountain, the expedition members descended to Tengboche, where they enjoyed the "thick" air and rested before the journey back to Kathmandu. When they finally arrived in the Nepalese capital in mid-June, they were astounded by the huge crowds waiting to greet them. Hillary and Tenzing were also shocked that most people wanted to know who had stepped on the summit first. The thought had never occurred to any of the other climbers, who thought of the two men as a team. Hillary and Tenzing agreed to say that they had reached the summit "almost together." (In his 1955 autobiography, Tenzing decided to put an end to the question: Hillary had stepped on the summit a few feet ahead of him.) From Kathmandu, the

In early July 1953, Hillary, Hunt, and Tenzing held a press conference at the Royal Geographical Society's head-quarters to explain the ascent.

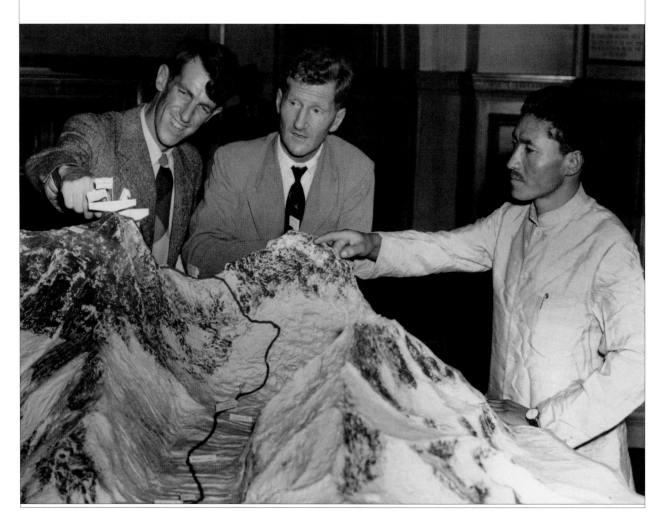

1953 EVEREST EXPEDITION PROFILE: TOM BOURDILLON

Tom Bourdillon, who was born in London on March 16, 1924, served as president of the Oxford University Mountaineering Club (which was founded, in part, by his father) while studying physics at the school. During World War II, he served in Greece and Egypt, and afterward he worked on rocket design for the British government. Bourdillon took part in the 1951 British reconnaissance expedition to Mount Everest and a 1952 expedition to the peak of Cho Oyu in the Himalayas. Together with his father, Dr. Robert Bourdillon, he designed the closed-circuit oxygen system that he and Evans used on their climb to the South Summit during the 1953 expedition. Three years later, on July 29, 1956, Bourdillon was killed in a climbing accident on the Jägihorn, a 10,518-foot (3,206 m) peak in Switzerland.

expedition members traveled to India and then to London, where they were greeted as heroes and honored at formal receptions. They met Queen Elizabeth II, who knighted Hillary and Hunt and presented Tenzing with the George Medal, Britain's highest civilian award for bravery.

In the years after their successful ascent of the world's highest peak, both Hillary and Tenzing returned to the Himalayas, though neither ever again climbed Everest. Tenzing served as a director at the Himalayan Mountaineering Institute in Darjeeling,

Famous French climber Chantal Mauduit attempted Everest in 1993 without the use of oxygen but with modern aids such as fixed ladders.

India, while Hillary set up the Himalayan Trust to build schools and hospitals for the Sherpas of Nepal, whom he visited often. The Sherpa porters had worried that once Everest had been summited there would be no work for them, but they found themselves busier than ever, as people from around the world traveled to Nepal to make their own attempts on the huge peak.

Today, hundreds of people try to scale Everest every year, and as of 2010, about 3,000 climbers had reached the summit (many more than once), most of them aided by the fixed ropes and ladders that now line much of the route up the southern side of the mountain. With up to 75 people working their way to the peak in a single day, it can be hard to remember that Mount Everest's summit was once untrodden—and that two men were responsible for opening Chomolungma to the world.

TIMELINE

1914 — Tenzing Norgay is born in May to a Sherpa family from the Nepalese village of Thami.

1919 — Edmund Hillary is born in Auckland, New Zealand, on July 20.

1921 — The British mount the first-ever expedition to Mount Everest, exploring the mountain from the north side.

1922 — The second British Everest expedition reaches an altitude of 27,300 feet (8,321 m) on May 23, and seven Sherpas later die in an avalanche.

1924 — On June 8, George Mallory and Andrew Irvine disappear near the summit during the third British Everest expedition.

1933 — The fourth British expedition to Everest fails to climb much higher than the 1922 expedition.

1935 — In July, Tenzing Norgay joins the fifth British expedition to Everest as a porter.

1936 — In May, the sixth British expedition, again with Tenzing as porter, is forced off Everest by bad weather.

1938 — During the seventh British expedition, Tenzing and other members are caught in an avalanche but survive.

1947 — Tenzing leads Canadian-born Briton Earl Denman on an illegal attempt to climb Everest from the north.

1948 — On January 30, Hillary makes the first-ever successful ascent of the south ridge of Mount Cook in New Zealand.

1950 — A British-American expedition becomes the first to approach Everest from the south, through Nepal.

1951 — In May, Hillary makes his first trip to the Himalayas.

1951 — In September, Hillary joins the British reconnaissance mission to Everest, which spots a potential route up the mountain.

1952 — On May 28, Tenzing and Swiss climber Raymond Lambert reach about 28,000 feet (8,534 m) on Everest.

1952 — Hillary takes part in a training mission to the Himalayas in May and June, scaling several new peaks.

1952 — On September 11, John Hunt is invited to lead the 1953 British expedition to Everest.

1953 — The British expedition, along with hundreds of porters, begins the trek from Kathmandu to Everest on March 10.

1953 — Hillary and Tenzing rope together for the first time on April 26.

1953 — On May 14, most expedition members move to Advance Base Camp on the Western Cwm.

1953 — Charles Evans and Tom Bourdillon reach the South Summit of Everest, at 28,700 feet (8,748 m) on May 26.

1953 — At 11:30 A.M. on May 29, Hillary and Tenzing reach Everest's summit, at 29,035 feet (8,850 m).

ENDNOTES

AIR PRESSURE: downward pressure caused by the weight of the atmosphere, or air; at lower altitudes, the layer of air above is thicker, so air pressure is greater there than it is at higher altitudes

ALPINE CLUB: the first-ever club for mountaineers, founded in 1857 in London to promote the development of the sport and organize mountain-climbing expeditions

BRITISH EMPIRE: a group of colonies and territories around the world controlled by Great Britain from the late 1500s to the mid-1900s

BUDDHISM: an Asian religion based on the teachings of the Buddha, who held that by denying worldly desires, one could reach a state of enlightenment called nirvana

CEREBRAL EDEMA: a condition in which excessive fluid in the brain causes swelling, resulting in trouble walking and hallucinations; it can sometimes lead to death, if the victim is not immediately moved to a lower altitude

CORNICES: overhanging masses of snow or ice, often formed by the wind on mountain ridges

CRAMPONS: metal spikes fastened onto climbing boots to provide grip on ice and snow

GLACIER: a large, slow-moving mass of ice and snow that forms in mountains and in regions where more snow falls than can melt each year

JAMMED: climbed by wedging one's hands, feet, arms, and legs into any available cracks

MOLECULES: the smallest units of a substance that retain the characteristics of that substance

RECONNAISSANCE: a preliminary investigation or exploration to obtain information

ROYAL GEOGRAPHICAL SOCIETY: an organization founded in 1830 in London to support geographical research, education, and expeditions

SURVEYED: made measurements of a land area for the purposes of making a detailed map

WESTERNERS: people from the western part of the world, particularly Europe and North America

SELECTED BIBLIOGRAPHY

Clark, Liesl. *Everest: 50 Years on the Mountain*. DVD. Washington, D.C.: National Geographic Television & Film, 2003.

Coburn, Broughton. *Everest: Mountain Without Mercy*. Washington, D.C.: National Geographic Society, 1997.

Douglas, Ed. *Tenzing: Hero of Everest*. Washington, D.C.: National Geographic Society, 2003.

Hillary, Edmund. *Nothing Venture, Nothing Win*. New York: Coward, McCann & Geoghegan, 1975.

———. *View from the Summit*. New York: Pocket Books, 1999.

Hunt, John. *The Ascent of Everest*. Seattle, Wash.: The Mountaineers, 1998.

Johnston, Alexa. *Reaching the Summit: Edmund Hillary's Life of Adventure*. New York: DK Publishing, 2005.

Tenzing Norgay, with James Ramsey Ullman. *Tiger of the Snows: The Autobiography of Tenzing of Everest*. New York: G. P. Putnam's Sons, 1955.

FOR FURTHER READING

Masoff, Joy. *Everest: Reaching for the Sky*. New York: Scholastic Reference, 2002.

Platt, Richard. *Everest: Reaching the World's Highest Peak*. New York: DK Publishing, 2000.

Ramsay, Cynthia Russ. *Sir Edmund Hillary & the People of Everest*. Kansas City: Andrews McMeel Publishing, 2002.

Skreslet, Laurie. *To the Top of Everest*. Tonawanda, N.Y.: Kids Can Press, 2001.